Nazism and the Pastors

A Study of the Ideas of Three

Deutsche Christen Groups

American Academy of Religion

Dissertation Series

edited by

H. Ganse Little, Jr.

Number 14

NAZISM AND THE PASTORS

A STUDY OF THE IDEAS OF THREE *DEUTSCHE CHRISTEN* GROUPS

by

JAMES A. ZABEL

SCHOLARS PRESS
Missoula, Montana

NAZISM AND THE PASTORS
STUDY OF THE IDEAS OF THREE *DEUTSCHE CHRISTEN* GROUPS

BY

James A. Zabel

Published by

SCHOLARS PRESS

for

The American Academy of Religion

Distributed by

SCHOLARS PRESS
University of Montana
Missoula, Montana 59801

NAZISM AND THE PASTORS
A STUDY OF THE IDEAS OF THREE *DEUTSCHE CHRISTEN* GROUF

BY

James A. Zabel
School of the Ozarks College
Point Lookout, Missouri 65726

Ph.D., 1971
The University of Chicago

Advisors:
Martin Marty
William McNeill
William McGrath

Copyright © 1976

by

The American Academy of Religion

Library of Congress Cataloging in Publication Data

Zabel, James A
    Nazism and the pastors.

    (Dissertation series - American Academy of Religion ;
no. 14)
    Bibliography: p.
    1. Church and state in Germany — 1933-1945.
2. National socialism. 3. Deutsche Christen (National-
kirchliche Einung) 4. Glaubensbewegung "Deutsche
Christen." 5. Luther-Deutsche (Reformatorische
Reichskirche) I. American Academy of Religion.
II. Title. III. Series: American Academy of Religion.
Dissertation series - American Academy of Religion ;
no. 14.
BR856.Z23   261.7'0943   75-30607
ISBN 0-89130-040-6

PRINTED IN THE UNITED STATES OF AMERICA

1 2 3 4 5

Printing Department
University of Montana
Missoula, Montana 59801

To my Parents

TABLE OF CONTENTS

ACKNOWLEDGEMENTS

The author owes a great deal to many people, without whose encouragement and help this dissertation would not have been possible. Special recognition goes to Professors William McGrath, William McNeill, and Martin Marty, my thesis advisers, whose constructive criticisms aided the progress of this work immeasurably. Professor Leonard Krieger also deserves special thanks for having introduced me to the topic. I am grateful to Professor Donald Lach for his continuing guidance and encouragement during my studies at the University of Chicago.

Miss Helen Smith, director of the University of Chicago Interlibrary Loan Service, very kindly helped locate numerous materials used in this work. Many of the primary sources which were utilized came from the Union Theological Seminary Library in New York City, and for its staff's willingness to lend materials, I am grateful.

My wife, Janet, showed continual confidence in me throughout my graduate study and, in particular, helped with the dissertation by spending many months proofreading and typing. For this, I cannot adequately express my appreciation. My parents provided support and encouragement throughout my academic career and I therefore gratefully dedicate this work to them.

INTRODUCTION

One of the striking characteristics of modern European nationalism is that the nation has been transformed into a religious object. Indeed, one might say that for many modern citizens, the nation has usurped the functions that churches traditionally have performed. Ever since the French Revolution, the nation has had its own sacred celebrations in the guise of memorial holidays, with appropriate ritual and symbol, its own saints represented by political heroes, and its own concept of what made up the community of believers, variously termed the race, *le peuple*, and *das Volk*. Writing in 1934 about the concept of the totalitarian state, the ultimate expression of nationalism, Paul Tillich observed that it was designed to create security and reintegration. "It is the 'fullness of time,' in the religious sense of the term....It has received mystic consecration and stands, not merely as the earthly representative of God, as Hegel conceived it, but actually as God on earth."[1]

Religion and nationalism have an ideological interconnectedness that has been effectively pointed out, in the German case, in the relationship bewteen pietism and the rise of nationalism in the late 18th and early 19th centuries. Faced with the destruction of older medieval and scholastic ties in the Enlightenment, and the secularization of life, the German "enlightened Pietist" cast around for a point through which his emotionalism and practical Christian nature could find an outlet. The nation provided this stable point.[2] In the 20th century, the relationship between religion and nationalism continued into the Nazi period, and there found one of its most strident and awesome portrayals. National Socialism was, for many of those who supported it, a religious experience of the deepest sort. It is no accident that the 1920's and 1930's, a period of renascent German nationalism, saw a variety of national-minded religious groups rise and flourish. Some of the new religious movements were not Christian, and based their platforms on the deeds of historical and mythical Germanic heroes. But certainly the stronger new religious formulations were those that based themselves on more traditional Christian concepts on the one hand, while affirming, at the same time, the German ways.

What follows is a study of some of these latter groups. Defined in the most general way, the term "German Christians" (*Deutsche Christen*) denotes Protestant (i.e., Evangelical Lutheran) Christians who willingly affirmed national renewal of a Volkish sort, particularly as represented by Hitler and the National Socialist movement. These German Protestants viewed the Third Reich as a reestablishment of Christian values. It is difficult to ascertain the precise importance of the German Christians to the rise and furtherance of Nazism, but one can be certain that theirs was no small contribution.[3] In 1933, two-thirds of German citizens still considered themselves Evangelical Lutheran, and in July of the same year, a vast majority of those who participated in the national church synod elections voted for German Christian candidates. The German Christian victory in the 1933 church elections did not, however, provide a stabilizing point of unity for all German Protestants. The bloom on the rose of church unity under the German Christians faded, and their only lasting church-political contribution was conflict and a sharpening of antagonistic viewpoints that disrupted the Protestant churches until after 1945. It remains a debatable point whether the chaotic situation in the Protestant Church was advantageous to the goals of Nazism (that is, if the eventual goal of Nazism was to destroy Christianity), or provided a continually embarrassing point of weakness in the process of *Gleichschaltung*. But there is another side to the German Christian phenomenon, that of the ideas put forth by the groups. In the latter case, there can be no doubt that German Christians provided ideological briefs for the rise and maintenance of Nazism that encouraged almost total church support for the regime.

If one scans the historical work completed to date on the German Christian question, it is obvious that, for the most part, historians have spent their time outlining the organizational growth and vicissitudes of the various German Christian movements. An outstanding work of scholarship by an East

German historian, Kurt Meier, is more than adequate in tracing the institutional development of the German Christians, at both the national level and throughout the various *Landeskirchen*.[4] Hans Buchheim has also included a survey of German Christian groups in his book dealing with Third Reich religious movements.[5] However, although German Christian ideology is of more than biographical significance, systematic ideological analysis has thus far dealt only with individual issues.[6] What remains untreated is the overall ideological picture of the German Christian movement with its wide variety.[7]

What follows aims not at being exhaustive, but analytical --an effort to bring order into an extremely complex topic. The results of research show that three types of German Christian temperament fed into the larger picture of German Christian ideology--conservative, opportunistic, and radical or revolutionary. Each of the three groups, represented respectively by the *Christlich-Deutsche Bewegung* (CDB), the *Glaubensbewegung Deutsche Christen* (GDC), and the *Kirchenbewegung Deutsche Christen* (KDC), was concerned with a number of key issues. Admittedly, the issues overlap the movements. Anti-Semitism, for example, was found in all three, but with widely varying intensity. As much as possible, however, such issues will be analyzed with very little repetition in order to show diversity in the larger picture of German Christian ideology.

Various sources have been utilized. Background material includes the numerous secondary works written by German and non-German contemporary observers as well as by historians writing after the fall of the Third Reich. In addition, the theological and church-political milieu was reflected in various non-German Christian theological journals of the 1920's and 1930's. German Christian periodicals were basic to the research, including the CDB journal *Glaube und Volk*, the GDC journal *Evangelium im dritten Reich*, and the KDC publication *Briefe an deutsche Christen*. Finally, related German Christian literature was utilized--books and pamphlets, many of which were once part of the *Hauptarchiv der NSDAP*, but are now held at Union Theological Seminary Library in New York.

Even the general outline of the church situation in Nazi Germany is not well known by many modern historians. This analysis of German Christian ideology is introduced, therefore, with chapters summarizing the church situation after Germany's defeat in World War I, and the chronological development of the German Christian movements to 1940. The following chapters concern the ideological analysis of the three German Christian groups and cover the years 1931 to 1937. A final summary will bring the ideas together in a unified picture of German Christian ideology in general.

NOTES

1. Paul Tillich, "The Totalitarian State and the Claims of the Church," *Social Research*, I, No. 4 (1934), 417-18.

2. This is the thesis of Koppel S. Pinson in *Pietism as a Factor in the Rise of German Nationalism* (New York: Columbia University Press, 1934), succinctly best stated on pp. 26-27. Franklin Hamlin Littell, *The German Phoenix: Men and Movements in the Church in Germany* (Garden City, New York: Doubleday & Company, Inc., 1960), p. 17, agrees with Pinson and blames a continuing lack of Christian response to the bad side of German nationalism on the abandonment, by pietists, of the discipline of existing religious bodies and their creeds.

3. Kurt Meier, *Die Deutschen Christen: Das Bild einer Bewegung im Kirchenkampf des Dritten Reiches* (Göttingen: Vandenhoeck & Ruprecht, 1964), p. xii. While pointing out the suspect nature of the available sources, Meier believes that the German Christian organizations never had over 1,000,000 official members. In mid-1934, the *Reichsbewegung Deutsche Christen* could claim about 600,000, and toward the end of 1936, the *Bund fur Deutsches Christentum* numbered about 250,000.

4. *Ibid*. I am greatly indebted to this work and to other secondary materials for the organizational overview that is presented in Chapters I and II, by way of introduction to my topic.

5. Hans Buchheim, *Glaubenskrise im Dritten Reich: Drei Kapitel nationalsozialistischer Religionspolitik* (Stuttgart: Deutsche Verlags-Anstalt, 1953), pp. 41-156.

6. Two representative examples are Wolfgang Tilgner, *Volksnomostheologie und Schöpfungsglaube: Ein Beitrag zur Geschichte des Kirchenkampfes* (Göttingen: Vandenhoeck & Ruprecht, 1966), and Carsten Nicolaisen, *Die Auseinandersetzungen um das alte Testament im Kirchenkampf, 1933-1945* (Ph. D. dissertation, University of Hamburg, 1966).

7. The most recent and easily available work in English on the German church struggle, and which includes a view of the German Christians, is John S. Conway, *The Nazi Persecution of the Churches, 1933-45* (New York: Basic Books, Inc., 1968).

PART I

GENERAL BACKGROUND OF THE GERMAN CHRISTIAN MOVEMENT

CHAPTER I: THE GERMAN EVANGELICAL CHURCH--1918-1933

The Protestant churches in Germany never felt at home in
the Weimar Republic. The defeat of 1918, a democratic government dominated by Social Democrats and the Catholic Center Party, and the loss of their special position in the German state
prevented Protestants from developing a sense of belonging to
what they thought was an imposed foreign regime. Thus, the
joyful response of German Protestantism to the accession of
Hitler in 1933 is understandable only when one sees the reasons
in the feeling of *anomie* that pervaded the Church during the
years of democratic experiment.

The end of World War I brought radical and immediate re-
percussions in the Protestant churches. With the fall of the
German princely houses, the Protestant churches lost their former privileged status. With the end of the principle of *summus
episcopus*, the close relationship of churches to governments
simply collapsed. After 1918, some churches adopted bishops
for their leadership. This was the case in Saxony, Hanover,
Braunschweig, Nassau, the Mecklenburgs, and Schleswig-Holstein.
But in Prussia there was much opposition to the episcopal concept, and that church took on a governing body consisting of a
General Synod and four General Superintendents.[1] The twenty-
eight *Landeskirchen*, with all their localisms, lack of unity,
and 19th century traditions of being loyal, bureaucratic sub-
ordinates, were in no position to assert an independent or
forceful role in the new state. The churches varied greatly in
size. The Old Prussian Union Church included about half of all
German Protestants in its eighteen million members; Saxony had
four and one-half million members, while Hanover had two and
one-half million. Of the remaining churches, only five had
more than one million each--Würtemberg, Thuringia, Bavaria,
Schleswig-Holstein, and Hamburg.[2] The fact that the Prussian
Church claimed such a large share of German Protestants was of
strategic importance in 1933 when the German Christians made

their bid for church control. But in 1918, there was no real unity in the German Protestant outlook.

German Protestants were aware of their lack of unity, and in 1922 at Wittenburg the twenty-eight churches agreed to a Federation (*Deutsche Evangelische Kirchenbund*) or loose amalgamation with an executive committee and President (the latter also the chief administrative official of the Prussian Church), a Federal Council made up of representatives of individual church governments, and a synodical assembly. The Federation had no authority over questions of faith or over the constitutions and administration of individual *Landeskirchen*. It was empowered to look after common Protestant interests in foreign countries and in the German nation in general, and to be involved in religious education and works of charity, but only when the various churches initiated the action. The Federation's sphere of influence was limited by localisms, but the possibility existed for a gradual unification of churches, especially in educational and missionary functions.[3]

The Weimar Constitution was a compromise document in regard to church-state relations. In November 1918, the Social Democratic government of Prussia issued a decree calling for the institution of secular schools, basing the elimination of prayers and religious instruction on the concept that religious belief was an entirely free and individual practice.[4] But the Catholic Church, with its political influence represented by the Center Party, was not prepared to allow this to happen. The Reich Constitution of August 11, 1919 was a compromise between the Socialists and the Center, and presented neither the real separation of church and state (which the Social Democrats wanted), nor *Staatskirchentum* (which conservative elements desired). Two concurrent principles were stated in the constitution: (1) separation of church and state, and (2) the continued recognition of religious historical development and the will of the faithful to be recognized.[5] Article 137 stated: "There is no state Church," and affirmed the privilege of all religious societies to organize as public corporations, if they could offer some guarantee of permanence, but gave them rights to tax money in relationship to official tax lists.[6]

The school question provided a thorny issue that was never satisfactorily dealt with throughout the republican era. Social Democrats wished to ban all religious instruction from schools, while some German liberals tried to accommodate the churchmen with the concept of the *Simultanschule*.[7] Again, there was a constitutional compromise with the Center. Article 146 allowed for religious instruction in public schools if "those responsible for the education of the young" desired it, and if it did not prejudice a well-ordered scheme of education. The details were to be worked out by state legislation. But the concept of unified national educational principles was further weakened by article 147 which allowed for the licensing and funding of private elementary schools in areas where the local public schools did not administer to the religious needs of a confession--even if that confession were a minority. Article 149 established religious instruction as a regular classroom subject, except in secular schools, with regulatory legislation to follow.[8] The overall result was that the question of religion in the schools continued on much the same basis as in pre-1918 Germany, and any single concept of nation-wide standards for common schools was impossible. Various projects for streamlining the schools were proposed during the 1920's, but opinion was never sufficiently unified to put them into practice.

The Weimar Constitution did not solve church-state questions in a national way. As in the school question, the churches in general used various means of adjusting their relationships with the states. Some states signed concordats with both the Catholic and Protestant Churches; with the Protestants, for example, in Braunschweig (1923), Bavaria (1924), Prussia (1931), and Baden (1932).[9] The individual Protestant churches adjusted their relationships to the various states in accordance with historical practices, while blaming the national government for abandoning a positive stance toward the churches and for being tainted with the "godlessness" of Social Democracy.

The identification of the Weimar Republic with Social Democracy damned the government in the eyes of many Protestants. The decade of the 1920's was a period in which the

Protestant churches lost a sizable part of their membership.
The defections continued to come from two sectors of German
society: industrial labor, especially in Saxony and the Prussian cities, and parts of the cultured class who were attracted
by the aristocratic, heroic, new non-Christian religions
preached by such people as Hermann Wirth, Wilhelm Hauer, and
the Ludendorffs.[10] Perhaps as many as 2,420,000 Germans re-
nounced their Protestant church membership between 1918 and
1931.[11] Protestant clergy, many of whom were monarchists,
could scarcely have had anything less than suspicion for the
Social Democrats who encouraged the exodus from the church.
Parenthetically, the Nazi accession in 1933 had the effect of
reversing this trend for several years.

Besides the formal statements and practical results of the
Weimar Constitution, there were more intangible forces working
on Protestants, and on Protestant clergy in particular. One
might term this the area of psychological despair. Outside of
a small group of Religious Socialists, most Protestant clergy
felt they had no political power in the new regime. Perhaps
the feeling was more apparent than real; Protestant clergy had,
to a large extent, been bureaucratic servants of the state
since the beginning of the 19th century. Still, the princely
regimes were at least assumed to have the good of the Protestant outlook at heart, and ministers had felt that they were
part of the establishment. That feeling was absent after 1918.

Anti-Catholic sentiment was particularly high among
Weimar-era Protestants. It is ironic that Catholics, who had
suffered under Bismarck, and who found it necessary to form a
political party for self-protection, now, along with the other
previously suspect group, the Social Democrats, had well-oiled
political machinery. The majority Protestants, however,
struggled along without ever finding a suitable unified political expression. After 1918, there occurred in Germany what was
called the "monastic springtide" when new religious orders,
convents, and Catholic schools were established. Catholic
bishops had some influence through the Center Party and seemed
to be able to work as well with democratic governments as with
the monarchical ones. The Protestant concordats came only after similar documents were signed with the Roman Church.[12] In

every area, the Protestant churches seemed to take a secondary
position to the Catholics. The result was that there were frequent accusations by Protestants of "political Catholicism."
At a *Kirchenbund* meeting in 1924, the imperial colors were displayed and one of the speakers demanded that Germany, which was
then standing "*unter Römischem Einfluss*," had to be shown the
way back to the Reformation.[13] In the Reich presidential elections of 1925, most Protestants, afraid of the Catholic Center
politics of the candidate Wilhelm Marx, voted for Hindenburg.[14]

Post-war inflation hit the Protestant churches very hard
also. Churches and church institutions lost their endowments,
foreign and home missions were hard-hit, and ministers' salar-
ies were often reduced to a subsistence level. In addition,
fewer young men were going into the Protestant ministry, and
once prestigious theological schools stagnated for lack of
financial backing.[15]

The psychological implications of Germany's defeat in the
war were evident in a large degree among Protestant clergy in
the 1920's. They felt keenly that 1918 had been a humiliating
experience. German Protestant churches had actively supported
the war and the old regime. Only a very few saw the new po-
tentialities for the Church in the Weimar Republic. Otto
Dibelius, General Superintendent of the Old Prussian Union
Church, was one of the few, and felt that the fall of *Staatskirchentum* might actually be giving the churches a new lease on
life. In addition, he took the unpopular position that war was
against the will of God. Religious Socialists, too, saw that
the social involvement of the churches was an important area
that unfortunately had been largely ignored by Lutherans of
earlier times.[16] But the more characteristic Protestant viewpoint is shown by one of the speeches given at the first German
Evangelical *Kirchentag* in Dresden in 1919 which concluded that
because of the war, everything the Protestants and their fathers held dear was surrounded by enemies. The Reformation had
to be recalled to reestablish the close relationship of Protestantism with the state. The separation of church and state was
said to have put the churches in severe danger.[17]

The state of mind of many of the German clergy can be seen
in a *cause célèbre* in the latter part of the 1920's. In

November 1928, in Magdeburg, a young minister named Günther
Dehn preached a sermon entitled "The Church and the Reconciliation of the Nations." Dehn, once a member of the Social Democrats and later a student of Karl Barth's, argued that only a
purely defensive war was justifiable. Although Dehn did not
support unconditional pacifism, he said that it was wrong to
romanticize fighting. He also objected to the installation of
war memorials in churches, saying that this ought to be left
to civil authorities. His sermon aroused an immediate storm of
protest, and when he was appointed as Professor of Practical
Theology at Heidelberg in 1930, the faculty voted to rescind
his call. The Prussian Minister of Culture, however, appointed
him to a position at the University of Halle where opposition
to Dehn was also strong. Nazi students protested, as did some
of the theological professors there, and Dehn found it almost
impossible to lecture in the classroom or to preach in the
chapel.[18] One response, voiced by a member of the *Christlich-
Deutsche Bewegung*, to the disorders at Halle, recognized that
the students there had been unruly, but pointed out that Dehn
was wrong for not recognizing that war is justifiable as a political tool of last resort "...for establishing justice between peoples who, in this world of sin, can also be destroyed
through so-called peaceful means."[19] Emanuel Hirsch, a famous
theologian and German Christian, combined an attack on Günther
Dehn with one on Karl Barth:

> A "harmless" affair you [Barth] call the question of
> commemorative plaques in the churches. But you have
> never known the feeling of a German mother, who has to
> consider seriously the possibility that the bones of
> her son have been thrown on a manure heap by some
> Belgian farmer, nor the countless German mothers,
> sisters, and wives who have seen nothing more of their
> beloved sons than a little note from the company com-
> mander and an official casualty list, or at best, a
> photograph of a nameless mass grave....[20]

These examples point up the kind of emotional patriotism that
was an integral part of German Protestantism of the post-war
period.

The general feeling among Protestant churchmen was that
the Church had no real place in the Weimar Republic. There was
talk from the pulpits of the "Versailles treason," and German
patriotic songs were sung during the Ruhr crisis of 1923.[21]

Toward the end of the decade, S. A. (*Sturmabteilung* or "storm troopers") and *Stahlhelm* formations began to show up in church, marching in as groups in full uniform. Theological journals, especially in the early 1930's, presented articles which voiced dissatisfaction with the national and moral values of the demo-cratic experiment. One Heidelberg theology professor wistfully noted the basic difference between pre-war "patriotism" and post-war "nationalism." He saw the Weimar government as only a remnant-state (*Reststaat*), without values, without freedom, and without power. He contrasted it with the "positive" experience of the war which affirmed the values of camaraderie, struggle as a basic element of life, and the intangible yet real fruit-fulness of sacrifice. The author concluded by calling for a clear statement from the church affirming the revelatory values of Volk and state.[22]

Alongside the political dissatisfaction, however, there were various new theological and churchly movements. Indeed, in terms of theology, the Weimar Republic-era can be charac-terized as a time of ferment. Not all observers were sympathe-tic to the spate of theological experimentation that was taking place. Heinrich Rendtorff, Professor at Kiel and later founder of the *Christlich-Deutsche Bewegung*, warned of the dangers of theological involvement, that he had seen in recent books that dealt with "...the monistic movement, the belief in proletarian socialism,...the youth movement, naturalism and eroticism, oc-cultism, Keyserling and Spengler in their relativism, as well as the in-breaking waves in German intellectual life of Jewish, Germanic, and Eastern beliefs...."[23] But new theological ten-dencies continued to be explored.

Probably the most meaningful of the theologians of the period was the Swiss Karl Barth, whose book *Commentary on Ro-mans* (1919) attacked the *Kulturprotestantismus* that was preva-lent in German theology, and countered the ideas of people like Ernst Troeltsch and other 19th and 20th century theologians who had stressed the historical-critical analysis of religion and Christianity's relationship to various historical eras. Barth denied such "hyphenated Christianity" as a false identification of Christian faith with cultural, social, or political progress, and posited in its place what Kierkegaard called the "'infinite

qualitative distinction' between time and eternity": God as
the "completely other."[24] The opposition to the attempts at
Gleichschaltung of the churches during the Nazi regime, and
thus, at the same time, the opposition to the German Christians, relied greatly on Barthian dialectical theology and its
unwillingness to interpret post-Biblical history as the continuing demonstration of God's revelation.[25]

A number of other church movements flourished in the
1920's. Between 1917 and the 400th anniversary of the Augsburg
Confession in 1930, Karl Holl and others revived an interest in
Luther to free Protestant thinking from the relativistic cultural theology that was considered to be a casualty of the war.
By returning to the Bible and the Reformation confessions, the
promoters of the "Luther-Renaissance" hoped to counteract an
overly academic and historical-critical tone of theology that
dominated German theological schools, and to get back to what
was seen as the solid unalterable principles of faith that
would appeal to a civilization too much infected by a feeling
of relativity in all things.[26]

A high church movement was also active in the Weimar Republic period, but was not very popular with most Protestants.
Stressing the "catholicity" of the Church, this group, whose
leader was Friedrich Heiler, hoped for the renewal of the sac-
ramental character of the church service. Throughout the
1920's and 1930's, its periodical showed a curious interest in
both ecumenicity and in the nationalist movements of the time.[27]
A more important movement, perhaps, was the *Berneuchener Kon-
ferenz* associated with Karl Ritter and Wilhelm Stählin which
aimed at a renewal of church liturgy and the cleansing of
church songs of "subjective" pietistic and romantic influences.[28]

Youth groups were very popular in post-war Germany. For
the Protestants, *Neuland* and *Jungevangelischen* provided the
framework for athletics, choral singing, and the presentation
of plays. Many of these groups were hothouses for the development of Volkish Christianity, and their influence was felt in
some of the later German Christian groups--notably in the
Thuringian German Christians.

In response to the problems of modern industrial labor, a handful of Protestant ministers, including Günther Dehn and Paul Tillich, formed a group of Religious Socialists. Although they participated in church politics, their influence was very small and served more as a center for attack from other church groups than as a rallying point.

Among all the theological and ideological movements in the Protestant church of the 1920's, there are two that deserve more than passing notice for their influence on later German Christian movements. They are the *Bund für Deutsche Kirche* and the ideas associated with Wilhelm Stapel in *Deutsches Volkstum*.

The *Bund für Deutsche Kirche* was founded in June 1921, at the Arndt-Hochschule in Berlin by *Studienrat* Joachim Kurd Niedlich. The intellectuals associated with it included Pastor Friedrich Andersen of Flensburg; the editor of Richard Wagner's *Bayreuther Blätter*, Hans von Wolzogen; Professor Adolf Bartels; and the cultural historian and religious theoretician Max Maurenbrecher. After Niedlich died in 1928, the movement split, with one branch hoping to get involved in mass propaganda. The *Bund* greeted the founding of the *Glaubensbewegung Deutsche Christen* in 1932, and while maintaining its own organization, it often campaigned for their candidates in church elections. The *Bund* made its strongest impression in Schleswig-Holstein.[29]

The ideas of the *Bund für Deutsche Kirche* revolved around two centers: the possibility of seeing Christ in heroic "Nordic" terms, and the corollary of this, that the way to achieve a Germanic Christianity was the radical purging of all judaistic tendencies in religion. One of the more important books representing the *Bund* viewpoint was Friedrich Andersen's *Der deutsche Heiland* (The German Savior).[30] In this book, the influence of modern liberal theology is immediately obvious. Andersen identifies Christianity with the principle of progress, and Christ fits into his theory of "great men" (others are Socrates and Giordano Bruno) characterized by their loneliness, sorrow, and struggle to overcome.[31] Andersen's book is replete with references to modern theologians and philosophers --Harnack, Treitschke, Wagner, Chamberlain, Kierkegaard,

10

Schleiermacher, to name only a few--, and it is from them that
he claims to get his "corrected picture" of Jesus. Churches
are wrong, he says, to portray a lamb-like Jesus instead of a
heroic Christ. The latter he finds to have been correctly
pointed out by H. Stewart Chamberlain who affirmed Christ's
Kampfeslust.[32] Andersen would also reduce Christianity (as he
said Schleiermacher did) to one locus--the person Christ who
does not need any "foreign underpinnings" (the Old Testament)
and who was not a Jew, but an Indo-European.[33] The bulk of
Andersen's argument is pure anti-Semitism. Very early in the
book he chose for his theme Treitschke's words: "*Die Juden sind
unser Unglück.*"[34] Christianity and Judaism are opposite poles.
"It will never be possible to have a real connection of the
two, for in their innermost essences they are like fire and
water." While the Christian God is a God of love, the Jewish
God is a vengeful God and an unjust, partisan being. Jewish
religion is based on fear rather than love, and its highest
value is to become rich. In short, Judaism is crassly materialistic and never gets beyond earthly concerns (*Diesseitig-
keit*). Christianity, however, appreciates the meaning of the
eternal (*Jenseitigkeit*), which Andersen said is in the Indo-
Germanic character that one can see in such worthies as Plato
and Kant who were able to believe in the non-visible, ideal
world--something Judaism can never do.[35] Andersen follows this
up with a lengthy analysis of "Judaism as it really is" which
includes not only elaboration of the alleged Jewish religious
immaturity, but also the modern dangers of Judaism as a capi-
talistic, internationalist, political power. For the Christian
churches the only answer is to be seen in a cleansing of church
usages to "return to Jesus as the basis and fount of a living
Christianity."[36] This can be accomplished only by taking the
step of the "*verdeutschung*" (Germanicization) of Christianity
by completely discarding the Old Testament and those parts of
the New Testament that are tainted by Jewish influences.[37]

The *Bund für Deutsche Kirche* had connections with the
later German Christians in several ways. As noted above, the
Bund helped elect German Christian candidates to church positions and some members also belonged to the *Glaubensbewegung
Deutsche Christen*. Reinhold Krause, whose rabidly anti-Semitic

speech of November 1933, split the German Christians, came out
of the *Bund*.[38] Those *Glaubensbewegung Deutsche Christen* writers who were mindful of their historical origins credited the
Bund with having opened up important new areas. Arnold Dannenmann, the official historian of the *Glaubensbewegung* agreed
that the German Christian church ought to be more mindful of
the Volkish elements of religion, but found the *Bund* to have
based its teachings falsely on liberal, religious-historical
research.[39] Friedrich Wieneke, a theologian very early involved with both the *Christlich-Deutsche Bewegung* and the
Glaubensbewegung Deutsche Christen, also had some favorable
things to say about *Bund* ideas: "Here appeared for the first
time the will to make really meaningful Germanness (*wirklich
artgemässes Deutschtum*) the bearer of the Biblical Gospel."
Wieneke found one *Bund* member, Max Maurenbrecher, the most influential: "One can see in Maurenbrecher the guardian of the
threshold [*Schwellenhüter*] for the German Christian movement of
our day." Maurenbrecher was less radical than most *Bund* members, however, and Wieneke had the same opinion as Dannenmann
concerning the failings of *Bund* ideas.[40] The fact that the
Bund members saw Christ in the German way as a hero and *Führer*-
personality, along with their affirmation of Luther as the
"German prophet," made them significant precursors of the
Glaubensbewegung Deutsche Christen, said another German Christian observer. However, the difference was that the German
Christians based their ideas on the Lutheran confessions.
"They [the *Glaubensbewegung Deutsche Christen*] are a conservative movement," while the *Bund* relied too heavily on relativis-
tic liberal theology.[41]

Partial disclaimers of *Glaubensbewegung Deutsche Christen*
ideologists should not hide the fact that *Bund* concepts were
very influential on German Christian ideas. Almost every German Christian group had ideas that had already been voiced by
the *Bund für Deutsche Kirche*. The concept of the Germanic
church, "heroic" Christianity, the search in history for the
roots of German piety, these and other ideas recurred in German
Christian ideology over and over. The most important ideas
that were carried over are those two which have been noted as

central to the *Bund für Deutsche Kirche* religious view: a German type (*artgemäss*) of theology, and anti-Semitism.

Wilhelm Stapel was another important influence on the ideas of German Christians. Not a professional theologian, Stapel combined a journalistic style with a theology of nationalism. He was the editor and a major contributor to the periodical *Deutsches Volkstum* throughout the 1920's, and until 1938 when his independent nature got him into trouble with the Nazi regime.[42] Although his early life (up to the turn of the century) showed a strong dual influence of conservative Lutheranism and a "Prussian" cast of mind that relied heavily on the concept of the duty of the state citizen and an "idealistic-Fichtean education ideal," his reading of some of Friedrich Naumann's works convinced him of the importance of *Volkstum* and Volkish theology that did not rely on traditional *Staatskirchentum*. These, plus a wide-ranging interest in Germanic art and literature, show the variety of influences that must be kept in mind when looking at his theological ruminations.[43] Stapel was, was, finally, an early supporter of Hitler for whom he wrote two books that tried to show the compatibility of Christianity and National Socialism.[44]

Stapel viewed Christianity and Germanism as inseparable due to their historical confluence, but sharply denied that the ethics (*Sitten*) of the Germans or of any other Volk were "Christian." Christianity is not an ethos or way of life; it is rather *the* religion, the mode of completion of the various *Nomoi* of the peoples of the earth, based on faith alone. The German *Nomos* was an ethic of heroism (*Heldenethik*), born out of the view that the world is characterized by struggle.[45] Biblical events, especially the Sermon on the Mount, have no general validity as paradigms for the ethical or legal behavior of Christians. They were relevant ethically only to a small circle of disciples and preached love only as *Agape*--the *Nomos* of the Kingdom of Heaven.[46] Stapel combined his disdain for "Christian ethics" with a strident militarism, the latter a theme that continued to be important with German Christians.

> To better man morally is the task of education, but
> not of religion. The meaning of Christianity is not
> to transform men into braver earthly citizens, but
> rather to save them from the forces of the devil and

from everlasting death. For spreading virtue through
word and example, a union for ethical culture is sufficient; the eternal God does not need to let himself
be crucified by men to achieve this. Actually, if
Christ had allowed himself to be nailed to the cross
for the sake of the spreading of pacifism, then one
could justly speak (as some now unjustly do) of the
"bankruptcy of Christianity."[47]

Stapel denied that Christ, the apostles, or the Reformation
leaders damned war as such. The pacifistic ideal did not grow
out of Christianity, but out of the Enlightenment. "Pacifism
is nothing else than the ideal of security of the enlightened
bourgeois who does not want to be disturbed in his life style
and pleasures."[48] Christ came not to fulfill the Jewish law
(Old Testament) alone, but to help us fulfill our values on the
basis of our racial, Volkish-community *Nomos*.

> We were born into a certain natural and historical
> community, without making the decision ourselves.
> The great natural life-community of every man is his
> Volk....With body and soul, he belongs to his Volk
> whether he will or not. He is and always remains a
> part of the greater life--"Volk." ...Just as my life
> is for my Volk, so is my religious life, the service
> of God, also for my Volk. What would it gain me to
> be blessed, if my Volk were damned?...Jesus felt and
> thought this way. He clearly said that he was sent
> to his Jewish people....And if he really sent his
> disciples abroad [*in die Fremde*]...he sent them to
> the other "peoples" [*Völker*], not to "men" [*Menschen*].
> To him service to God was always a Volk matter [*Volks-
> angelegenheit*].[49]

The most important Biblical story for Stapel was that of the
tower of Babel which, he says, shows how mankind was saved by
differentiation into Volk-nations.[50] Stories and practices of
the pagan gods of the pre-Christian Germans have, for Stapel,
as much validity as the Old Testament as a matrix for Christianity. They made up the "*Krypta*" below the cathedral of
Christianity for the German People. Pre-Christian gods (for
all peoples) were the equivalent of "God the Father" or the God
of Creation.[51]

> Because there are many religions, there are many earthly
> moralities [*Sittlichkeiten*]. In these moralities, the
> expired national religions live on. The *Nomoi* of the
> pre- and sub-Christian national religions are examples
> of God's mercy [*Erbarmungen Gottes*]....The national
> religions are thus, seen from a sacred history view-
> point, the presuppositions of Christianity.[52]

Stapel's theology resulted in some interesting by-products.
The Old Testament was, of course, of little value to all
peoples except Jews, although he distinguished between the
"Jewish *Nomos*" and the "words of the prophets" (*Prophetenworte*),
and thereby found a justification for keeping the Bible intact.[53] In addition, one's highest duty was not to any kind of
Christian ethics, which are non-existent, but to the national
Nomos or national religion. The command of obedience to the
Volk-state, which is the logical result, was thus not based on
the Lutheran concept of the state as an order of God created to
control the chaos of selfish and sinful men, but rather on a
positive affirmation of the ethical, norm-giving value of the
Volk. Parenthetically, Stapel denies in his most widely-read
book that ethical Christian statesmanship is possible, but says
the truly moral statesman is the man who acts to further the
values of the Volk *Nomos*. Stapel posited his belief that the
German Volk had a mission to establish and maintain a European
Nomos under German leadership. He called it "Imperium Teu-
tonicum."[54]

Stapel's theological constructions were very useful to the
reemergent nationalism that was an undercurrent in the 1920's
and a stark reality of the Hitlerian period. For those who accepted his ideas, there were no barriers to being theoretically
Christian on the one hand and agreeing with the most unchristian acts on the other. The effects of Stapel's ideas can be
seen in every German Christian group. Some picked up his belief that Christianity was essentially the completion and development of primeval German ways, while others found pacifism
to be patently unchristian. Stapel's limitations on the value
of the Old Testament, though not necessarily resting entirely
on anti-Semitic presuppositions on his part, reinforced that
important aspect of German Christian ideas.[55]

Scanning the place of the Protestant churches in the Weimar Republic, one can see a two-fold situation. On the one
hand, the Protestant churches felt little sympathy for the new
regime which seemed at odds with the values of a Lutheran
people. The Protestant churches were bound up with the forms
of a vanquished Germany and its Bismarckian values of blood and
iron and simple, heroic piety. The secular artificiality of

the new Germany, its military weakness, its lack of an historical sense of the German traditions--these could not provide
the warmth and security that Protestantism in Germany was seeking. On the other hand, the 1920's in Germany were not years
of stagnation in the churches. In the realm of ideas, German
religious thinkers were exploring a large number of avenues--
some traditional, some radically new. It is out of this dual
experience of "cultural despair" and ideological ferment, that
German Christian ideas arose.

NOTES

1. Karl Kupisch, *Zwischen Idealismus und Massendemokratie: Eine Geschichte der evangelischen Kirche in Deutschland von 1815-1945* (Berlin: Lettner Verlag, 1955), p. 150.

2. James Hastings Nichols, *History of Christianity, 1650-1950: Secularization of the West* (New York: The Ronald Press Company, 1956), p. 383.

3. Charles S. MacFarland, *The New Church and the New Germany: A Study of Church and State* (New York: The Macmillan Company, 1934), pp. 22-23.

4. Herbart Raab, ed., *Kirche und Staat* (Munich: Deutscher Taschenbuch Verlag, 1966), pp. 275-76.

5. *Ibid.*, p. 125.

6. *Ibid.*, pp. 280-81, and Heinrich Oppenheimer, *The Constitution of the German Republic* (London: Stevens and Sons, Limited, 1923), pp. 249-50.

7. Erich Eyck, *A History of the Weimar Republic* (Cambridge: Harvard University Press, 1962), p. 150.

8. Raab, *Kirche und Staat*, pp. 281-82, and Oppenheimer, *Constitution*, pp. 251-52.

9. Raab, *Kirche und Staat*, p. 127.

10. Nichols, *Christianity*, pp. 384-85.

11. Paul F. Douglass, *God Among the Germans* (Philadelphia: University of Pennsylvania Press, 1935), p. 278. This statistic may be somewhat suspect as it is said to be quoted from a Roman Catholic source. A reliable Protestant source puts the number of withdrawals from the Protestant church between 1919 and 1925 at 1,383,914. "Kirchenaustrittsbewegung," *Die Religion in Geschichte und Gegenwart* (6 vols., 2d ed.; Tübingen: J. C. B. Mohr Verlag, 1927-32), Vol. III, pp. 828-29.

12. Waldemar Gurian, *Hitler and the Christians*, trans. by E. F. Peeler (London: Sheed & Ward, 1936), p. 35.

13. Kupisch, *Idealismus und Massendemokratie*, p. 180.

14. Eyck, *Weimar Republic*, p. 336.

15. Nichols, *Christianity*, pp. 377, 381.

16. Kupisch, *Idealismus und Massendemokratie*, pp. 181-82.

17. Raab, *Kirche und Staat*, pp. 277-78. This is a paraphrase of a speech entitled "Kirche und Monarchie" by one Dr. Moeller.

18

18.   Arthur C. Cochrane, *The Church's Confession under Hitler* (Philadelphia: The Westminster Press, 1962), pp. 51-52. There is also an account in Kupisch, *Idealismus und Massendemokratie*, pp. 182-184.

19.   "Zum Fall Günther Dehn," *Glaube und Volk*, I, No. 2 (1932), 29.

20.   Emanuel Hirsch, "Offener Brief an Karl Barth," *Deutsches Volkstum*, ed. by Wilhelm Stapel and Albrecht Günther, No. I (April, 1932), p. 267.

21.   Kupisch, *Idealismus und Massendemokratie*, p. 179.

22.   Heinz-Dietrich Wendland, "Nationalismus und christliche Erneuerung," *Christentum und Wissenschaft*, VII (1931), 208-09, 218.

23.   "Praktisches Theologie," *Die Theologie der Gegenwart*, XXIII, No. 8 (1929), 231.

24.   Karl Barth, *The Epistle to the Romans* (Oxford: Oxford University Press, 1933), pp. 10, 115.

25.   Nevertheless, one of Barth's most famous colleagues, Friedrich Gogarten, was for a time associated with the conservative branch of the German Christians.

26.   Andrew L. Drummond, *German Protestantism Since Luther* (London: The Epworth Press, 1951), pp. 151-53. Also Kupisch, *Idealismus und Massendemokratie*, pp. 161-65.

27.   Accounts of the High Church Movement are found in Kupisch, *Idealismus und Massendemokratie*, p. 152, and Ludwig A. Veit, *Die Kirche im Zeitalter des Individualismus: 1648 bis zur Gegenwart* (Freiburg: Herder & Co., 1933), p. 438. The journal of the High Church Movement was *Die Hochkirche* (after 1934 called *Eine Heilige Kirche*). Ambivalence toward the Nazi movement can be seen in an issue of the journal which presented one article strongly condemning the pagan and anti-Semitic character of National Socialism, and another article written by a High Church adherent who was also a Nazi. Until the mid-1930's, the former was more characteristic of the High Church people than the latter. "Christentum und Nationalsozialismus," *Die Hochkirche*, XIV, No. 6, (1932), 212-14.

28.   Kupisch, *Idealismus und Massendemokratie*, p. 152.

29.   Meier, *Deutschen Christen*, pp. 320-21 [footnote 123]. Other accounts may be found in the "Deutschkirche" article in *Evangelisches Kirchenlexicon: Kirchlich-theologisches Handwörterbuch* (Göttingen: 1956), I, 874-5, in Buchheim, *Glaubenskrise*, pp. 45-46, and in Günther Van Norden, *Kirche in der Krise* (Düsseldorf: Presseverband der Evangelischen Kirche im Rheinland, 1963), pp. 25-27.

30.   Friedrich Andersen, *Der deutsche Heiland* (Munich: Deutscher Volksverlag, 1921), is based on and revised from an earlier book by Andersen called *Anticlericus* (1907).

31.   *Ibid.*, pp. 10, 15.

32.   *Ibid.*, pp. 19-20.

33.   *Ibid.*, pp. 28-37.   Andersen's arguments concerning Jesus' racial heritage are taken from various sources such as Friedrich Delitzsch, a late 19th century Old Testament scholar, and H. Stewart Chamberlain, the infamous racialist-philosopher. Jesus' parents, Andersen says, were Jewish converts.

34.   *Ibid.*, p. 5.

35.   *Ibid.*, pp. 59-62.

36.   *Ibid.*, p. 151.

37.   *Ibid.*, pp. 123, 148-151.

38.   Nicolaisen, *Auseinandersetzungen*, pp. 27-28.

39.   Arnold Dannenmann, *Die Geschichte der Glaubensbewegung "Deutsche Christen"* (Dresden: Oskar Günther Verlag, [1933]), pp. 11-12.

40.   Friedrich Wieneke, *Die Glaubensbewegung "Deutsche Christen*," No. 2 of *Schriftenreihe der "Deutschen Christen"*, ed. by Joachim Hossenfelder (Soldin: H. Madrasch, 1933), p. 8. For the ideas of Max Maurenbrecher, see his *Der Heiland der Deutschen: Der Weg der Volkstum schaffenden Kirche* (2nd edition; Göttingen: Vandenhoeck & Ruprecht, 1933).   Maurenbrecher separated from the *Bund für Deutsche Kirche* when he decided that he believed in the Old Testament as Holy Scripture insofar as it foretold the coming of Christ.   His Old Testament views are presented by Nicolaisen, *Auseinandersetzungen*, pp. 32-35.

41.   Constantin Grossmann, *Deutsche Christen--Ein Volksbuch: Wegweiser durch die Glaubensbewegung unserer Zeit* (Dresden: Verlag E. am Ende, 1934), pp. 24-25.

42.   Background information and secondary analyses of Stapel's theology are presented in Tilgner, *Volksnomostheologie*, pp. 89-127, and Jean F. Neurohr, *Der Mythos vom dritten Reich: Zur Geistesgeschichte des Nationalsozialismus* (Stuttgart: J. G. Cotta, 1957), pp. 172-76.

43.   Tilgner, *Volksnomostheologie*, pp. 89-92.

44.   Wilhelm Stapel, *Sechs Kapitel über Christentum und Nationalsozialismus* (Hamburg: Hanseatische Verlagsanstalt, 1931), and *Die Kirche Christi und der Staat Hitlers* (Hamburg: Hanseatische Verlagsanstalt, 1933).

45.   Stapel, "Deutschtum und Christentum," *Deutsches Volkstum*, No. 4 (1925), pp. 251-52.

46.   Stapel, *Sechs Kapitel*, pp. 18-19.

20

47. Stapel, "Deutschtum und Christentum," *Deutsches Volkstum*, No. 4 (1925), pp. 254-55.

48. Stapel, *Sechs Kapitel*, pp. 20-21.

49. Stapel, "Das Deutschtum und die Kirchenspaltung," *Deutsches Volkstum*, No. 1 (1921), p. 1.

50. "The dispersal of mankind into linguistic and morally [*sittlich*] differentiated peoples was an example of God's goodness." Stapel, "Eine Theologie des Nationalismus," *Deutsches Volkstum*, No. 1 (May, 1932), p. 365.

51. Stapel, "Der Teufel und die Heiden," *Deutsches Volkstum*, No. 2 (October, 1934), p. 876.

52. Stapel, "Eine Theologie des Nationalismus," *Deutsches Volkstum*, No. 1 (May, 1932), p. 364.

53. Stapel, *Sechs Kapitel*, pp. 14-15.

54. Stapel, *Der christliche Staatsmann: Eine Theologie des Nationalismus* (Hamburg: Hanseatische Verlagsanstalt, 1932). A completely adequate summary of the thesis of the book can be found in "Eine Theologie des Nationalismus," *Deutsches Volkstum*, No. 1 (May, 1932), pp. 363-65.

55. In the 1930's, Stapel took part in some German Christian activities. For instance, in October of 1935, he participated in a "theological convention" of the *Reichsbewegung Deutsche Christen* in Wittenberg. *Christentum und Wissenschaft*, XI, (1935), 426.

CHAPTER II: DEUTSCHE CHRISTEN CHRONOLOGICAL DEVELOPMENT

AND THE *KIRCHENKAMPF*--1927-40

An overview of German Christian development between the
late 1920's and 1940 resembles an hourglass figure with a mid-
point reached in 1933.   The German Christian phenomenon pro-
gressed from diversity to unity and back again to diversity.
The fact that German Christians only found unity in the fever-
ish few months just preceding and following Hitler's take-over,
points up the many different types of people involved in German
Christian activities.   Because the purpose here is to provide a
typology of ideas, the discussion of the organizational background will stress a similar typology--isolating the three
types of German Christians: conservative, opportunistic, and
radical.

In addition to the three major movements presented here,
there were other German Christian splinter groups.   But in most
cases, their impact was small and they can be grouped with one
or another of the three major organizations.   Such, for instance, is the case of the "Saxon German Christian" movement
which declared its autonomy at the end of 1933 but ideologically developed very quickly in the direction of the Thuringian
group, the *Kirchenbewegung Deutsche Christen*.

The conservative group under study is represented by the
Christlich-Deutsche Bewegung (hereinafter referred to as the
CDB), founded in 1930, and dissolved in the fall of 1933.[1]
Werner Wilm, a provincial youth pastor from Brandenburg,
gathered around him a group of like-minded people--one von
Kleist-Schmenzin who was an estate owner, Bruno Doehring who
was a Prussian court pastor at the outbreak of the First World
War, university professors such as Emanuel Hirsch, Heinrich
Bornkamm, and Paul Althaus, and one of the later leading
Glaubensbewegung Deutsche Christen ideologists, Friedrich
Wieneke.   In 1932, Heinrich Rendtorff, *Landesbischof* of Meck-
lenburg, took over the leadership of the movement.   What is immediately noticeable is that almost all of these people were
from what might be termed an "upper class" background.   No

doubt this was a major factor in the coloring of the prevailing ideas of the CDB. Conservative Lutheran university professors, an estate owner, a Hohenzollern court preacher, a state church bishop whose early childhood was spent in the companionship of the children of Hohenzollern nobility--these leaders reflected the types of people involved in the CDB.[2]

Politically, the CDB was conservative and closer to the Nationalist Party (DNVP) and the paramilitary organization, *Stahlhelm*, than to the Nazis, although Friedrich Wieneke is an exception. The CDB hoped to combat the influence of the Social Democratic and Center Parties, to point up their opposition to the "war-guilt lies" and the Versailles Treaty, and to protect Lutheran Christianity against the new *ersatz* religions--especially the Ludendorffs' pagan *Tannenbergbund*.[3] Althaus and Hirsch voiced their despair at the international political situation as it pertained to Germany in a declaration of 1931:

> ...The German nation was forced into a war that it did not want, and robbed by a dictated peace of participation in the space [*Raum*] and goods of the earth which it needs simply to be able to breathe and live. It is being bled white by war contributions that go by the lying name of reparations....Under the guise of peace, Germany's enemies are continuing to wage the war against the German people and are thus through this falsification, poisoning the world situation to the point where justice and trust are becoming impossible.[4]

The platform of the CDB affirmed love of Volk and country which grew out of the "depths of the blood and heart, and hardened in the glow of war, forged in the sorrow of fate and hatred of the enemy, broadened in the world-historical task of the German Volk and state..."[5] At the same time, the CDB platform placed the movement on firm orthodox grounds and emphasized that the movement for German freedom would come only when the nation found its way back to the Gospel.

> We learned the hard way, that neither faith in the state nor the economy, neither faith in parties nor movements, neither faith in race nor the good will of German men, can save the German Volk. We learned in the dark depths of this bitter experience, that the cross of Christ is the deepest, yes the only, meaning for our fate.[6]

These words, characterized by their conservative Lutheran belief in the sinfulness of all earthly things, are in contrast

to other German Christian groups. The CDB ideas are presented
as a halfway house on the road to German Christianity. It is
significant that they are the only German Christian group to
put "Christian" before "German" in the name of their movement.

The first issue of *Glaube und Volk*, the periodical of the
CDB, appeared in January of 1932. Another church journal noted
its birth with these words:

> This periodical, which will appear monthly, hopes to
> take a position against the undermining of the German
> Christian Volk-life that is creeping in on the one
> side through the atheistic movement [*Gottlosenbeweg-
> ung*], and on the other side in Volkish attitudes.
> Against both, it intends to affirm true Christianity
> and pure Volkishness, and at the same time serve the
> awakening freedom movement, so that it does not split
> apart over these important decisions.[7]

This attempt to steer a cautious middle way characterizes the
history of the CDB. When church elections came up, the editors
of *Glaube und Volk* were of little specific help to their readers. "We ask, that only those Christians be elected who feel
themselves duty-bound by God to the service of their Volk....
The Church can and must only be bound to God and not to any human [*menschlich*], political, economic or other authority."[8]
Even the editors had to note that some of the readers had objected to this lack of a firm stand.[9]

The CDB did not actively support the Nazis before 1933
(distinct, that is, from the other nationalist groups), and in
some ways were unsuited to be the enthusiastic supporters that
the other German Christian groups became. But the CDB, by its
indecisiveness, was still of value to Nazi designs, just as the
German Nationalist Party was in the political sphere, because
the CDB strengthened the influence of national-Volkish thought
on conservative Lutherans. Those CDB members who were willing
to be more directly supportive of Hitler joined the *Glaubensbewegung Deutsche Christen*. Hirsch and Althaus joined, as did
Wieneke. Writing about the conservatism of the CDB, Wieneke
noted, "It [the CDB] was unable to become a decisive factor in
the German freedom struggle because the Volk thoughts of the
CDB continued to be more Prussian-conservative, and recognized
too little the essence of the racial Volk in the sense of a
divine order of creation."[10] Even in the heat of German

Christian success in the middle of 1933, Rendtorff steered the
CDB into a "wait-and-see" position regarding church politics,
hoping for the hour when the balanced view of the CDB would be
recognized by all.[11] The opportunity never arose however. As
early as April of 1933, Mecklenburg Nazis tried to replace
Rendtorff's state church leadership with more enthusiastic
German Christians. Although the early attempts failed, the
hounding continued, and Rendtorff dejectedly left his post on
January 6, 1934, and took up a pastorate. He was replaced as
Landesbischof by the leader of Mecklenburg's GDC.[12] Although
the story of Rendtorff's church problems is not told in the CDB
periodical (there is only one notice in passing that since his
activities were taken up elsewhere, Rendtorff's usual column
was being postponed), clearly the CDB was at an end. Rendtorff
and Wilm dissolved the organization on September 6, 1933.[13]
The journal continued until the end of the year with what were
obviously "fill-in" articles.

The CDB as an organization did not survive the more forceful attacks of the Nazi period, although some individuals continued to present the CDB viewpoint. While supporting Volkish
renewal and, in 1933, the Nazi movement, the CDB members were
too indecisive to suit their German Christian colleagues.
Nevertheless, the CDB represents the way conservatives could be
used for more radical ends.

The *Glaubensbewegung Deutsche Christen* (hereinafter referred to as the GDC), the group characterized as ideologically
opportunistic, shows a two-fold organizational character. On
the one hand, it is a distinct group of German Christians,
called into existence by the Nazi Party, but with its own set
of ideas. On the other hand, for about one year (late 1932 to
November of 1933), the GDC was also a composite organization,
gathering under one roof the entire spectrum of German Christian groups for the purpose of a common front designed to support early Nazi aims regarding the churches. While it is required of the historian that he note both aspects of the GDC,
the ideological analysis which follows is limited to the nar-
rower group with a definite ideological center.

The GDC was founded in June of 1932, in Berlin by Wilhelm
Kube, the Nazi Party delegation leader in the Prussian *Landtag*.

Since 1930, Kube had made contacts with Friedrich Wieneke and a *Neumark* pastor Karl Eckert, an *"Alter Kämpfer"* in the Party. The army chaplain, Ludwig Müller, later German Christian *Reichsbischof*, was also an early supporter of this movement. Unable to rely on the CDB because of its indecisiveness and lack of racial prejudice, Kube decided to set up a movement that would organize pastors for pro-Nazi campaigns in church elections and combat the influence of the *Christlich-Soziales Volksdienst* (Religious Socialists). Kube, along with Pastor Joachim Hossenfelder (later at the center of the GDC) and Professor Gensichen of Halle were so successful in this endeavor that in November of 1932, one-third of the seats in the Prussian Union Church synod were won by the *Evangelische National-sozialisten* list of candidates.[14]

The GDC movement was first based in Berlin, and although it later spread out over the entire Reich, it kept a city-oriented stamp. Academic prestige was supplied by the early adherence of Professors Fabricius and Stolzenburg of the University of Berlin,[15] and later in 1932, both Paul Althaus and Emanuel Hirsch also joined. If the *Christlich-Deutsche Bewegung* was characterized by its elite social base, the GDC generally reflected a much lower stratum--in fact, a leveling tendency and an egalitarian stance may be noted. Wieneke pointed out that faith movements come secretly out of the depths of society, not from the heights of *Kultur*.[16] Other GDC ideologists minimized social differences when faced with national concerns. Often this was attributed to the war experience. "The Fatherland--that means wife and child, comrades in the same front-area, in the same trenches. All differences that once had separated man--class, birth, title--they all fell."[17] With the exceptions already noted of Hirsch and Althaus, few of the GDC members could claim a national reputation. The GDC members were the "S. A." (storm troopers) of the German Christian movement.

A platform, written by Hossenfelder, was published in May of 1932, demanding a new order in the church. It called for national unity of the twenty-eight *Landeskirchen*, took its position on the basis of "positive Christianity" (point 24 of the Nazi program), and rejected Marxism, the Communist International,

26

Christian Socialism, pacifism, and Freemasonry. Most importantly, it called for the churches to help cleanse the German
Nation of the foreign blood of Jews.[18]

By September of 1932, the GDC was a highly structured organization. The organization of Prussia alone had well-defined
offices for a whole variety of church questions. Offices were
established for such areas as the press, religious education,
propaganda, youth, "personal questions," national questions,
missions, and Germans abroad [Auslandsdeutschtum].[19] The GDC
periodical, Evangelium im dritten Reich, first appeared October
16, 1932.

The GDC proved to be of particular value to the Nazi Party
in 1932 and 1933 because it was, as already noted, an opportunistic group. Unlike the Christlich-Deutsche Bewegung with
its indecisiveness, or the third movement, the Kirchenbewegung
Deutsche Christen, with its enthusiastic but unpredictable nature, the GDC always was able to put its ideology in a secondary place--below the party line.

The third major group, the Thuringian Kirchenbewegung
Deutsche Christen (hereinafter referred to as the KDC), could
trace its organizational origins back to 1927. It remained
local until about 1932 (when the title Kirchenbewegung was officially adopted). Centered in the Wiera valley of Thuringia,
the movement was led by two pastors, Siegfried Leffler and
Julius Leutheuser, who had a strong background in student
marching groups. They had fled the Bavarian Evangelical-
Lutheran Church in 1927 because their Nazi beliefs had brought
them into doctrinal conflicts with the conservative Lutheran
leadership there. Thuringia, whose church was a relatively
new amalgamation of several smaller churches, did not demand
the same kind of rigorous orthodoxy.[20]

The area of Thuringia in which the two settled was both
agricultural and industrial. With methods that can only be
called "revivalist," Leffler and Leutheuser traveled around the
Wiera valley, holding lively emotional services and discussions, appealing largely to farmers and to artisans (Handwerk-
er) who were not class conscious. Socially, the movement attracted lower strata, and the ideological results reflect this
fact. Confessional differences, even between Catholics and

Protestants, were played down in favor of a "German Church,"
Hitler was seen as a divine appearance, and the values of *Bau-erntum* and nature for religious practice were not overlooked.

In 1931, the KDC took part in Thuringian church elections,
and this marks the first time the term *Deutsche Christen* was
used in church politics. They won five of the sixteen seats at
issue.[21] In July of 1932, the KDC periodical, *Briefe an
Deutsche Christen*, first appeared.

Unorthodox in the extreme, and highly enthusiastic about
Hitler and Nazism, the core of the KDC was the most durable of
the German Christian groups. Thuringia, significantly, was the
site of Hitler's first major electoral breakthrough,[22] and this
pro-Nazi stance was reflected in KDC activity which had a long
life in Thuringia. The "Leffler movement" survived under various names until 1940.

After mid-1932, the *Glaubensbewegung Deutsche Christen* began to consider itself a national organization and began to
make contacts with other like-minded groups. During the autumn, the GDC and the *Kirchenbewegung Deutsche Christen* merged,
arrangements were made for simultaneous membership in the GDC
and the *Christlich-Deutsche Bewegung* as well as in the GDC and
the *Bund für deutsche Kirche*, and contacts were made with German Christian groups throughout the nation--in Silesia, in Hanover (*Arbeitsgemeinschaft nationalsozialistischer Pfarrer*),
Baden (*Kirchliche Vereinigung für positives Christentum und
deutsches Volkstum*), and in Nassau (*Christlich-Nationale Be-
kennerbund*).[23] For about a year, until November of 1933, the
German Christian groups presented a united front. The facade
of unity actually covered a wide divergence of ideological
stances, but allowed for important Protestant support of Hitler
when he most needed it.

When Hitler came to power at the end of January of 1933,
there were few Protestant churchmen who did not greet him enthusiastically. For several months, Hitler was able to ride
the wave of Protestant support. The easy early successes in
unification of the German Protestant churches and the begin-
nings of church *Gleichschaltung* reflected the fact that through

most of the spring and summer of 1933, Protestants overwhelm-
ingly surged toward German Christian concepts of what the
church ought to be, politically and ideologically. One observer, looking back from early 1934, after the enthusiasm had
broken apart, noted that support for the Nazis and the German
Christians had come from every quarter of the church. Not only
did the church-conservative groups, "outspoken pietists and *Ge-
meinschaftsleute*," join up, but even many of those around Barth
and the "theology of crisis," as well as some who had once been
Marxists.[24] The National Socialist German Christians seemed to
be fulfilling a role that the church had not succeeded in doing
for some time, i.e., bringing church and Volk to a better understanding of each other.[25]

Hitler's pronouncements during the early months of 1933
were encouraging to frustrated church people. On March 23,
Hitler spoke to the *Reichstag* of the regime's attitude toward
the churches:

> The national regime sees in the two Christian confes-
> sions the most important factors for the conservation
> of our Volkishness. The arrangements made between
> them and the various states will be respected. Their
> rights will not be touched. It is expected and hoped,
> however, that the work of the national and moral re-
> newal of our Volk, which is the goal of the govern-
> ment, will conversely receive the same respect....The
> national government will define and ensure the Chris-
> tian confessions their due influence in school and
> education. Their [the government's] concern is for
> the correct coexistence of state and church. The
> struggle against a materialistic world interpretation
> and for the construction of a true Volk community
> serves equally the interests of the German nation
> as those of our Christian faith....The rights of the
> churches will not be made smaller, their relation-
> ship to the state not changed.[26]

Many Germans saw in the political experience God's call to
bring the churches into line in a unified way to back up the
national renewal. Plans for uniting the Protestant state
churches now rapidly went forward. Between May 16 and 20,
some church leaders met at Loccum cloister and issued a mani-
festo which included what were later to be the essential points
of the new German Evangelical Church constitution.

> Through God's intercession, our beloved German Father-
> land has experienced a mighty exaltation. In this
> turning point in history we hear, as faithful

evangelical Christians, the call of God to a closing
of ranks and a return, the call also for a single
German Evangelical Church....The confessions are its
unalterable basis....The spatial splintering of German Protestantism will be set aside, but energetic
state churches are welcome co-workers. A national
bishop [*Reichsbischof*] of the Lutheran confession
stands at its head. At his side will work a spiritual ministry....Christ comes again and brings an
eternal completion in the majesty of his Kingdom![27]

In early April, the GDC held its first national convention
in Berlin, at which Goering, Frick, and Kube represented the
Nazi Party. The goal of a Reich-wide Protestant Church was
shared by many Germans, and brought the membership in the GDC
to new heights. During the same time, Ludwig Müller and Joachim Hossenfelder were consolidating their positions in the
good graces of the Nazi Party and as leaders of the German
Christians. Hitler appointed Müller his "Representative for
Evangelical Church Affairs" on April 25, perhaps hoping that
the ex-military chaplain could bridle the more unruly elements
of the GDC, while forming the churches into willing instruments
of the Party. Hossenfelder, who was *Reichsleiter* of the GDC,
was also given a post in the Ministry of Cults. In May, Müller
was given a stronger position in the GDC when he was appointed
its "Protector" (*Schirmherr*).[28] At this point in 1933, relationships between the Nazi Party and the GDC were still very
cordial and continued to be so until the autumn.

On May 16, the GDC presented a new platform written by
Professor Fezer of Tübingen and offering a milder tone that
more moderate Protestants could accept. Recognizing the national political renewal, the document called for a similar
movement in the church. To reach the goal of providing adequately for the German Volk, a new German Evangelical Church
constitution was called for that would reject church government
based on the democratic system of election and replace this
with "unified leadership under a spiritual *Führer* who will meet
and personally be responsible for great decisions..." The
Reformation confessions were supported, but it was asked that
they be applied to the "burning questions of the present in the
sense of a radical turning away from all erroneous teachings,
mammonism, Bolshevism, and unchristian pacifism." Racism was
toned down, although the program supported the work of

"missions to the pagans" while recognizing the variations of peoples and races as a God-willed order. A "comradely Volk community" was called for because "God has given us responsibility not only for ourselves, but also for our neighbors."[29] The mildness of the Fezer Platform provided a middle road that large numbers of German Protestants could follow.

Since the beginning of May, 1933, President Kapler of the *Kirchenbund*, Bishop Marahrens of Hanover (representing the Lutherans), and Pastor Hermann Hesse (for the Reformed Church), had been working on a new church constitution for the entire Reich. Anticipating the creation of the office of Reich bishop, the representatives of all the state churches met at Eisenach in May, and after several votes, chose Friedrich von Bodelschwingh, a well-known director of an institution for epileptics at Bethel, over the German Christian candidate, Ludwig Müller. Bodelschwingh modestly accepted the position only after objecting that he would rather have the less pretentious title of "deacon."[30]

The German Christians, however, were not prepared to accept this decision. Their opportunity to circumvent the election of Bodelschwingh came when Kapler resigned his dual position as leader of the *Kirchenbund* and of the Prussian Union Church. Thereupon, the Prussian Minister of Cults named a Nazi Jurist, August Jäger, "*Staatskommissar* for Prussian Church Affairs." Church officials were dismissed throughout the Prussian Church and replaced by German Christian sympathizers. Believing the situation to be unacceptable, Bodelschwingh resigned June 24. Four days later Ludwig Müller and the SA took over the buildings of the *Kirchenbund* in Berlin, and the committee working on the church constitution was dissolved and replaced by a new group consisting of four Lutheran bishops, four members of the GDC, August Jäger, and a few others from the Prussian Church.[31] Müller justified these unusual moves with the following declaration:

> The German Evangelical Church has been called into an emergency situation; the absolutely necessary unity of Volk and church is in danger. This emergency situation calls for extraordinary measures. With the agreement of the State Commissioner for the Prussian Evangelical State Church, I am taking on, for the good of the Church and its Gospel, the title of

Authorized Agent [*Bevollmächtiger*] of the Reich
Chancellor for the leadership of the Evangelical
Kirchenbund...[32]

A new constitution was adopted on July 14. It provided
for a Lutheran Reich bishop who would be aided by a three-man
"Spiritual Ministry" (one Lutheran, one Reformed, and one
United), and a National Synod whose representatives would be
sent from the state churches (two-thirds) and also elected from
the total church (one-third). Church laws would be a joint affair of the Spiritual Ministry and the Synod.[33] Elections to
the Synod were to be held on July 23. The Party called for all
of its Protestant members to cast their votes for the GDC candidates.[34] Hitler himself broadcast over the radio the eve of
the elections, and though carefully dissociating himself from
confessional comments, asked that the German Christians be supported.[35] The German Christians won everywhere as expected,
claiming almost two-thirds of all votes cast. On August 4, the
Senate of the Prussian Union Church elected Ludwig Müller as
its President and gave him the title "*Landesbischof*." A month
later the state synod confirmed this decision, adopted an
"Aryan paragraph" in its by-laws, and superseded the General
Superintendencies by carving up the Prussian Church into ten
bishoprics--each held by a German Christian luminary.[36] As the
Prussian Church had half of Germany's Protestants in its membership, its control by the GDC was an important step in the
attempt at *Gleichschaltung* of the churches. On September 27,
the first national German Evangelical Church Synod met at Wittenberg. Müller was formally elected as *Reichsbischof* and
chose his "Spiritual Ministry" which included the thirty-four
year old Hossenfelder for the United Congregations, fifty-two
year old Bishop Schöffel of Hamburg for the Lutherans, and
thirty-one year old Pastor Weber of Elberfeld for the Reformed.[37] Adopted at the same time was an "Aryan paragraph"
modeled on the Prussian Church example which had stated that,

> Who is not of Aryan background or is married to some-
> one of non-Aryan background cannot be called as either
> a pastor or officer of the general church structure.
> Pastors and officers of Aryan parentage, who have en-
> tered into marriage with a person of non-Aryan parent-
> age, will be dismissed.

This injunction could be circumvented only for those who had been pastors or church officials before August 1, 1914, or who had fought on the front during the war or lost fathers or sons in the war.[38] The Aryan paragraph, along with the disdain for many of the German Christian personalities, was the instigation for the founding, by Martin Niemöller and friends, of the opposition group (*Pfarrernotbund*) that fought German Christian politics and was the kernel of what later became known as the "Confessional Church."

Church unity was short-lived and by late September of 1933, what once appeared to be irreversible German Christian success began to show signs of cracking. One of the most important events in German Christian development took place on November 13, in the Berlin *Sportpalast* where 20,000 German Christians had gathered to hear speeches from leaders of the GDC. It was a militant atmosphere, and measures were adopted by vote that were especially harsh in their anti-Semitism. One of the featured speakers, who had come to the GDC from the *Bund für deutsche Kirche*. In a speech that was continually interrupted by applause, Krause called for

> the completion of Martin Luther's goal in a second
> German Reformation, the result of which will not be an
> authoritarian pastoral church with its confessionally-
> characterized bonds; rather, only a German Volk church
> can result, that has enough room for the whole spec-
> trum of a relevant [*artgemässen*] experiencing of God,
> while at the same time in its outer form is built in
> such a completely German way as is obviously neces-
> sary in the Third Reich.

Krause believed that only very radical methods could accomplish this goal.

> ...The first step toward this becoming relevant is
> the freeing from all things unGerman in the service
> of God and confessions, a freeing from the Old Tes-
> tament with its Jewish reward-morality, from these
> stories of cattle herders and pimps [*Viehhändler-
> und Zuhältergeschichten*]. People have rightfully
> pointed out this book as one of the most question-
> able books of world history....If we National Social-
> ists are ashamed to buy a tie from a Jew then we
> must also rightfully feel ashamed to accept from
> Jews something that is supposed to speak to our soul,
> to our innermost religious being....It will also be
> necessary for our state church to be concerned with
> distancing itself openly from all disfigured and

counter-faithful accounts of the New Testament and
reject basically the whole scapegoat theology and
theology of inferiority [*Sündenbock- und Minder-
wertigkeitstheologie*] of the Rabbi Paul....[39]

After the excitement of the meeting died down, the next
few days found German Christian members everywhere in a complete state of confusion. Krause's ideas were not in the main-
stream of German Christian thought (Krause himself soon moved
into non-Christian religious areas and founded a new group, the
Glaubensbewegung Deutsche Volkskirche), but the victims were
the movement and leaders of the GDC who had allowed the drift
toward Krause to take place.

Even the Nazi Party began to realize that the GDC was becoming more of a liability than an asset in bringing about
church quiescence, and in a series of actions, the Party established a stance of neutrality.[40] On November 27, the Nazi
press issued a statement slapping the hands of the GDC:

National Socialism is the outlook of the whole Volk....
It is therefore erroneous if church groups believe that
they alone represent National Socialism, or if they
make use of this concept for the carrying on of theological argumentation....The National Socialist movement has always said that it will not be a religious
movement, and the Führer has always denied that he
would want to be a religious Reformer.[41]

The more moderate members of the GDC also reacted strongly
to the events of November 13. Reich bishop Müller, who had
been trying to control more extreme GDC leaders since September, now forced Krause to resign his church office, and on November 15, Müller ordered that all Evangelical Churches were to
adhere to the Bible and the Reformation confessions, and to
stay out of politics.[42] During the next month, the GDC rapidly
disintegrated into a host of smaller groups. The German Christian *Landesbischof* of Saxony led a group out, changed its name
to *Volksmissionarische Bewegung Sachsens*, and adopted a new
platform. The Bavarian German Christian pastors left about the
same time, as did those in Wurttemburg. Most importantly, virtually all of the "name" theologians dissociated themselves
from German Christian activities. These included Professors
Fezer, Weiser, Rückert, and G. Kittel from Tübingen, Heinrich

Bornkamm and Ernst Haenchen of Giessen, several from the University of Halle, and Friedrich Gogarten.[43]

Müller, in a desperate move to maintain the dignity of his office, used Hossenfelder as a scapegoat and fired him from his position as member of the Reich bishop's Spiritual Ministry and *Reichsleiter* of the GDC. Müller himself resigned as *Schirmherr* of the GDC on December 6.[44]

At the end of 1933, German Christian affairs were in bad shape. The GDC had been abandoned even by its "protector," although this did not mean that Müller had abandoned his pro-Nazi position. On December 20, Müller handed over the 600,000 member "Evangelical Youth" church group to Baldur von Schirach, leader of the "Hitler Youth," justifying the move because "the new unity of our Volk must be ensured according to the will of the *Führer* through a unified education of our youth." It would be an injustice, Müller pointed out, to deprive Protestant youth of working for the good of the Volk. The parents should encourage their children in the transition. "Tell them that they will do a great service to their Savior and Master if they conduct themselves as virtuous boys and girls."[45]

The year 1933 was the central year for the German Christian movement, as it was for German political affairs. The legacy of the activities of 1933 was not what the German Christians had hoped. Instead of a German Evangelical Church united behind the political regime, the lasting result of the GDC was that church affairs were to be chaotic until 1945, and a constant embarrassment for the Nazi regime.

The German Christians were by no means at an end after 1933, but branched out again into splinter groups, more correctly representative of the variety of ideas present in German Christianity. What the Krause speech and its aftermath showed more than anything else was that the GDC as a church-political unified front was weak because it did not represent a unified ideological stance. After 1933, no German Christian group ever again had the official support of the Nazi Party, but some of them were hopeful that the relationship could be reconstructed, and all remained committed, in their various ways, to Hitler.

At the end of 1933, the GDC got a new leadership, new name, and new platform. The jurist Christian Kinder changed

the name to *Reichsbewegung Deutsche Christen* (hereinafter referred to as the RDC) and with it changed the nature of the
movement. The third platform of the GDC had been suitable for
a *Kampfeszeit*, but not for the job ahead which was one of consolidation of the German Evangelical Church.[46] The bulk of the
new RDC platform consisted of the "Twenty-eight Theses" which
had been drawn up for the Saxon state church after the Krause
affair. Placing the movement on the basis of the "positive
Christianity" of the Nazi Party Program, the theses affirmed a
separation, but not neutrality, of church and state. The importance of blood and race were recognized, as was the Aryan
paragraph of the church by-laws, but this was tempered by saying that "the Christian of another race is not a Christian of a
lower rank, but simply a Christian of a different type." It is,
however, God's commandment that race be kept pure, and interracial marriages are especially to be forbidden. The bases of
the church are the Bible and confessions, but "the Old Testament does not have the same value" (as the New Testament), and
the Reformation confessions were noted to be bound up with the
questions of particular historical circumstances. "Not back to
the faith of the fathers, but forward in the faith of the
fathers!" The Volk church is to turn away from liberalism in
theology, neo-orthodoxy, or attempts to replace Christianity
with religion based on the race experience.[47] The RDC was a
compromise between affirmation of the Nazi experience, and the
moderate, traditional Lutheran beliefs. Kinder went to great
lengths to show that no one was to be forced to adhere to any
or all of the RDC principles.[48] Actually, the moderate ideas
of the RDC also made it a very boring program, and the RDC de-
clined in influence.[49]

Late in 1934, Joachim Hossenfelder and Friedrich Wieneke
tried a comeback with a new organization, the *Kampf- und
Glaubensbewegung Deutsche Christen*, which, however, did not
have the support of the Nazi Party and was unable to gain much
influence, except in northern Germany, with its attempts to
build up militant German Christian cells based on the *Führerprinzip.*[50]

Another German Christian movement was centered in Bremen
and headed by the State Bishop Heinz Weidemann, who had

ambitions of being *Reichsleiter* of a renewed German Christian
movement. When conflicts over his church-political position
arose in the RDC in mid-1935, he founded his own organization--
the "*Niederdeutsch Deutsche Christen*" (also called "*Kommende
Kirche*"). In some ways, the ideas of this movement were close
to those of the *Kirchenbewegung Deutsche Christen*, especially
as to the question of playing down confessional differences between German Catholics and Protestants, and the desire for a
new Reformation.[51] Weidemann's ideas remained on paper, however, and his influence never got much beyond Bremen.

Meanwhile, larger Protestant church developments were taking place in Germany. With the failure of the GDC to bring
unity to the churches, the unwillingness of certain state
churches to toe the Reich Bishop's line, the outright refusal
of some Confessionals to work with German Christian leaders,
and the foundation of a "Provisional Church Government" by non-
German Christian Lutheran bishops, Hitler and his aides decided
to put the church question "on ice."[52] On July 16, 1935, Hanns
Kerrl, a long-time supporter of Hitler, was authorized to deal
with church concerns through a new "Ministry of Church Affairs."
Kerrl knew that the GDC and Müller had failed in the all-
important task of unifying the Protestant churches, and after
wiping the slate clean by offering amnesty to all pastoral dis-
sidents, he set up a series of Committees [*Kirchenausschüsse*]--
a national one, and several for state churches.[53] General
Superintendent Zoellner, who was respected in all quarters of
the church and had no German Christian background, was appointed as chairman of the national committee. Zoellner tried to
appeal to both the German Christian and Confessional sides in
the church controversy. In his call to unity, the two positions were both represented.

> ...The absolute basis of the German Evangelical Church
> is the Gospel of Jesus Christ, as it is set forth in
> the Holy Bible and newly interpreted in the confes-
> sions of the Reformation. All the works of the Church,
> including its theology and its structure, must serve
> the announcements of this Gospel.
> Out of this unity of faith we admonish and ask
> the Evangelical congregation to stand in interces-
> sion, faith, and obedience, with the Volk, Reich,
> and *Führer*. We affirm the National Socialist de-
> velopment of the people on the basis of Race, Blood,

and Soil. We affirm the will for freedom, national
worth, and socialistic sacrificial readiness for
life-long devotion to the Volk community. We recognize therein the God-given truth of our German Volk.[54]

This combination really satisfied neither side, however. Constant criticism by Confessional leaders resulted in Kerrl's
calling in the police to confiscate funds of the Confessional
movement and to impose censorship on Confessional publications.
Both propagandizing and special training of seminarians were
proscribed on December 2, 1935.[55] On the other hand, Zoellner
did not feel that he got the full support of the government
either, and resigned his position on February 12, 1937.

The German Christian relations with the church committees
took two directions. The RDC decided to cooperate fully and
was, in return, found to be free of errors by a theological
committee of the Reich Church Committee. But the Thuringian
German Christian movement (the KDC) did not receive the same
imprimatur and was roundly condemned because its "...false
identification of Volk and church arises from a false identification of Volk history and sacred history [Heilsgeschichte]."[56]
Kurt Meier has shown how this selectivity was designed to undermine the German Christian state church regimes still in
power in Thuringia and Mecklenburg.[57] The actual result was,
however, the end of RDC influence among dedicated German Christians who thought that there had been a sell-out to church
moderates, and a general German Christian move closer to KDC
leadership, because the KDC was seen as the unjustly accused
scapegoat. In short, convinced German Christians no longer had
any use for the luke-warm ideas of the RDC, and those who had
once been moderate German Christians found the Church Committee
situation as congenial as RDC membership.

In the autumn of 1935, leadership of the RDC was assumed
by Wilhelm Rehm whose moderate rule lasted until the end of
1938. With his resignation in October, 1938, the RDC collapsed
and was replaced by the "Luther-Deutschen," an organization
that can be identified as "German Christian" only with difficulty.[58]

The future for a viable German Christian outlook after
1933 was with what previously had been a very limited organization, geographically speaking. The Thuringian German Christian

movement (the KDC) was one of the groups that split from the
GDC shortly after Krause's speech of November, 1933. But certainly the leaders of the KDC had different reasons from most
for steering an independent course. Ideologically, the KDC
never put a premium on orthodoxy, and the ideas presented by
Krause were not the object of their attack. On November 24, an
open letter from Siegfried Leffler to Hossenfelder clearly put
the blame for unrest in the church on the emphasis placed by
the GDC on power politics in the church.

> And that you confess yourselves clearly to stand on
> the Bible, we value that highly in a time when the new
> can only develop on the certain tracks of the apostolic
> prophetic history of the past. But we need more than
> declarations and assurances; the world today asks the
> question: what is Christ? And to that you have thus
> far had only one answer: a purely church-political one.
>   You have toppled old church princes! Certainly,
> that had to be! And you and your Berlin friends have
> grabbed up bishoprics and bishops' thrones. But you
> really have brought nothing else.[59]

On December 11, 1933, the KDC issued its own platform,
which is basically different from any other German Christian
ideas. The German Christian is to believe simply in the Savior
Jesus Christ, the power of his cross and resurrection. "Jesus'
life and death teaches us that the way of struggle is at the
same time the way of love and the way to life." God has put
Germans in their community of blood and faith. "Germany is our
task, Christ our power!" God reveals himself in the Bible and
in the faith experiences of our forefathers. "The Old Testament is an example of divine Volk education," and has value because it helps us to understand Christ. "As is the case for
every people, our Volk has been given its own appropriate [art-
eigenes] law created by the eternal God. It won expression in
the Führer Adolf Hitler and in the National Socialistic state
that he formed." The German law can be fulfilled in the faithful German congregation [Gemeinde]. "In it alone does the
Savior come to the German Volk and give us the power of faith.
Out of this union [Gemeinde] of German Christians shall grow,
in the National Socialist state of Adolf Hitler, the 'German
Christian National Church' [Deutsche Christliche National-
kirche] that will embrace the entire Volk."[60]

If the RDC was steadily dying in the years after 1933, the KDC was picking up German Christian support throughout the Reich. The "Old Guard" of the German Christian membership was disenchanted by the moderate course plotted by the post-Krause RDC, and gravitated toward Leffler and Leutheuser who, it was thought, had maintained contact with the old values of German Christianity. Almost everywhere interest in KDC affairs rose in proportion to the decline in influence of the RDC. German Christian bishops and church officials who had been installed in their positions in the halcyon days of 1933 felt increasingly threatened, especially after the institution of church committee government. With the RDC out of church politics and actually supporting Zoellner's governmental structures, ambitious German Christian leaders found it necessary to support the KDC.[61]

In 1935, there were abortive attempts to unite the KDC and the RDC--attempts to reestablish a unified German Christian organization. After discussions between Kinder for the RDC and Leffler, a jointly-signed announcement was published on July 13, 1935.

> We have the great common work, the great common goal: the cordial [herzensmässige] uniting of all Germans into a Christian community [Christusgemeinde] of Germans. Rising above all the things that separate us, we have put ourselves together in the same service. Honor to the living God demands that of us. We are brought to this position by love of our Volk....[62]

Leffler was under the impression that he would become Reichsleiter of the new German Christian movement, but Kinder was in no position to make such promises. Kinder was replaced by Wilhelm Rehm as leader of the RDC, and Rehm cut off the negotiations with the KDC and supported the formation of the church committee structure. Leffler angrily accused the RDC of playing politics and not being serious about the one "Christian congregation of Germans." "The people throughout the land have been waiting for bread; the church politicians have given them stones."[63] Never again would the KDC try, or need, a reconciliation with the RDC.

The KDC emerged from the mid-1930's as the center of a new national German Christian organization. In the spring of 1936,

Leffler made contacts with Hossenfelder and Weidemann of Brem-
en. The three formed what was known as a *Führerring*. Soon
thereafter, the Saxon German Christian group, under their leader Walter Grundmann, also gained entrance to the group (in June,
1936, the Saxon German Christians officially became part of the
KDC). During the summer, the addition of groups from Mecklenburg, the Rhineland, Anhalt, and the *Gau* of Greater Berlin,
caused a change of the name of the administrators to *Führer-
kreis*. Rules for affiliation were loose (Hossenfelder kept his
group more independent than the rest) but Leffler's KDC was the
recognized center of the new confederation.[64]

In November of 1936, the development continued, and the
Bund für deutsches Christentum was formed, more for church-
political and legal interests than for ideological reasons.
Comprised of the state churches of Thuringia, Mecklenburg, Lü-
beck, and Anhalt, with the looser contacts in Bremen and Olden-
burg, the *Bund* was centered in Berlin.[65]

The KDC and some others were not satisfied with just an
organizational unity of German Christianity, but hoped for
ideological coordination as well. Leffler and his associates
founded the *Nationalkirchliche Bewegung Deutsche Christen*
(hereinafter referred to as the NKBDC) in early June of 1937.
The Baden German Christians had already agreed to join; others
in the Rhineland, Wurttemburg, and Mecklenburg followed soon
thereafter, and most of those who had been in the *Bund* (excluding Weidemann's group) eventually also joined.[66] The program
(*Leitsätze*) stressed the transconfessional hopes of the movement as well as the call for the setting aside of Jewish and
foreign ideas in the church. Christ was characterized as the
deadly enemy of Judaism.[67] The emphasis on anti-Semitism reflected, no doubt, an accommodation to the many groups involved
in the organization. Although there was anti-Semitism present
in earlier KDC publications, it had not earlier been an integral part of their ideology.

In the larger German Protestant Church situation, the
later years of the 1930's were characterized by lack of policy
on the part of the state. The Reich Church Committee had been
attacked from both German Christian and Confessional sides--
though both attackers found it impossible to get unanimity of

opinion within their own ranks regarding cooperation or non-cooperation. In addition, the political *Gauleiter* of two states (Sauckel of Thuringia and Hildebrandt of Mecklenburg) supported the KDC against Church Committee attacks. Even Kerrl, head of the Reich Church Ministry, could not make up his mind which side to support. After Zoellner resigned, and the Church Committee structure collapsed, Hitler ordered on March 15, 1937, that churches would have to decide for themselves, through elections, their future form of government. The elections were postponed twice and never held.[68] After 1937, a Nazi jurist, one Dr. Werner, was appointed President of the Reich Church and of the Prussian Church, and with the help of the German Christian bishop Schulz and Lutheran bishop Marahrens of Hanover, church affairs were loosely administered with decreasing tension.

The high-point of the influence of the KDC was reached in March of 1939, when members of the NKBDC and "middle" groups of Protestant pastors and laity came together to sign the so-called "Godesberg Declaration." After duly noting that Hitler had brought Germany out of slavery to freedom and majestic greatness, the document condemned church strife, but found that it at least reflected a new awakening of religious life. The main part of the declaration consisted of three points. First, to the question of the correct relationship of the Nazi world outlook and the Christian religion, it was answered that Nazism had led the work of Martin Luther forward and helped the German people again to a true understanding of Christian faith. Second, as to the question of the relationship of Judaism and Christianity, the answer was that "the Christian faith is the unbridgeable religious opposite of Judaism." Finally, to the question of the "internationalism" of Christianity, it was asserted that "International Churchdom of a Roman or Genevan type is a political degeneration of Christianity."[69] Although the term "National Church" did not appear in the document, it shows the influence of KDC ideas.

One of the projects which came out of the Declaration was the establishment on May 6, 1939, of the "Institute for the Research and Elimination of Jewish Influences in German Church Life [*Institut zur Erforschung und Beseitigung des jüdischen*

42

Einflusses auf das deutsche kirchliche Leben]." Professor
Walter Grundmann of Jena opened the first meeting with this
statement:

> The German hour, in which we find ourselves, is an
> epochal time of world-wide significance, in which the
> final and deepest question will be asked. For the
> given religion of the German people [Christianity]
> that today has to prove its life value and life power,
> the question is, how does it stand toward that enemy[70]
> of German life and the renewal of the West--Judaism.

It is astounding how many well-known scholars participated from
virtually every theological school in Germany, including among
others, Professors Bertram of Giessen, Hempel and Wobbermin of
Berlin, and Gerhard Kittel of Tübingen.[71] The Institute was
the last unified effort of the German Christians. With the
coming of the war, other affairs besides church interests took
the time of German Christian members. After June of 1941, German Christian periodicals were not allowed to appear. This
signalled, for all practical purposes, the end of the German
Christian development.

The chronological development of the German Christians
shows in itself a certain typological development. Only a very
fragile unity existed in 1933, and the events of November of
that year showed how diverse the groups really were. The lack
of unity in German Christian church-political goals ultimately
reflects very different ideological interest. German Christian
ideas spanned a wide spectrum and thereby attracted quite different personalities, both in intellectual and social terms.
Although a wide variety of ideas can be collectively classified
as "*Deutsche Christen*," it is possible to distinguish three
different ideological types--conservatives, opportunists, and
revolutionaries. These types existed simultaneously as early
as 1932, but there was also a chronological movement from the
predominance of conservative to the acceptance of starkly radical ideas. The order of presentation here is thus not simply
a typological one, but also reflective of an historical trend.
Usually, individual ideologists maintained their basic stances
throughout; conservatives, for instance, became less vocal as
German Christian ideas moved to the left. But in a few cases,
ideologists accommodated their ideas to new circumstances.

When this is the case, they must be presented in their several
idea-realms.[72]

What follows is an ideological analysis of three types of
German Christian groups. The first group, the CDB, dealt with
three characteristic ideas: the necessary connection of Lutheran Protestantism and *Deutschtum*, theology and order, and war
and anti-pacifism. In the working out of these concepts, this
group showed itself to be thoroughly conservative--theological-
ly and politically.

The ideas of the second type of German Christians, represented here by the GDC, centered on "Positive Christianity,"
the possibility of utilizing the *Führerprinzip* in the church
along with its call for Protestant church unity, and its characteristic views regarding anti-Semitism and the Old Testament.
The ideas that the GDC offered paralleled its political depen-
dency and exhibited a strong stamp of opportunism.

Finally, ideological radicalism is represented by the KDC
whose views showed its members' interest in such concepts as
the revelation of God in modern and contemporary history, natural and agricultural imagery in religion, and the desire for
a non-denominational German church.

The hope is to present ideological types rather than detailed information on the ideologists themselves. To eliminate
unnecessary complexity, details concerning the background of
individual ideologists can be found following the text in a
chapter of short biographies.

1. As many of the important members did not affiliate until early 1932 when the journal *Glaube und Volk* (Hereinafter shortened in footnotes to *GuV*) was started, one could say that 1932-33 is a more accurate gauge of the CDB's life span.

2. Rendtorff was one of six pupils chosen to be classmates of the Kaiser's brother's son (Prince Heinrich's son, Waldemar). His father was President of the *Gustav-Adolf Verein* (missionary activities among Catholic Germans), and his uncle, Adolf Schlatter, taught New Testament courses at Tübingen. Paul Toaspern, ed., *Arbeiter in Gottes Ernte: Heinrich Rendtorff. Leben und Werk* (Berlin: Christlicher Zeitschriftenverlag, 1963), pp. 14-16.

3. Buchheim, *Glaubenskrise*, p. 60.

4. Paul Althaus and Emanuel Hirsch, "Evangelische Kirche und Völkerverständigung: Eine Erklärung," *Theologische Blätter*, X, No. 6 (June, 1931), 177-78.

5. "Richtlinien der 'Christlich-deutschen Bewegung,'" *GuV*, I, No. 5 (May 15, 1932), 78-79. The platform is more readily available in Hermann Sasse, ed., *Kirchliches Jahrbuch für die evangelischen Landeskirchen Deutschlands*, LIX, (1932), 75-76.

6. *Ibid.*

7. *Allgemeine Evangelische-Lutherische Kirchenzeitung*, LXV, No. 4 (January 22, 1932), 114.

8. "Die Christlich-deutsche Bewegung zur Kirchenpolitik," *GuV*, I, No. 7 (July 15, 1932), 112.

9. "Nachwort," *GuV*, I, No. 7 (July 15, 1932), 112.

10. Wieneke, *Glaubensbewegung*, p. 9.

11. Heinrich Rendtorff, "Die Christlich-Deutsche Bewegung zum kirchlichen Lage," *GuV*, II, No. 6 (June 15, 1933), 102-05.

12. Meier, *Deutschen Christen*, pp. 84-85.

13. *GuV*, II, No. 9 (September 15, 1933), 178.

14. The story of the early development of the GDC (to 1933) is easily available in Buchheim, *Glaubenskrise*, pp. 70-78, and Meier, *Deutschen Christen*, pp. 10ff. The "official" German Christian accounts are Wieneke, *Glaubensbewegung*, pp. 5-12, and Dannenmann, *Geschichte*, pp. 14ff.

15. Wieneke, *Glaubensbewegung*, p. 12.

16. *Ibid.*, p. 6.

17. Walter Grundmann, *Gott und Nation: Ein evangelisches Wort zum Wollen des Nationalsozialismus und zu Rosenbergs Sinndeutung* (2d ed.; Berlin: Furche-Verlag, 1933), p. 12.

18. Hossenfelder's *Richtlinien* can be found in several places: Joachim Beckmann, ed., *Kirchliches Jahrbuch für die Evangelische Kirche in Deutschland*, LX-LXXI (1933-34), 4-6; Joachim Hossenfelder, *Unser Kampf*, No. 1 of *Schriftenreihe der "Deutsche Christen,"* (Berlin-Charlottenburg: Max Grevemeyer Verlag, 1933), pp. 6-7; Dannenmann, *Geschichte*, pp. 37-41; *Die Christliche Welt*, XLVI, No. 17 (September 3, 1932), 807-08; Cochrane, *Church's Confessions*, pp. 222-23 (in English).

19. Footnote in Meier, *Deutschen Christen*, p. 316.

20. Biographical information on Leffler and Leutheuser is from a footnote in Meier, *Deutschen Christen*, pp. 312-13. The story of the early development of the KDC can be found in Meier, *Deutschen Christen*, pp. 2-10, Buchheim, *Glaubenskrise*, pp. 48-59, and Van Norden, *Kirche*, p. 25.

21. Meier, *Deutschen Christen*, pp. 3,6.

22. David Schoenbaum, *Hitler's Social Revolution: Class and Status in Nazi Germany 1933-1939* (Garden City, New York: Anchor Books, Doubleday & Company, Inc., 1967), p. 34.

23. Meier, *Deutschen Christen*, p. 13.

24. Hermann Mulert, "Kirchliche Leben des Jahres 1933," in *Die Christliche Welt*, XLVIII, No. 1 (January 1, 1934), 14. Mulert described Asmussen, Hans Beyer, Fezer, and Gogarten as among the "theology of crisis" people who were swept up by the Nazi fever, though, it should be noted, for some it was a short infatuation, and all of the above named left the German Christians by the end of 1933.

25. *Ibid.*, pp. 13-14.

26. *Allgemeine Evangelische-Lutherische Kirchenzeitung*, LXVI, No. 14 (April 7, 1933), 331. Also in Beckmann, *Kirchliches Jahrbuch*, p. 13.

27. Beckmann, *Kirchliches Jahrbuch*, pp. 15-16.

28. Buchheim, *Glaubenskrise*, pp. 94-95.

29. Kurt Dietrich Schmidt, *Die Bekenntnisse und grundsätzlichen Äusserungen zur Kirchenfrage des Jahres 1933* (Göttingen: Vandenhoeck & Ruprecht, 1934), pp. 143-44. Also in *Allgemeine Evangelische-Lutherische Kirchenzeitung*, LXVI, No. 21 (May 26, 1933), 496-97; *Die Christliche Welt*, XLVII, No. 11 (June 3, 1933), 525-26; Andreas Duhm, *Der Kampf um die deutsche Kirche: Eine Kirchengeschichte des Jahres 1933-34, dargestellt für das evangelische Volk* (Gotha: Leopold Klotz Verlag, [1934]), pp. 102-04.

30. Buchheim, *Glaubenskrise*, pp. 98-102.

31. *Ibid.*, pp. 106-10.

32. Beckmann, *Kirchliches Jahrbuch*, p. 17.

33. For a German Christian analysis of the new church constitution, see Duhm, *Kampf*, pp. 41-48.

34. *Völkischer Beobachter*, July 19, 1933, p. 1.

35. Beckmann, *Kirchliches Jahrbuch*, pp. 21-22.

36. Buchheim, *Glaubenskrise*, p. 120. Hossenfelder became Bishop of Brandenburg; see Meier, *Deutschen Christen*, p.27.

37. Buchheim, *Glaubenskrise*, p. 121.

38. Beckmann, *Kirchliches Jahrbuch*, pp. 24-25.

39. Duhm, *Kampf*, pp. 84-85.

40. Conway, *Nazi Persecution*, pp. 54-55.

41. Meier, *Deutschen Christen*, p. 52.

42. Buchheim, *Glaubenskrise*, p. 131.

43. Meier, *Deutschen Christen*, pp. 44, 48. For the reasons for leaving the GDC, see "Warum die drei Tübinger Professoren aus den 'Deutschen Christen' austraten," *Allgemeine Evangelische-Lutherische Kirchenzeitung*, LXVI, No. 49 (December 8, 1933), 1146-48.

44. Buchheim, *Glaubenskrise*, pp. 141, 144.

45. Beckmann, *Kirchliches Jahrbuch*, pp. 33-35.

46. Schmidt, *Bekenntnisse* 1933, pp. 176-77.

47. Beckmann, *Kirchliches Jahrbuch*, pp. 30-32.

48. Meier, *Deutschen Christen*, p. 63. This is the theme of Christian Kinder's retrospective book, *Volk vor Gott: Mein Dienst an der Deutschen Evangelischen Kirche* (Hamburg: Hanseatische Verlagsanstalt, 1935).

49. In a series of geographical surveys of the various state churches, Meier, *Deutschen Christen*, very effectively shows how the RDC lost control of the German Christian-minded people to other groups.

50. Meier, *Deutschen Christen*, pp. 93-101.

51. Heinz Weidemann's development and ideas are summarized in Meier, *Deutschen Christen*, pp. 100-05. A collection of his essays, articles, and sermons, taken from the periodical *Kommende Kirche*, may be found in *So sieht die kommende Kirche aus* (3d ed.; Bremen: Verlag Kommende Kirche, 1940).

48

52. Wilhelm Stapel, "Zur Neuordnung der evangelischen Kirche," *Deutsches Volkstum*, (November, 1935), p. 864.

53. This account is from Conway, *Nazi Persecution*, pp. 128-139.

54. Beckmann, *Kirchliches Jahrbuch*, p. 104.

55. Stewart Herman, *It's Your Souls We Want* (Philadelphia: Muhlenburg Press, 1943), p. 149.

56. Texts of the RDC position and of the Committee response to both the RDC and the KDC are in "Reichskirchenausschuss und Deutsche Christen," *Die Christliche Welt*, L, No. 14 (July 18, 1936), 650-66.

57. Meier, *Deutschen Christen*, pp. 138-39.

58. On the *Luther-Deutschen*, see *ibid.*, pp. 258-66.

59. The letter was originally published in the November 23 edition of *Gothaer Beobachter*, reprinted in Duhm, *Kampf*, pp. 124-29, and Buchheim, *Glaubenskrise*, pp. 140-42.

60. *Briefe an Deutsche Christen*, III, No. 1 (January, 1934), 9. Also in Beckmann, *Kirchliches Jahrbuch*, pp. 32-33.

61. For a church-by-church overview of this development, see Meier, *Deutschen Christen*, pp. 76-92.

62. *Briefe an Deutsche Christen*, IV, No. 15 (August 1, 1935), 177.

63. Siegfried Leffler, "Der Weg der Deutschen Christen," *Briefe an Deutsche Christen*, IV, No. 15 (September 15, 1935), 210b. See also the account in Meier, *Deutsche Christen*, pp. 105-109.

64. Meier, *Deutschen Christen*, pp. 145-47.

65. *Ibid.*, pp. 147-48.

66. *Ibid.*, pp. 219-25.

67. *Nationalkirche (Briefe an Deutsche Christen)*, VI, No. 30 (July 25, 1937), 237.

68. Meier, *Deutschen Christen*, pp. 209-18.

69. Document reprinted in Leon Poliakov and Josef Wulf, *Das Dritte Reich und seine Denker: Dokumente* (Berlin-Grunewald: Verlags-GmbH, 1959), pp. 191-93. Among the non-NKBDC people who signed the document were Professors Ellwein, Schomerus, and Helmut Kittel. The instigation for the document seems to have been a call from the Archbishop of Canterbury for a world-wide church appeal to keep peace in the world, and for a "...church clearinghouse for the counteracting of the misuse of religion for political ends."

70.   Quoted in Meier, *Deutschen Christen*, pp. 290-91.   For
the collected results of the Institute's first year of research,
see Walter Grundmann, ed., *Christentum und Judentum: Studien
zur Erforschung ihres gegenseitigen Verhältnisses--Sitzungs-
berichte der ersten Arbeitstagung des Institutes...vom 1. bis
3. März 1940 in Wittenberg* (Leipzig: Verlag Georg Wigand,
1940).

71.   Meier, *Deutschen Christen*, p. 291.

72.   Walter Grundmann, Emanuel Hirsch, and *Reichsbischof*
Ludwig Müller are examples.   The latter two were, at different
times in their careers, associated with the CDB, the GDC, and
the KDC.

PART II

THE *CHRISTLICH-DEUTSCHE BEWEGUNG*

CHAPTER III: THE NECESSARY CONNECTION OF
LUTHERAN PROTESTANTISM AND *DEUTSCHTUM*

Conservative German Christians, with historical references
always in their minds, characteristically juxtaposed Lutheran
Protestantism and Germanness. They were traditionalists who
defended the interrelationship of "throne and altar," of German
history, and of the historically developed church. In most
cases, these German Christians were not anticipating a Hitler-
ian-type revolution, but rather a return to what was thought to
be the traditions of their fathers. Nevertheless, the conservative thread was an important part of the fabric of National
Socialism. The yearning for affirmation of God and country led
to the blurring of distinctions between the two spheres to the
point where the nation and its renewal could take on religious
colorings. In the late 1920's and early 1930's when *Christlich-
Deutsche Bewegung* (CDB) members and other conservatives were
writing, the relating of Lutheranism to *Deutschtum* reflected
both a positive position and a defensive stance. The conservatives saw various enemies of the happy coexistence of Christianity and nation, and these enemies were counteracted by
showing how Lutheranism was the most German of historical ap-
pearances.

The goal of the CDB was to show that it **was** impossible to
think of German *Volkstum* without thinking of the Lutheran evangelical faith. "The peculiar form that Christianity has taken
on in its evangelical aspect derives from the meeting of German
humanity with the Gospel." The Reformation was the way the
Western peoples reached their own interpretation of the Christian message. "But this breakthrough took place in the German
Saxon blood and carried the stamp of all the liveliness of the
German Volk Ways."[1] It is possible to speak of the "congenial-
ity of Luther and Germanness." Lutheranism was, in fact, "the
German form of religion."[2]

52

For the conservative, the greatest contribution of Luther was his return to the Bible and his transformation of it into a relevant piece of literature.

> The meaning of Protestantism for the German type and growth rests, in the first instance, on placing the Bible as a German Volk book [*deutsches Volkbuch*] with its living, critical, and ever-renewing power, back into the life of our Volk.[3]

The conservatives provided the only German Christian example where the Bible in its timelessness was maintained and presented as the unalterable guidepost for contemporary living. It is a mark of the conservative German Christian mentality that the overcoming of cultural and national problems could come about only through a return to the Reformation confessions and especially to the Bible. "But when all is said [about the surface problems of one's daily life], we must still go further; individual men, as opposed to the masses and the slaves to newspapers or parties, will mature when the Bible again becomes a familiar book around the house. For this book frees one, because it can break through all human traditions and panaceas, because it places one before God and thereby gives the individual life its completely personal existence."[4] The problems of modern times would inevitably dissolve if one could only get back to the faith of the fathers. The traditional faith based on the Bible alone is prior to action. "We do not question whether the Lutheran confession is still appropriate to the present, but rather...whether the present is appropriate to Christ!"[5] To weaken the Biblicist aspect of Lutheranism would be to weaken Germanism. "In German Lutheranism the German essence (*Wesen*) unfolds most clearly," and German Lutheranism meant, for the conservatives, a renewed heeding of the Bible and the Reformation Confessions.[6]

But Luther's contributions went beyond Biblicism, they said. In his strengthening of the German language through his translation of the Bible, he furthered the self-consciousness of Germans as a national group. Goethe was correct, said one conservative German Christian, when he said, "The Germans first became a Volk through Luther."[7] One could not conceive of the great post-Lutheran German culture without Luther's prior

greatness. One after another of the CDB writers showed how
German poets and philosophers were imbued with Lutheran ideas.

> The young theologian Fichte conceived of the moral
> world as the only reality, and set up, in the place
> of the sensational attractions of the prevalent world-
> view of English-French theoreticians of perception,
> the I as the supporting mid-point of the cosmos. Only
> on the Lutheran soil could a philosophy have been vic-
> torious that set up as a basic fact the metaphysical
> results of the strong responsibility of the I. Kant's
> sublime law, that the moral allows no connection with
> the natural desires of men for good fortune, was only
> taken over from Luther's deeper commandment that is
> called for out of the fulfilling of the law "in love
> and freedom." ...The valiant affirmation of this
> world that Leibniz voiced in the statement that it
> was the best of all possible, and the overflowing
> "yes" to fate that Nietzsche also voiced out of a
> much deeper view of its torn-apart reality, stand
> under Luther's great shadow.[8]

The successes of German statecraft also had a basis in the
Reformation. "The ethos of German statecraft--Brandenburg-
Prussian--that has decisively marked the German life-constitu-
tion and intellect since the breakdown of the old Germanness
in the Thirty Years' War and up to the World War, completely
derived from evangelical Christianity."[9] Bismarck, the "Christian Statesman," by making man's earthly existence more secure,
had also fulfilled God's commandment as interpreted in a
Lutheran-Reformation way.[10]

The apologies for Lutheranism were sometimes connected
with a strong anti-Catholic bias, explainable not only because
of the hatred of Catholic politics in the Weimar Republic, but
also as a phenomenon with a four-hundred year old history. The
conservatives' anti-Catholic sentiment was based on both political and religious grounds.

> The meaning of Luther, who gave the German Bible to
> the German people, is that he cleared the way to God
> of Jesuitical-Papal barricades, and with his actions
> certainly saved Germany from declining into the for-
> eign ways of the Habsburg Spanish Empire. Without
> this liberation, the German intellectual heroes like
> Schiller and Goethe, Kant, Herder, and the others,
> could never have been, nor the Prussian kingdom and
> the Prussian state.[11]

Germany, as a Lutheran land, had been spared the lack of intellectual freedom that Catholicism had inflicted elsewhere.

"Germany was never the land of mass movements, of intellectual
uniformity and disciplining. None of the great Catholic orders
was founded on German soil."[12]   As late as 1936, long after the
political Catholicism of the Center had disappeared, the conservatives were still attacking Catholicism on religious bases.
In a pamphlet that was designed to counteract those groups
which denied that the weak, "imposed" Christianity had a place
in the new heroic Germany, Heinrich Bornkamm noted,

> We should not forget that it was an already altered
> Catholic picture of Christ that came to the Germans
> with the Catholic Church...and carried the Germans
> with it into a legalistic, moralistic practice of
> religion....The tragedy of the Christianization of
> the Germans is not that they became Christians, but
> that they became Catholic Christians and were not
> given the pure and original Gospel.[13]

Undoubtedly, anti-Catholic statements could be found in
other branches of the German Christians, but for the conservatives within the CDB, it was an integral element of their
thought—and had been an aspect of conservative Lutheranism for
a long period of time before the 1920's. The "Evangelical
Union" and *Gustav-Adolf Verein* of the late 19th century, with
which conservative Protestants had been associated, had been
imbued with anti-Catholic sentiment and had contributed to such
conversion attempts as Georg von Schönerer's Pan-German, anti-
Catholic, pro-Hohenzollern *Los-von-Rom* movement in Austria.[14]
For the members of the CDB, it was part of their conservative
viewpoint to continue an antipathy toward Roman Catholicism.

The connecting of Lutheranism and *Deutschtum* was partly a
defensive stance. Modern civilization had spawned a number of
competing ideologies, each claiming to be the legitimate representative of the needs of the German soul. The conservatives
were fearful that the traditional Protestant Christian faith of
Germany, which had already shown signs of weakness for more
than a century, would continue to decline. It was necessary to
show that Lutheranism still offered something more than the
newcomers, and that German history was nothing less than
"...the show-place of a sinister spiritual struggle...."[15]

The CDB ideologists mistrusted German mysticism. Paul
Althaus, in an attempt to discredit the modern religious mysticism of Alfred Rosenberg, Jakob Hauer, and Hermann Wirth,

denied that the history of German Volk piety had been basically along the mystical lines of Meister Eckhardt. German piety would be unthinkable without Luther. "Wittenberg was the greatest hour of our history."[16] Heinrich Bornkamm also observed that Luther was the epitome of the German soul. Though he incorporated the thought of Gottschalk, Meister Eckhardt, and Tauler into his own, Luther knew that mysticism did not go far enough. German Christianity was not to be a cult of weakness nor of "suffering soulfulness" (*Leidensseligkeit*).[17] The CDB was a self-consciously orthodox movement and, unlike other German Christian movements, was not attracted significantly into more unstructured religious concepts.

Generally, the CDB was also sceptical of liberal theology or theological tampering. Although some of the members were well-known theologians (Heinrich Bornkamm, Paul Althaus, Emanuel Hirsch), they were theologically conservative and were associated with the post-war "Luther Renaissance" which was a reaction to what they saw to be overly speculative and culturally-bound 19th century Protestant theology. There is an element of generational conflict involved in the CDB theological position. The dividing point was World War I. The pre-war situation had been characterized by a theological liberalism that had strayed away from conservative and orthodox Lutheran teachings. But the younger and older generations had now split. "The reason for this is perfectly clear: the lost World War and the resultant suffering forced the younger generation to criticism of the older, and the upheaval in thinking, especially perhaps in perceptiveness, is noticeable in all areas of spiritual life." Questions of Biblical criticism now took second place behind a search for simple, certain piety.[18] Future theological work would have to stand firmly on the Bible and Reformation bases and forego theological tampering.[19] What some of the CDB members feared was abstraction and systematic rationalism in religion.

> Against the inclination of the pre-war era to undo
> theology into a pale historicized or psychologized
> science of religion [*Religionswissenschaft*], the
> post-war time has followed with the necessary reac-
> tion to a resolute turning to systematics. Already,
> however, the danger can be noted of a one-sided
> reliance on systematics, which results when one

> distances himself from concrete reality and values
> too little the meaning of history as the ever new
> revelation of God.[20]

This over-reliance on systematics on the one hand and liberal
theological speculation on the other was not limited, in the
view of the CDB, to the universities. The CDB had little use
for the attempts to identify German religion with only margin-
ally Christian ideas which were associated with the *Bund für
deutsche Kirche*. The problem of the BDK was that it was too
much imbued with liberal theology and modern Enlightenment
reasoning. "And this faith in the goodness of man--even of
the German man--this faith in the perfectibility of man--even
of the Nordic man--is for us really no longer possible." The
BDK thesis, that man can experience God in his own mind (*Geist*),
was seen as basically false. Furthermore, the BDK did not support Luther, said the conservatives, by claiming that it wanted
to complete what he had started.[21] Even the well-known theologian Emanuel Hirsch had little respect for the idea that human reason ultimately was of value in the religious sphere.

> ...No, reason and freedom are in themselves not unity-
> creating things, but rather are characterized by mani-
> foldness and opposition. Why is this? Because rea-
> son and freedom have in themselves no binding author-
> ity. Reason is, in its living historical movement, a
> restless, critical thing. What it seizes on, it dips
> into its own peculiar delight of discussion....That is
> the great contradiction on which the regal dream of
> philosophy as science [*Wissenschaft*] has shattered.[22]

What liberal theology and its successors had really done, the
CDB writers thought, was to knock the essential props (the
Bible and Reformation faith) out from under German Christianity. Luther and Lutheran piety had to be reestablished as the
only true partners of the German ways. No doubt it was true
that 19th century Biblical criticism and liberal theological
scholarship did not suffice for a generation that had lived
through a world war that seemed to them to demand a return to
sure footings. The CDB denial of liberal theology and the
critical method was, however, an overreaction.

One of the familiar aspects of German nationalism after
World War I was its condemnation of "Bolshevism"--a term that
lacked exact definition, but was associated with a

Marxistic-materialistic-godless concept of life. The CDB feared Bolshevism as a force in a modern civilization that was determined to undermine Christianity. In a sermon opening the new year, 1931, Heinrich Rendtorff warned that Bolshevism was always standing right outside the door with its goals of fighting conscience, the service of love, and belief in God. Germans were faced with the question: "For God or against God?"[23] In his "call to arms" in the first edition of *Glaube und Volk*, Rendtorff stressed that the struggle for the Volk would be led against Bolshevism.

> It is there, it lurks on our eastern frontier....It knows only the one goal of world revolution. It knows only one means for reaching this goal: the nameless masses led by terror....In politics and business, in the press and the arts, in education and marriage—a great sliding and upheaval.[24]

It is interesting that Rendtorff distinguished between Bolshevism and Marxism—the latter was the "bridge by which the spirit of Bolshevism comes to Central and Western Europe."[25] The distinction was evidently drawn because the two words meant two different things. Marxism was a fairly specific concept that represented a formal economic-historical viewpoint and was possible of definition, while Bolshevism was a catch-all word that could include a whole series of cultural problems and fears. When another CDB member presented his own analysis of the goals of the CDB, he also used both words: "We fight against anti-Christian Bolshevism; against anti-Churchly Marxism..."[26] The reaction of CDB writers to the word "Bolshevism" was not of a rational sort and can only be compared to the irrational use in other times and places of such words as "bourgeois imperialism" and "Communist." Nevertheless, the idea of Bolshevism was one that conjured up in the minds of German Christians the idea of a force that was determined to destroy Christian principles, root and branch. By bolstering Christian ideas with a strong nationalism, the conservative German Christians hoped to build up their defenses against the mysterious sinister forces which Bolshevism represented.

The post-war period was a time when theological ferment occurred not only in the churches, but also outside the Christian context. Men like Professor J. W. Hauer of Tübingen,

Arthur Bonus, and Herman Wirth actually overthrew Christian
concepts, replacing them with various interpretations of "German faith" which usually included emphases on the freedom of
the will and the peculiar spiritual strengths of the German
Volk. The claimed antecedents of these groups were people such
as Paul de Lagarde, Houston Stewart Chamberlain, and Friedrich
Nietzsche, though the last-named was probably greatly misunder-
stood. The most influential of the "German faith" groups was
the Tannenberg Bund led by General Erich Ludendorff and his
wife; it was bitterly and explicitly anti-Christian. This
group and the pagan religious ideologist, Alfred Rosenberg,
presented religions that purported to rely on the blood and
that were strongly imbued with anti-Semitism.[27] Most of the
pagan movements were associated with extreme nationalism and
with Nazism.

Although most Nazis did not subscribe to the new *ersatz*
religions, there was a fear among many church people, including
members of the CDB, that the forces of national renewal were
sliding into this enemy's camp. It became all the more important to show how the various "German faiths" were really much
less German than Lutheranism was. In 1931, an early writer for
the CDB asked whether there were perhaps too many "self-
reliant" men in the national movement. Faced with the attempts
of some to found Volkish or Germanic religions or to cut out
the unGerman aspects from Christianity, the special task of the
CDB was to bring the living God into nationalist circles. This
was every bit as important as wooing German workers away from
Marxism and materialism.[28] Much of Professor Althaus' polemical writing was done to combat a pagan or Volkish religion that
put "*volkisch*" before "God" and claimed that Christianity was
only a transient episode in German history.[29] What bothered
the CDB writers about the *ersatz* religions was that these religions completely passed over the negative, sinful side of man.
"On this basis the Christian faith is opposed to the 'Germanic
faith.' ...It is not weakness nor mistakenness that separates
man and God, but sin."[30] Again, the falseness of the *ersatz*
religions was found in their over-reliance on modern ideas of
man's self-sufficiency.

One way of counteracting the new paganism was to appeal
to history and to honored historical personages such as Ernst
Moritz Arndt, Karl Stein, and Bismarck who seemed to combine
the best of Lutheranism and Germanness. One professor quickly
traced the happy relationship of *Deutschtum* and Christianity
back to the 4th century to show the impossibility of rejecting
1500 years of historical development.[31] As already mentioned,
the CDB ideologists were fond of analyzing the inner connections of the Lutheran concepts and the ideas of the greatest
of the German thinkers, and cataloging the German poets and
thinkers who were Lutheran pastors' sons and had been trained
in theology.[32] The favorite example of the combination of
Lutheran piety and *Deutschtum*, often quoted by the conservative
CDB writer, was Bismarck, who seemed to bring together the best
of simple piety with a determined patriotism and responsible
statesmanship. Rendtorff quoted Bismarck as saying, "Politics
means listening to God's step through world history, then
springing up and attempting to catch on to a corner of His
cloak."[33] Bismarck was the ideal example of the "Christian
statesman" who knew that all earthly human actions bore the
mark of sin, but who also knew his responsibility as a Lutheran
Christian to further the state order.[34]

But the surface events of history had their limits for the
CDB ideologists who tried also to show the spiritual interconnectedness of German history, the Lutheran picture of God, and
the Gospel. Rendtorff presented the very problem of Volk existence as a problem of a relationship to God: "A Volk is only
then really a Volk, living and healthy and strong within, when
it sees and affirms its Volkishness from the depth of its conscience, when it lives its history before and under God, when
it believes. Hence faith and Volk [*Glaube und Volk*]."[35]
Emanuel Hirsch had long before established his position that
the God of the Gospel was also the God of nature and of history.
When discussing the nation and its mores [*Sittlichkeit*], he
noted, "as elsewhere, so also on this point we sense that the
God of conscience [*Gewissen*] is also the Lord of nature and
history."[36] A decade later, Paul Althaus, in a similar vein,
wrote that the German Volk, hearing the statement, "'I am the
Lord thy God,'--the God of the Old and New Covenant...'" could

assume that this was applicable to the German experience, and
that it was this God,

> ...who sent you the words of the Gospel and built its
> church among you, who made your way difficult and
> tiring, who awakened Martin Luther among you and
> made his faith strong in you, who led you back through
> prophets and heroes out of self-denial, for whom your
> forefathers waged the War of Liberation, who sent you
> freedom from your enemies, who built for you the
> house of the Reich, who caused you to fall from the
> heights and then so miraculously raised you up again,
> who gave you responsibility and service far beyond
> your borders--I am the Lord thy God![37]

It is perhaps not unusual to conceive of an omnipotent
creator God as maintaining an interest in the development of
what he created. The danger for the German Christians was that
they claimed to know the design, and interpreted German history
accordingly. Not surprisingly, the movement for national renewal in the 1920's and Hitler's revolution in 1933 evoked the
response from CDB ideologists that this, too, reflected the
movement of God in history for the better. Both Althaus and
Hirsch believed that peoples and nations had their hour
[*Stunde*] when God's will touched the mundane course of history.
The trick was to recognize the event and make the most of it--
the nation might otherwise miss its cue.

> Evangelical men and women! We stand in a fateful
> hour of our Volk and our church. We feel their
> responsibility. Woe to us if the Volkish movement
> and the church fail to embrace one another as the
> worker movement and the church have not done....It
> would be the death knell of our Volkishness [*Volks-
> tum*], it would be the renunciation by the churches
> of their duty to penetrate into the world, to en-
> sure that the whole Volk be answerable before God.[38]

Hirsch had already long before noted that even a great nation
was offered its chance only once in its development. It was
necessary to be ready with the requisite special power and will
to fulfill the call.[39] For Hirsch the hour came with the National Socialist revolution.

> The present hour makes us responsible for our theology
> and church. God will ask us sometime whether we, in
> this time of secularism and atheism and erroneous be-
> lief, have shown our Volk the God of the Gospel as
> the one with whom this hour is faced and with whom
> we intend to go a new way.[40]

The Nazi experience, Hirsch believed, had given the Germans
their opportunity to see God at work in history.

> We have for the first time since the Reformation ex-
> perienced a turning point in German history in the
> great movement of Volk renewal and reconstruction,
> that is not consciously derived from evangelical
> Christianity or its depths of belief. But this
> movement is not therefore faithless; no, it has its
> certain grounding in a meeting with the living God
> who is the Lord of history, who calls to the nations
> to serve him, each in its own way.[41]

The Protestant churches could not continue their work "as if
nothing had happened." The freeing of the Volk, the breakthrough to a new historical age, meant at the same time a freeing and breakthrough of evangelical Christianity.[42]

The interpretation of history as the visible movement of
God in human affairs was a concept that could easily get out of
control. The German Christians of Thuringia (*Kirchenbewegung
Deutsche Christen*), as will be shown below, knew no restraints
on this tendency. But the CDB generally maintained its conservative outlook. When Volk and faith were combined, these
ideologists were careful to steer away from pagan overexuberance. Never did blood or nation become deities in themselves.
One of the expressed goals of the CDB was to guard against "impure nationalism that tends to distort and corrupt. Do some
ban the pagan spooks of destroyed spirits just to put new pagan
gods in their place--gods of flesh and blood?"[43] The official
platform of the CDB warned that only the Christian faith could
ultimately save the German--the "school of hard knocks" had
shown the futility of faith in parties, race, and the good will
of Germans.[44] An article that analyzed the *Tannenbergbund*
stated in no uncertain terms that Ludendorff's Nordic paganism
was of great danger, especially to the German youth, and that
his military record had given him an audience for his religious
views that he certainly did not deserve.[45] Yet there were admittedly those who strained at the bit--among them, Paul Althaus, and especially Emanuel Hirsch. For them the distinction
between divine and earthly revelation sometimes was not so
clearly drawn. "The Protestant Christian hears one and the
same God, whether he faces the call of the God of the Gospel,

or, in the great holy storm of present-day Volk happenings, finds the call of the Lord of history."[46]

The CDB ideologists believed that the German Volk and the Protestant faith needed each other to survive. They were to travel the same road and protect each other against Bolshevism, Marxism, secularism, false individualism, impure nationalism, and against a theology that tried to separate the evangelical God from the God that had brought Germany through her history. These were defensive positions, born out of a fear for survival of Lutheran Christianity. Something more substantial, more positive, had to be presented to shore up the defense. CDB ideologists thus showed how (in their view) Luther's concepts equalled German concepts (as opposed to "Western" concepts) in their inner sense. Theological ecumenism was not viable, as one writer pointed out:

> But the intellectual discussion with other nations who were in the war, perhaps still more the initial attempts with them in the setting of the so-called ecumenical movement, have convinced us that piety is not in its basics everywhere the same; that it is not just different individual non-essential dogmatic teachings that are different, but rather piety itself--the concept of the relationship of men to God--that is interpreted very differently and can actually be diametrically opposed.[47]

Lutheran concepts as interpreted by the CDB ideologists were correspondent with German concepts on a number of points. They both shared a sense of the value of community.

> Protestant community thinking, in the form of Luther's picture of the Church of God, has its mission not only in the social, but also in the churchly split of our Volk. The congregation of mutually representative priesthood [*des füreinander stellvertretenden Priestertums*] is the only hope in view of the splintered Volk community.[48]

Community was seen as a concept that did not contradict, but rather found true expression in, the Lutheran belief in the "priesthood of all believers." "The I [*Ich*] of the German man became educated to a free responsibility within the community. Not personal experience, rather the great holy acts of God were sung in the church hymns."[49]

The Lutherans and Germans were said to share a similar sense of fate and were willing to make decisions, trusting in

the eventual justification, even if these decisions seemed
"hard and dreadful."[50] The good German Lutheran furthered the
well-being of his Volk, family, and state authority, even
though he knew his actions would have on them the fate of all
earthly doings--the taint of sin and death.[51] This aspect of
the conservative position was, of course, basic to the CDB view
of earthly law and order.

Another idea, often presented by Paul Althaus, among
others, is that the Lutheran personal, unmediated relationship
to God was somehow of a peculiarly German origin, tied up with
the concept of leadership [Führertum]. "In the Lutheran belief
in the 'freedom of the Christian man' is grounded the Protes-
tant-German Führer ideal of a free conscience answerable only
to God."[52] But this aspect of the interrelationship of the
Germans and their religion even antedated the Protestant Reformation. Althaus tried to show how Reformation Protestantism
was the only natural way that Germans could face God.

> The important thing is just this: in the German soul
> lives the yearning, from the times of Heliand [a 9th
> century, Old Saxon epic poem about Christ] to the
> Reformation, to grasp this Gospel in thoroughly per-
> sonal connections in the "evangelical" you [Du] of
> pure trust, in the Protestant I [Ich] of personal
> responsibility and freedom. The first is obvious
> in the way that Germans conceive of the reality of
> God and the form of Jesus Christ. It corresponds in
> its depths to the Germanic type and makes the German
> and the Biblical, including Old Testament thought--
> which many Volkish-minded people misunderstand--so
> kindred to each other: that God is not simply the
> highest being, nor an idea, nor exclusively a law-
> giver, but the living master of history who operates
> and creates in the present. Or one might take the
> relation of the German soul to Christ: in life es-
> sence, in law, the personal relationships of fidelity
> and obedience play an important role. Everywhere
> the German sees these relationships.[53]

Although the Gospel was brought from outside, the Germans found
in it the possibility of understanding anew the German concepts
of "...Führertum, obedience [Gefolgschaft], free devotion,
trust, all the personal traits of the Germanic life-order."[54]
A year after Hitler came to power, Althaus still found it necessary to parry the attacks of anti-Christian religious groups
by pointing up the German Christian indebtedness to Nordic
Piety. Referring to the Icelandic Sagas, he noted that Germans

must believe that God is a personal friend and that Christ, as interpreted in the Lutheran-German way, fulfills this yearning for the strong *"Freund-Gott."*[55]   In the political sphere also of the late 1920's and 1930's, many Germans were yearning for someone who would represent both a friend and a center of authority.

On the other hand, both the German essence and the Lutheran religion were said to share a love of freedom. "In German Lutheranism the German essence unfolds most clearly. The German drive for freedom through the propagation of freedom of conscience...is mirrored in Lutheran church songs."[56] But it was the "German idea of freedom" that most CDB writers had in mind, and it had nothing to do with modern liberalism. Freedom to Emanuel Hirsch, for instance, resided in duty and in honor of one's God-given national order. Freedom was the affirmation of order, community, and societal obligation, not the limitation of the same.

> Were freedom to violate the *Nomos*, it would deny in
> so doing the demanded fulfilling of the god-set *Horos*
> itself, and would not be freedom, but demonism.
> That is the real meaning of the struggle today
> against individualism and liberalism....The struggle
> proceeds against the individual decision, making
> honor a delusion, to be a self-empowered individual
> and want to follow no flag, therewith separating
> one's freedom from his own honor that is given in
> community life--the honor of free enclosure and
> participation within the confines of the *Nomos*, the
> honor of leadership and following, that both serve
> the whole. He who does not hear the call of the
> flag cannot know what freedom is.[57]

This definition of freedom Hirsch finds as far back as Socrates (one of the few non-German examples he uses) who suffered judgment and death as a free man rendering honor to his national *Nomos*. Today, says Hirsch, it is the army officer who has this same deep concept of freedom as responsibility.[58] Freedom is a term that can be defined in many ways. The conservative German Christians pointed out that Lutheran belief and German traditions sought freedom, but it was a freedom of honor and of responsibility to the national community that was talked about.

Both the German essence and Lutheran Christianity appreciate the importance of strength in their respective viewpoints,--so said some of the conservative German Christian

ideologists. The emphasis on the German characteristic of
strength in religion is to be found more readily, however, in
conservative German Christian writings of the post-1933 period.
This again reflects a countering of allegations, made by the
anti-Christian groups in German society, that Christianity was
too womanly and weak to be appropriate to the German character,
but also may be seen as a desperate attempt at accommodation to
the new regime. "Evangelical faith, where it is pure, became a
cultivation and strengthening of character, a loosening of man-
liness from the bonds of all-too-human, honor-endangering self-
seeking, a freedom from fear and prejudice to upright action."[59]
Heinrich Bornkamm, another conservative Lutheran, also noted
that Lutheran Christianity was characterized by strength, not
weakness. Faith is not easy, he pointed out.

> It is a war of life and death through which every one
> who is not blunted must pass. The man Christ died,
> as Luther said so well, in order that for us the
> fight would be fought already, so that the sign of
> defeat, the cross, was changed into a sign of vic-
> tory. We are all called into this struggle, but
> everyone by himself, just as everyone will be called
> into death alone.[60]

Perhaps these are familiar comments on the surface, for Protestant Christians, but the emphasis here on "war" and "struggle"
was deliberate. The call in the third and fourth decades of
this century in Germany was for "the good fight"--and the religion of the Germans had to be responsive to this desire. Althaus somewhat wistfully pointed out that it was only in struggle that Germany seemed to be able to find unity--"...that has
always been Germany's fate, in its outer and inner beings."
This meant not only that political unity had been born only in
strife, but that Protestantism shared the same character. "It
also is a battlefield. The German Volk is no fortunate Volk,
and the Protestant church is no fortunate church. Protestantism is always only possible as a fighting church [*kämpfende
Kirche*], struggling within itself and for the unity of spiritual life."[61]

Finally, the conservatives pointed out how Lutheran Protestantism and Germanism shared the same weaknesses, sorrows,
and joys. The finding of unity only in times of emergency has
already been noted. But the weaknesses were not overemphasized.

The point the CDB writers wanted to drive home was that even in modern times the church and the German Volk had experienced things together--war and defeat, inflation and rebuilding. The Protestant church could play an important part in bringing the German people together again.[62] Germanism and Lutheran Christianity had always been natural compatriots. With the CDB hoping to identify alleged personality traits of the German people with Lutheran Christianity, there was some confusion of the two.

What were the practical results for the CDB ideologists of the alleged symbiotic relationship between Lutheranism and *Deutschtum*? First, the CDB concept of the nation as based on Volkish concepts was reinforced, to the detriment of liberal democratic ideals. Love of country was seen as an organic natural law that grew in the heart like love of parents or love of God.[63] It is instructive that both Emanuel Hirsch and Friedrich Gogarten started their writing careers with studies of Fichte--the Fichte of the *Addresses to the German Nations*.[64] Althaus, too, explicitly accepted the Fichtean view of the Volk-nation:

> Volk is what we call the life-unity of men of a similar spiritual type [*seelischer Art*], that reaches out over clan and tribe, and through natural and intellectual continuing creation reaches across the centuries. This connecting "*Seelentum*"--Fichte called it national character--is what *Volkstum* is. It appears in the language of a people, but beyond that in its entire *Kultur*, in its poetry and thought, pictures and architecture, in its order and forms, in law and constitution, in its cults and churchdom.[65]

It was an easy step from this position, for some a prior assumption, that *Volk* or *Volkstum* was the creation of God and was to be maintained and honored by good Christians. In 1931, in one of the first publications of the CDB, Rendtorff tried to take a middle stand. Was *Volkstum* to be considered holy (E. M. Arndt's "Catechism" is quoted on this) or simply an accidental outer form? Rendtorff concluded that God does work through the nations (*Völker*) to do his work on earth. But at least Rendtorff voiced the possible dangers of overexuberance on the issue.[66] In an article written a year later, however, Paul Althaus had no doubts that "...*Volk* and *Volkstum* are God's creation and gift....We cannot think of Volkishness without thanking God. We see his creative will in the Volkish

differentiation of humanity."[67] Hans Schomerus dealt with the
question of Christianity and Germanness in a number of theses
and began by asserting that "*Volkstum* is a divine order of
creation in the same sense as marriage, family, and the authorities....I am created as German to Germans in the same duty-
bound sense as man to wife."[68] The logical result of this
thinking was that one must love his Volk to love God, and vice-
versa. One cannot be true to God without being a patriot.[69]
The idea was still voiced as late as 1937, when Heinrich Bornkamm showed how the total state was not contradictory to total
adherence to the Christian Kingdom of God. The Volk and Gospel
can serve each other well. Quoting someone else, Bornkamm said,
"He who does not love his Volk, which he sees, how much less
must he love God, whom he cannot see."[70]

Yet it is characteristic of the conservative German Christian that he tried to maintain some distinction between Volk
history and sacred history (*Heilsgeschichte*)--a distinction
that is blurred by other German Christian groups. Although God
had created the Volk and ordained the state, they were not in
themselves means to salvation, but "only the tools of God for
the preservation and unfolding of this earthly, sinful, unre-
deemed life."[71] Althaus was very critical of the Thuringian
and other radical German Christian groups which did not distinguish between the once-and-for-all nature of the Scriptures and
the continuing revelation of God in history. His view of the
Old Testament was, to be sure, partly a paradigm--the history
of how a Volk had worked out its relationship to God. But more
important to Althaus was the sacred meaning of the Old Testament as once-and-for-all revelation.[72] Other CDB ideologists
subscribed to similar views, and it is this holding back from
full acceptance of the German Volk as a vehicle for salvation
that gives them the conservative stamp.

But the CDB people did not stay out of political involvement. The Volkish question, touching as it did, to their
minds, on questions of God's creativeness and the Lutheran essence, was therefore a religious question. Althaus believed,
for instance, that the churches had been too silent when the
"Versailles lie" had been forced on Germany. The church should
not shrink from political preaching.

> She must point out how self-seeking and fear of
> sacrifice and lack of discipline is the ruin of the
> Volk, how a Volk that does not obey the sixth com-
> mandment dies, how ineluctable strong law executes
> the connection of guilt and punishment in the life
> of the nations, how God with fearful earnestness
> visits the sins of the fathers on their children
> unto the third and fourth generations, including in
> the political sphere. The church today ought also
> to speak concretely about how the lack of responsi-
> bility of post-war German parliamentarism brought
> our Volk to the edge of the precipice, that its bar-
> gaining and marketing of parties at the time of the
> greatest need of our country was sin. The smashing
> of parliamentarism is truly more than a profane
> revolutionary experience. The political here has
> an ethical depth and weight. The "crisis" of par-
> liamentarism was a judgment, pure judgment. The
> church is called upon to talk about it.[73]

The assertion that the Lutheran religion and the German Volk
were natural partners in the past and present made it incumbent
on the church to take up the Volkish question and try to direct
Germany's affairs in the right direction.

Although the CDB ideologists viewed the nation from a
Volkish rather than liberal vantage point, they lacked a strong
racial sense. There are many examples, in fact, of their criticism of the paganization of blood and race. Rendtorff warned
of well-meaning patriots going off the deep end: "Now they make
of their Volk a God, before which everything else pales and re-
treats. Now they assert that their blood will save them, and
no longer recognize the fine voice of the conscience, nor the
gentle but forceful power of faith."[74]

The tendency of the conservative German Christian was to
interpret Volk development as the happy result of actions of
great men guided by God, rather than as a racial thing. The
Volk was an historical, not a racial, experience. Rendtorff
favorably reviewed Max Maurenbrecher's book, *Der Heiland der
Deutschen*, because, among other things, it did not see the correct German road to religion and closeness to God in race, but
in a recollection of German history and concepts.[75] Arnold
Dannenmann, a GDC historian, pointed out later that the CDB
never really thought through the Volk concept in terms of the
racial concepts of Paul de Lagarde and Moeller van den Bruck.[76]
The greatness of the German Volk was told by CDB people in
terms of such individuals as Luther, the Prussian kings, Kant,

Fichte, and Bismarck--all of whom, it was believed, had furthered both the German Volk ways and Reformation Christianity.

A very important reflection of the restrained, conservative nature of the CDB was the relatively minor role that anti-
Semitism played in its thought. There is nothing in the historical, as opposed to racial, view of Volk development that
necessarily calls forth anti-Semitism. Certainly, the diligent
researcher can find occasional examples in most of the CDB
ideologists. Althaus, in 1927, reflected a cautious anti-
Semitism when he said that, "it is not a matter of hatred of
Jews....It has nothing to do with blood, nor even with the
religious belief of Judaism, rather with the threat of a completely fragmented and fragmenting urbanized [*grossstädtische*]
mentality, whose bearer seems now to be above all the Jewish
Volk."[77] Although this was an irrational statement arising
from cultural despondency, it was nevertheless cautious. More
instructive is that in the two years of *Glaube und Volk*'s existence, anti-Semitism appeared very seldom, and then in equiv-
ocal language. Typical of this "incidental anti-Semitism" was
the conclusion of one patriotic article that concentrated its
guns against France. France, it was asserted, was the tool of
the international Jewish Freemasonry lodge - "Grand Orient."[78]
In another example, national leaders were called upon to save
Germany from "...Jewish-Slavic bolshevism (Marxism) and Jewish-
French materialism."[79] In the entire two years of the existence of the journal there was only one article devoted with
venom essentially to anti-Semitism. It appeared after Hitler
was in power, and was written by a man who was at the same time
an authority on the "Jewish problem" for the GDC.[80]

The CDB view of the Old Testament also reflects ultimately
its members' lack of concentration on racial prejudice. Generally, the CDB members took the position that the Old Testament
was to be retained for German Christianity, and would be given
almost equal value to that given the New Testament. An early
example of CDB writing stated unequivocally, "the CDB sees in
the Bible of the Old and New Testaments the evidence of the
revelation of the living God, who is the master of all
peoples."[81] There were variations on this theme, of course.
Althaus tended to use the Old Testament pedagogically, asking

what lessons could be learned from the Hebrews to be applied to
the present, but there is no question that he saw it as
"...once-and-for-all, certain, historically-past, *perfectum
praesens*..." revelation.[82]   Hirsch, in his CDB days, concurred
with the revelatory value of the Old Testament, noting that the
Psalms were the prayerbook of Jesus Christ, that Jesus saw himself as the fulfillment of the prophecies, and that Christ and
the Kingdom of God were Old Testament concepts.[83]   Hans
Schomerus posited the two-pronged thesis that, "without the Old
Testament Christ for us would be a horrible and injudicious
riddle in history. Without Christ the Old Testament would be
a completely indifferent religious document."[84]

The end result of the attempt by the CDB to combine
Lutheranism and *Deutschtum* was conservative in nature. Looking
back to better times, fighting a constant battle against the
disintegrating forces of modern civilization, the CDB members
were psychologically prepared more for a return to a patriotic
and religious past than for a revolution that condemned the
evils of modernity while adopting the tools of the present--
racism, industrialism, mass psychology. Ultimately, however,
a combination of hope and resignation resulted in the CDB hesi-
tatingly supporting the national Volkish renewal represented by
Hitler. For reasons related to their social base and self-
conscious orthodoxy, the CDB, nevertheless, provided for the
possibility of conservative German Christianity.

NOTES

1. Emanuel Hirsch, *Deutsches Volkstum und evangelischer Glaube* (Hamburg: Hanseatische Verlagsanstalt, 1934), p. 5.

2. Paul Althaus, *Luther und das Deutschtum* (Leipzig, 1917), pp. 5, 7, as quoted in Tilgner, *Volksnomostheologie*, p. 181. Also see Althaus, "Protestantismus und deutsche Nationalerziehung," *Evangelium und Leben: Gesammelte Vorträge* (Gütersloh: Verlag von C. Bertelsmann, 1927), p. 92, where he says,""Protestantism of a Lutheran type stands, without degrading the universal meaning of its religious bases, as a breakthrough of the Germanic spirit [*Geist*] into the history of Christianity. It is in its essential lines, cognate to the German Volk type, including its weaknesses."

3. Althaus, *Evangelium und Leben*, p. 92.

4. *Ibid.*, p. 104.

5. von Arnim-Kröchlendorff, "Mit Luther zum Sieg," *Glaube und Volk* (hereinafter referred to as *GuV*), I, No. 5 (May 15, 1932), 74.

6. *Ibid.*, p. 75.

7. Heinrich Bornkamm, *Luther und der deutsche Geist* (Tübingen: Verlag von J. C. B. Mohr, 1934), p. 15.

8. *Ibid.*, pp. 16-17.

9. Hirsch, *Deutsches Volkstum*, p. 5.

10. Walter Machleidt, "Bismarck, der christliche Staatsmann," *GuV*, I, No. 10 (October 15, 1932), 158.

11. H. von Stackelberg, "Was heisst Glauben?" *GuV*, I, No. 8 (August 15, 1932), 124.

12. Althaus, *Evangelium und Leben*, p. 99.

13. Heinrich Bornkamm, *Christus und die Germanen* (Berlin: Verlag des evangelischen Bundes, 1936), p. 14.

14. Andrew Gladding Whiteside, *Austrian National Socialism before 1918* (The Hague: Martinus Nijhoff, 1962), p. 66. A study of the actual connections which undoubtedly exist between the *Los-von-Rom* movement and German Christian movements would be an interesting study of the history of their common ideas. Hitler, by the way, attributed the failure of von Schönerer's Pan-Germanism partly to its foolish attempts at Protestant proselytism in Catholic Austria. See *Mein Kampf* (Boston: Houghton Mifflin Company, 1943), pp. 109-19.

72

15. Heinrich Rendtorff, "Kampfaufgaben," *GuV*, I, No. 1 (January 1, 1932), 3.

16. Paul Althaus, *Christus und die deutsche Seele* (Gütersloh: Verlag C. Bertelsmann, 1934), pp. 23-24, 33.

17. Bornkamm, *Luther und der deutsche Geist*, pp. 7-8.

18. Johannes von Walter, "Heimatlose Theologen," *GuV*, I, No. 1 (January 1, 1932), 12.

19. Comments to this effect are made by von Arnim-Kröchlendorff, "Mit Luther zum Sieg," *GuV*, I, No. 5 (May 15, 1932), 74, and Althaus, *Christus und die deutsche Seele*, p. 32.

20. Gerhard Günther, "Zur Geschichte des deutschen Glaubens," *GuV*, I, No. 12 (December 15, 1932), 185.

21. Heinz Pflug, "Deutscher Gottesglaube," *GuV*, I, No. 4 (April 15, 1932), 57-58.

22. Emanuel Hirsch, *Die gegenwärtige geistige Lage im Spiegel philosophischer und theologischer Besinnung* (Göttingen: Vandenhoeck & Ruprecht, 1934), pp. 13-14.

23. Heinrich Rendtorff, "Wir wissen die Zeit," *Kirche im Kampf: Evangelische Rufe und Reden aus der Zeit des Kampfes um Deutschlands Erneuerung* (2d ed.; Schwerin i. Mecklenburg: Verlag Friedrich Bahn, 1934), pp. 46-47.

24. Rendtorff, "Kampfaufgaben," *GuV*, I, No. 1 (January, 1932), 2.

25. *Ibid.*

26. Superintendent Grell, "Neuer Most in neuen Schläuchen," *GuV*, I, No. 7 (July 15, 1932), 104.

27. Paul B. Means, *Things That Are Ceasar's: The Genesis of the German Church Conflict* (New York: Round Table Press, Inc., 1935), pp. 163-84, for a short discussion of the new paganism of the 1920's and 1930's.

28. Heinz Pflugk, *Die Christliche-deutsche Bewegung*, No. 2 of *Glaube und Volk: Schriftenreihe der Christliche-deutschen Bewegung* (Küstrin: Verlag Deutscher Osten, 1931), pp. 7-9.

29. Paul Althaus, "Das Evangelium deutsch," *GuV*, I, No. 3 (March 15, 1932), 42, and Althaus, *Christus und die deutsche Seele*, p. 18.

30. Pastor Hasse, "Glaube und Volkstum," *GuV*, I, No. 9 (September 15, 1932), 133.

31. Professor von Walter, "Die Annahme des Christentums durch die Germanen," *GuV*, I, No. 6 (June 15, 1932), 81-86.

32. Bornkamm, *Luther und der deutsche Geist*, p. 16.

33.   Rendtorff, *Kirche im Kampf*, p. 51.

34.   Machleidt, "Bismarck, der christliche Staatsmann," *GuV*, I, No. 10 (October 15, 1932), 158.

35.   Rendtorff, "Kampfaufgaben," *GuV*, I, No. 1 (January, 1932), 1.

36.   Emanuel Hirsch, *Die Liebe zum Vaterlande* (3d ed.; Langensalza: Herman Beyer & Söhne, 1924), p. 14.

37.   Paul Althaus, *Die deutsche Stunde der Kirche* (3d ed.; Göttingen: Vandenhoeck & Ruprecht, 1934), p. 20.

38.   Althaus, *Evangelium und Leben*, pp. 142-43.

39.   Hirsch, *Die Liebe zum Vaterlande*, p. 25.

40.   Hirsch, *Die gegenwärtige geistige Lage*, p. 135.

41.   Hirsch, *Deutsches Volkstum*, p. 7.

42.   Hirsch, *Die gegenwärtige geistige Lage*, pp. 134, 139.

43.   Rendtorff, "Kampfaufgaben," *GuV*, I, No. 1 (January, 1932), 3. Also see Rendtorff's sceptical comments on race and religion in "Praktisches Theologie," *Die Theologie der Gegenwart*, XXV, No. 7 (July, 1931), 139.

44.   *GuV*, I, No. 5 (May 15, 1932), 78.

45.   Walther Machleidt, "Ludendorff als Feind des Reiches," *GuV*, I, No. 6 (June 15, 1932), 91.

46.   Hirsch, *Deutsches Volkstum*, p. 39.

47.   von Walter, "Heimatlose Theologen," *GuV*, I, No. 1 (January, 1932), 12.

48.   Althaus, *Evangelium und Leben*, p. 93.

49.   Bornkamm, *Luther und der deutsche Geist*, p. 5.

50.   Rendtorff, "Entscheidung," *GuV*, I, No. 3 (March 15, 1932), 33.

51.   Hans Schomerus, "Thesen über Christentum und Deutschtum," *GuV*, II, No. 1 (January 15, 1933), 16.

52.   Althaus, *Evangelium und Leben*, p. 93.

53.   *Ibid.*, p. 97.

54.   Althaus, "Das Evangelium deutsch," *GuV*, I, No. 3 (March 15, 1932), 42.

55.   Althaus, *Christus und die deutsche Seele*, pp. 7-9.

74

56. von Arnim-Kröchlendorff, "Mit Luther zum Sieg," *GuV*, I, No. 5 (May 15, 1932), 75.

57. Hirsch, *Die gegenwärtige geistige Lage*, pp. 40-41.

58. *Ibid.*, p. 41.

59. Hirsch, *Deutsches Volkstum*, p. 25.

60. Bornkamm, *Luther und der deutsche Geist*, p. 8.

61. Althaus, *Evangelium und Leben*, p. 105.

62. These sentiments are paraphrased from a 1930 sermon by Heinrich Rendtorff, "The Church Today," in *Kirche im Kampf*, p. 12.

63. Hirsch, *Die Liebe zum Vaterlande*, pp. 6-7.

64. Tilgner, *Volksnomostheologie*, p. 83.

65. Althaus, "Gott und Volk," *Allgemeine Evangelische-Lutherische Kirchenzeitung*, No. 31 (July 29, 1932), 723.

66. Heinrich Rendtorff, Das Wort Gottes über das Volk, No. 1 of *Glaube und Volk: Schriftenreihe der Christlich-deutschen Bewegung* (Küstrin: Verlag Deutscher Osten, 1931), pp. 3-7.

67. Althaus, "Gott und Volk," *Allgemeine Evangelische-Lutherische Kirchenzeitung*, pp. 725-26.

68. Hans Schomerus, "Thesen über Christentum und Deutschtum," *GuV*, II, No. 1 (January 15, 1933), 15.

69. Hirsch, *Die Liebe zum Vaterlande*, p. 20.

70. Heinrich Bornkamm, *Der Totalitätsanspruch des Evangeliums* (Berlin: Verlag des Evangelischen Bundes, 1937), p. 11.

71. Paul Althaus, *Kirche und Staat nach Lutherischer Lehre* (Leipzig: A. Deichertsche Verlagsbuchhandlung, 1935), p. 14.

72. Althaus, *Die deutsche Stunde*, p. 15.

73. *Ibid.*, p. 19.

74. Rendtorff, *Das Wort Gottes über das Volk*, p. 9.

75. Rendtorff, "Praktisches Theologie," *Die Theologie der Gegenwart*, XXV, No. 7 (July, 1931), 139.

76. Dannenmann, *Geschichte*, p. 16.

77. Althaus, *Evangelium und Leben*, p. 131.

78. Generalmajor Graf von der Goltz, "Zusammenarbeit," *GuV*, No. 2 (February, 1932), 28.

79. H. von Stackelberg, "Was heisst Glauben?" *GuV*, I, No. 8 (August 15, 1932), 124.

80. Gerhard Kittel, "Die Judenfrage im Lichte der Bibel," *GuV*, II, No. 8 (August 15, 1933), 152-55.

81. Pflugk, *Die Christliche-deutsche Bewegung*, p. 8.

82. Althaus, "Das Evangelium deutsche," *GuV*, I, No. 3 (March 15, 1932), 43. For an in-depth study of Althaus' and others' views of the Old Testament, see the chapter on German Christians in Nicolaisen, *Auseinandersetzungen*.

83. Hirsch, "Etwas von der christlichen Stellung zum alten Testament," *GuV*, I, No. 1 (January, 1932), 8.

84. Schomerus, "Thesen über Christentum und Deutschtum," *GuV*, II, No. 1 (January 15, 1933), 16.

CHAPTER IV: THEOLOGY AND ORDER

Political Order

The ideologists of the *Christlich-Deutsche Bewegung* exhibited characteristic hesitancy when dealing with the interrelationship of Lutheran theology and political order. They tried to uphold strict Lutheran concepts regarding the teachings about the separation of the Kingdom of God and the Earthly Kingdom, and about obedience to constituted state authority, but at the same time wanted to affirm the new nationalistic ground swell. Was the Church qualified to deal with questions of law and order as well as preach the Gospel? Did not obedience to the state apply to every state? The conservative German Christians combined wishful thinking and the authority of Lutheran teachings to answer these questions. As a result, the CDB contributed to the mandate to obey the new Nazi state, while justifying the failure to obey the same mandate when applied to the Weimar Republic.

The CDB ideologists believed that the Church was caught between internationalism, represented by the Weimar Republic, and Volkishness, represented by the new nationalist groups, especially the Nazis. The ecumenical and international interests of some Christian groups, for instance, indicated a misuse of Christianity.

> World peace, world conscience, world reconciliation,
> world brotherhood, world economy, are characteristic
> words that have attained an almost religious sound.
> It is only natural that here one always hears talk
> about the world, but not about God.[1]

But the same author warned of the Volkish paganization that reveals its humanistic tendencies of impure individualism by putting the German man and not God in the middle of the cosmos.[2] The same viewpoint characterized Rendtorff's writings. Speaking of the situation in Weimar Germany, he noted on the one hand the lack of patriotic feelings in a large part of the German people.

> No land on the earth is so rich in castles built in
> the air as the German land, none so rich with plans

77

78

and programs, systems, and ideologies, parties and
world outlooks--and none has so many people that are
blind toward their own Volk, who do not know and do
not wish to know the reality of their own life.[3]

On the other hand, there were also those who loved the German
Volk with their whole heart, but had forgotten their God.
"They made out of their love to the German Volk a blind pas-
sion. And now they became harsh and unjust toward anything of
a foreign sort."[4]

But if the CDB claimed to play a middle role in the ideological milieu of Germany, actually its sentiments were with
the Volkish and nationalist side. God, the CDB believed,
created the peoples of the earth in their distinctness. The
Volk order was not something accidental, but a life-order sent
by God.[5] "It is God's power that reaches, flows through, and
directs us as his creative gift in the history of our Volk."[6]
With these sentiments, it was incumbent on the CDB ideologists
to support the great Volkish movements. Some of the conservative German Christians imposed limits on their enthusiasm.
Rendtorff and Pflugk were characteristically thus reserved.
Pflugk combined acceptance of the national renewal forces with
a dose of caution.

> The *Christlich-deutsche Bewegung* takes the national
> will seriously. Therefore [the CDB] will struggle
> alongside these [nationally-minded] men in complete
> earnestness for obedience under the Lord God. On the
> other hand, however, we will not glorify nor falsely
> treat the national will in a religious way, nor make
> the evangelical church in any wise a vessel for na-
> tional movements. It ought only to cooperate in
> service, so that the German Volk might be guided to
> the reality of the living God.[7]

It was impossible always to maintain this reserved judgment. Because God's will could be seen in earthly orders (such
as the Volk, the family, and especially the state) and in the
events of the present, the church did have the responsibility
to speak out on current issues. Friedrich Gogarten, much of
whose writing in the 1920's was directed toward an analysis of
the Christian's relationship to the state, put the church's obligation in this way:

> What the church, and with it, Christianity today must
> do for the world is to help the world back to a
> recognition of the great orders [*Ordnungen*] in which

alone the world can have its life, and a knowledge
of which today has been so basically lost.[8]

The conservative German Christian position was dependent
on what was considered to be the orthodox and original Lutheran
interpretation of the meaning of earthly *Ordnungen*. What follows is not necessarily a true interpretation of Luther on the
state and Volk, but rather a presentation of the way CDB ideologists used him.

One who believes in a Creator-God is bound to special duties on earth. Emanuel Hirsch could say: "To be unreservedly
faithful to our country means to give up all other earthly relations and duties if the Fatherland demands it of us," but at
the same time deny that this could conflict with one's duties
to God as a Christian. On the contrary, he said, faithfulness
to God demands being true to one's earthly duty as a patriot.
The concept of God as creator makes a connection between heavenly and earthly duties.[9] Paul Althaus presented very similar
sentiments:

> The faith in God's creative will is at the basis of
> Volkish thought. Protestantism conceives of the con-
> nection of the Kingdom of God to *Volkstum* and coun-
> try, not as a relationship with two different values,
> but as the unconditional majesty of a certain his-
> torical responsibility which results from an earnest,
> unconditional sense of duty. It is on this basis
> that devotion to *Volkstum* and country are both based
> and purified. Earthly faithfulness only has its
> right when it derives from obedience to God; the re-
> verse is also true: obedience to God binds us to a
> certain earthly faithfulness.[10]

The editorial comments presented in *Glaube und Volk* often presented the same view:

> Because we regard history as God's history, the world
> as his creation, we believe that he is served if we
> desire to help our Volk to a life of order and free-
> dom; for this Volk is his creation as are all crea-
> tures and called by him to a life that is according
> to its kinds and needs.[11]

One should not get the impression, however, that CDB
ideologists were talking about social involvement of the
churches. Lutheranism has traditionally ignored the social implications of Christianity more than many other Christian denominations. Friedrich Gogarten was definite on this point.

Social involvement, in and for itself, could be a dangerous
thing. He asserted that one cannot talk of social ethics without talking about prior faith, even though the tendency since
the French Revolution had been the reverse.[12]   The great war
had shown the bankruptcy of this tendency toward self-reliance
and belief in the sovereignty of *Humanitas*. The study of
ethics had taken on a new meaning.[13]

> But is the church then continuing on the right track
> when it does what it has already done in these times,
> when it also begins now to work in the social areas,
> when it creates a social credo, in order to make its
> members duty-bound to a social-mindedness?
>   According to what I have already said, there can
> be no doubt that the only answer to this question is
> a hard, plain "No."[14]

An early article in *Glaube und Volk* devoted space to the call
for the salvation of German workers from the "golden calf" of
materialism. It was unfortunate, the author said, that before
the war many workers thought the church was only for the rich.
But now it appeared that the real danger was that some churchmen were thinking in dangerously socialistic terms. The cor-
rection of this mistaken view would come when workers recognized the value and God-sent nature of work. As materialism
and self-seeking crumbled, the worker would be taught again
"...that 'praying and working' belong together."[15]   This was
the limited extent of the ideas of the CDB on the worker and
his social problems, and it is not surprising, therefore, that
the CDB retained only an elite base.

Although the CDB people tended to slur the distinction between the church's mission and their Volkish, patriotic, and
state interests, they maintained a sharp distinction between
the church's mission and social involvement. They based the
distinction on the Lutheran teaching of the two kingdoms. On
the one hand, God worked in both realms, the heavenly and the
earthly. Subjective morality that works in the soul is incorporated in its objective manifestation in the earthly orders
and arrangements of Volk, state, and nation. On the other
hand, the CDB people could claim that the two-kingdoms teaching
also meant the church itself as the guardian of the gates to
the Kingdom of God really had nothing to do with the earthly
issues of society which were better left with the state.[16]

Parenthetically, one recent analyst of this position that
stressed the alliance of throne and altar but with their different respective spheres of influence, denies that the conservative German Christian position was reflective of either the
theology of Luther or Lutheranism, but was rather the result of
an historical development that started only in the late 18th
century.[17]

The state and the Volk were nevertheless orders of God.
The relevant questions for the CDB ideologists were what the
state and Volk were created for, and what attitude toward these
orders was demanded of the Christian, as a result. There were
two viewpoints. Friedrich Gogarten and Heinrich Bornkamm were
more state-oriented than Volk-oriented, while an ideologist
such as Emanuel Hirsch could apply his Lutheran philosophy to a
consideration of the Volk as the primary earthly order of God.
The nature of the emphasis made the latter a more radical interpretation, though still within the conservative camp.

The statist interpretation of Luther on order viewed the
state as an order of God that saves sinful man from the strife
and chaos that is his natural lot. Gogarten elaborated the
position in some detail in his 1932 work, *Politische Ethik*.
"The state is that order with which man seeks to protect himself against chaos and against the destructive force by which
his earthly existence is threatened, and including the force
and destruction that spring out of his own essence."[18] Gogarten presented his agreement with the peculiarly German interpretation of freedom which is consonant with the strengthening
of state authority. "When we remember what that evil is from
which the state protects us, and when we keep before our eyes
what that freedom is that the state ought to guarantee, then we
will see that there is no contradiction between the two."[19]
The state, by its authority to protect man from himself, was
said to "give man the possibility of being himself." The sign
of the state's authority is the sword. "That means, wherever
there is real authority, true state power, it has the right...
to demand things of its subjects. This right of state power
over the life of its subjects derives from the highest and proper task of state authority, to protect the life of its subjects."[20] It is only on this basis that the state can have its

justification. States are built on sand and not truly authoritative if constructed any other way. "If man knows nothing of this destructive power, what has here been called the evil, then he cannot know about the correct foundation of the state nor of its majesty."[21] Heinrich Bornkamm, writing in 1934, repeated the same ideas of the basis of state authority, but put a different twist on the argument by asserting that Luther was, above all, a realist.

> Luther was basically different from other philosophers of the state in that he did not derive the state from human wants or basic rights, nor from a state ideal or value system, rather from reality: the struggling and hatred in the world that would annihilate mankind without the dams of state power. There was no room in his view for state utopias, for the playful painting of a completed state in paradise. Where love and freedom rule there is no need for a state authority. But in this deranged world, God created the state, a miracle in the middle of destruction. The state alone makes possible the life of mankind. Therefore, it is, as God's work of creation, of a higher order than any individual life. It is previous to and superior to the individual, an ineluctable, fate power, that man did not seek out, but that actually first made him a man. Just as man cannot exist without a body, so mankind cannot exist without the state. Honor for authority is the only salvation of mankind from ruin.[22]

The conservative Lutheran view of the state's justification was presented over and over in the pages of *Glaube und Volk*. Althaus, for instance, distinguished between the state and the Kingdom of God by saying that the former, with its right of compulsion, was characterized by justice, while only the latter could be characterized by forgiving love.[23] Out of this view of the state there were two results. First, the state had every right to use force--"the sword"--to save man from himself. The citizen had no redress of his grievances on the basis of individual rights. Second, man's sin after the creation of earthly orders such as the state was at least partly defined as his unwillingness to submit to constituted authority. "For the sin that man does, is sin against creation, against the will of the creator."[24]

The emphasis on the state exhibited by Gogarten and others discussed above was de-emphasized by some other CDB ideologists in favor of an emphasis on the Volk as the most important political order of creation. Hans Schomerus grouped *Volkstum* with marriage, family, and authority (*Obrigkeit*) as orders that exhibited the goodness of God by maintaining the life of fallen, sinning men.[25] The CDB program also pointed out that "obedience to the call of our Volk is, for us, obedience to God; denial of this obedience is sin."[26] But some attention should be given to the characteristic ideas of Emanuel Hirsch which in their emphasis on the Volk are distinct from the "order maintenance" concepts of other conservatives. As early as 1924, in a polemical lecture to students at Göttingen, Hirsch defined the primary role of the state as being a matrix for the unfolding of Volkish potential. "If a Volk is to have its life unfold according to its own proper law, it must be circumscribed by an independent state. It must be free, otherwise foreign life becomes its master; the arena of its freedom is, however, the state."[27] Just before the accession of Hitler, an article by Hirsch in *Glaube und Volk* presented his theory of the "hidden sovereign"--Volkishness. The post-monarchical situation in Germany (that is, the system set up under the Weimar Constitution) gave citizens the authority of the sovereign. This, said Hirsch, the reformers in the 16th century had never dreamed of as a possibility. What the authority (*Obrigkeit*) was for the 16th century Lutherans, the Volk was for 20th century Germans.[28]

> ...The Volk...is the hidden, and therefore the true, sovereign. Every member of the Volk is, through his inclusion in the Volk, called to his place, and with the full power given him, is an interpreter and executor of the will of the hidden sovereign, to fulfill and form the true state. Every real or alleged force in the state must be tested and judged by the measure of how it conforms to the hidden sovereign....[29]

Hirsch theoretically allowed for political revolution (although he certainly disapproved of the concrete revolution of 1918) when there appears to be no way that the existing state can help the Volk toward the fulfilling of its life and tasks. In short, Hirsch came up with a different, albeit politically and religiously conservative, Protestant theory of the state, based on a 19th century, idealist concept of the Volk as a creation-order of God, with a continuing organic life. For Hirsch, it was the unfolding life-process of the Volk that was to be honored by good Christians, rather than state authority as such.

84

Hirsch was a conservative Lutheran who nevertheless believed
that the church had to allow for some change in its state-
teachings with changing times. "[The truth is that]...not the
protection from chaos, but rather the building up and fulfilling of the life and task of our Volk is the service that gives
the state its true majesty."[30] Unlike most other CDB members,
Hirsch did not ignore the element of race in his teachings.
The Volkishness which was to unfold in the congenial state was
based on feelings in one's blood. Gogarten, with his more
statist and traditional views, accused Hirsch of stressing the
Bios over divine grace.[31]

It ought to be pointed out briefly that conservative German Christians also recognized orders besides the state and
Volk. It was in the conservative interest to mention now and
then such orders as marriage and family. Their importance lies
mainly in the fear that some CDB members felt that modern Western civilization, with its ideas about the ability of man to
legislate his own morality, was undermining the bases of these
divine orders.[32]

The overriding emphasis that comes out of CDB writings on
the divine order of the state (excluding Hirsch's ideas concerning the Volk which provide a stepping stone to the ideas of
other German Christian groups) is on the absolutely central
position of sin. No written work of Rendtorff or Gogarten, for
instance, could conceivably be read without noting their pervasive pessimism toward man's basic nature. Rendtorff devoted
several articles in *Glaube und Volk* to presenting the reality
of sin. "Sin? Sin simply exists in the life of all men....It
poisons and destroys the life of the individual as well as that
of the community, the nations as the world....There is only one
sin, and this sin is: distancing oneself from God, life without
God."[33] Max Weber has somewhere pointed out that political ru-
lers are pained by such concepts as original sin. The pessi-
mistic outlook of the CDB colored its relationship toward, and
affirmation of, Nazism. It was not as possible for the CDB as
for the other German Christian groups to be completely positive
about national Volkish renewal. But in the balance, the conservative German Christian position regarding state authority,
combined with admitted or unadmitted wishful thinking, helped

overthrow one form of authority for another. The question that
must be answered is how the CDB members, most of whom were alleged supporters of the Lutheran mandate to obey the constituted state authority, nevertheless worked to undermine the authority of the Weimar Republic.

The Weimar Republic, to the minds of CDB ideologists, was
far from being a satisfactory example of a state order. Althaus cataloged a variety of ills that he saw around him.

> ...The present in Germany appears everywhere to be
> painfully degenerate. Our Volk has lost itself, so
> we hear. Lost itself to civilization, lost to foreign
> ways. Lost to civilization: that means rational or-
> ganization instead of living organicism, splintering
> into the mass instead of membership in the Volk body,
> a "society" [Gesellschaft] of unbound individuals in-
> stead of organic community [Gemeinschaft], uprooted-
> ness and homelessness, in outer and inner ways, in-
> stead of outer and inner indigenousness [Bodenständig-
> keit], disinheritedness instead of life in the tradi-
> tions of our fathers; in many respects one can say:
> "fatherless, motherless, without family tree," without
> history...the big city is certainly the symbol of our
> entire times!...But the foreign is also a power in
> the homeland: the takeover by foreign influences of
> our literature, theater, art, fashions, and celebra-
> tions, of party ways and of public life, our abandon-
> ment to Volkless money powers....[34]

Sin comes from not heeding God, and for the conservative German
Christians this specifically included losing sight of the ways
of their fathers. The decade of the 1920's in Germany was a
time in which there was much that was new and difficult for
many Germans to understand--new political forms, new social and
economic realities of a drastic sort, new ideas about public
and private morality. Much was condemned by the conservative
German Christians simply on the basis of its untraditional or
"unGerman" nature.

One of the more frequent complaints by CDB writers was
that aspects of the Weimar situation revealed that people had
an incorrect idea of freedom. "The individual man is supposed
to be 'free,' i.e., he is supposed to abandon himself to his
own arbitrariness. The state exists [now] for the purpose of
providing for the welfare of as many individuals as possible."
But what this democracy usually means is the dissolution of the
Volk community.[35] In a sermon in 1930, Rendtorff noted that in

the area of conscience, individualism was also not an absolute.
"Luther's freedom of conscience is not fetterless I-seeking,
but the strongest of ties."[36] "False individualism," which
passed for freedom, was characterized as a separation from God.
The unbound individual with all his drives had become the ideal
of modern times--radical individualism was the new pagan god to
which everything had been sacrificed. Thus the CDB ideologists
could claim that the tendency toward freedom, that they believed had increasingly characterized European thought and
politics since the French Revolution, was not only unwise, but
sacrilege, because it denied the greater community order established by God. "The drive of men toward unconnectedness [with
the community], toward self-glorification, is in its innermost
essence the drive to make oneself independent of God, the master of all life....The [question of] political, esthetic, ethical, and economic individualism is only the question of religious individualism."[37] The German nation lost its religious
faith and church because the door was opened, by liberal religious theorists, among others, to seeing man as the increasingly self-reliant master of history.[38] Some of the writers
saw an inherent paradox in the modern demands for freedom. No
doubt there is some truth to what Gogarten, for instance, noted
about modern man and his apparent inability to cope with freedom.

> It is precisely this modern man who is enslaved under
> an enormous despotism; this man who has based his
> whole life, his whole life outlook and order, on
> freedom, on the self-glorification of the individual
> man. This man, who looks at himself and his entire
> life as his own free action over which he therefore
> also has free disposal, and concerning which he is
> answerable to no one; it is precisely this man who
> endures a tyranny as no other man before him. And
> it is his own action that enslaved him. He is
> locked up in the delusion of his freedom. And every
> nameless hidden fear that has rushed him into his
> prison and the nonsensical faith in freedom and
> self-reliance in which he seeks his security in the
> fearful insecurity of this world, they hold him
> in the grip of this sinister despot.[39]

Emanuel Hirsch, too, was sceptical of freedom, especially in
the form that he believed it had developed in having abandoned
the ideas of early 19th century German Idealist thought. The

emptiness of the present concept of freedom, its arbitrariness, had convinced many observers, he said, that the necessary end result of the whole development was a dictatorship of the masses of the type that Nietzsche had predicted. Hirsch did not seem to have a specific dictator in mind.[40] Admittedly, the talk of false individualism or incorrect concepts of freedom dealt with various emphases. Some of the CDB ideologists were referring to political, some to ideological or philosophical, some to religious, and some even to economic examples of man's overreliance on his own powers. But together they reflect the conservative's concern with the modern tendency toward discreteness and individualism in human affairs and the attendant move away from dependence on religion and church for providing answers to man's needs in all areas. The important thing for all discussions of the unhappy turn of modern-day concepts of freedom was that the Weimar Republic became identified with the decadent, overly-individualistic freedom that conservative German Christian ideologists could not tolerate.

Another black mark against the Weimar Republic was that the order requisite in a correctly-conceived state was lacking. The earlier German sense of position in social ranking, order in government, and respect for law seemed to have no reflection in the new state. One after another of the CDB writers complained of the chaos in politics. They had little respect for elective parliamentary government. In a pre-election note in *Glaube und Volk* in October of 1932, an editor noted the apparent helplessness of the parliamentary parties to get anything done. "It is really not so important, how the voting comes out; Parliament is no longer considered the place for political decision....In the political as well as the economic area, new creations are necessary."[41] In the next month's issue, the same writer spoke despairingly of the disorder of the state caused by agitators who drowned out the quieter voices of the Volk.

> A Volk that lives in the chaotic disorder of the age
> of the masses can often not hear the quieter voice
> of the Volk over the shrill cries of the agitators.
> The order in the Volk can today only be created by
> the state. For this task it is necessary to again
> have a state whose authority is worthy of faith. All
> authority comes from God. Men cannot bestow authority.

> The people likewise cannot bestow authority through
> elections; it must merit it through its objective
> performance.[42]

At this point, however, the author was still calling for the
German people to line up behind Reich President von Hindenburg.
Another twist to the problems of politics in the Weimar Republic was that they were based again on what has already been described as the false idea of freedom. The liberalism which the
CDB member saw as the basis of the constitution and political
life of the state worked *against* the state--to limit its control over the individual member. For the conservative Protestant who saw the state as a creation of God designed to protect
man against his own evil nature, the throwing-off of control
was anathema. Put in other terms, the saying, "the state that
governs least, governs best" was not considered by the conservative German Christians to be a healthy interpretation of political freedom. One CDB analyst made the distinction between
democracy (which he could accept under his own definition) and
liberalism. Liberal politics, he said, has always meant politics against the state. German democracy of the post-war period could have been non-liberal.

> For a democracy does not mean a lasting compromise
> between different opinions, but rather the rule of
> the Volk as a totality and unity; not the decision
> of the majority is the mark of democracy, but the
> decision of the *Volkheit*, whereby the *Volkheit* does
> not mean the sum of some living or even enfranchised
> peoples, but the unity of those who have lived, those
> who are living, and those who will live. It is espe-
> cially not necessary for the essence of democracy,
> that the expression of the political will must follow
> from general elections.[43]

This example by itself shows to what extent conservative German
Christian ideologists were willing to abdicate their right to
objective political participation for the reconstruction of
order. Friedrich Gogarten voiced similar sentiments to those
presented above when he drew the distinctions between a state
properly conceived and a "society" [*Gesellschaft*] such as the
one the Weimar Republic represented.[44] Another aspect of the
order issue was the very elemental one of what the conservatives saw as a breakdown of law and order generally. The concern over criminality that seems out of control is a concern

that arises at many points and places in history. In words
that sound familiar today, Heinz Pflugk complained that the
libertarian atmosphere of the Weimar Republic made it appear
that more thought was given to the rights of criminals than to
the rights of their victims.[45] The significance of the CDB observation of the lack of order in the Weimar Republic was that
it knocked the one essential prop out from under the conservative Lutheran interpretation of a state's *raison d'être*. A
state that did not seem to provide order was no state at all.
This was the really important issue in the CDB decision to turn
away from the Weimar democracy.

Another aspect of the Weimar Republic that CDB ideologists
did not like was its materialism (usually blamed on Marxism)
and its mechanization of life. Gogarten believed that modern
men had been separated from others at least partly by the "an-
onymous powers" of capital and the economy. Slavery to the
mechanistic age was not simply obvious in the factory, however;
it had insinuated itself into all aspects of society and had
replaced all interhuman connections with mechanistic organizations.[46] Gogarten noted something that has continued to be a
complaint of modern man--that men are used as things, not as
human beings.[47] Economic dislocation was also blamed on the
Weimar Republic. Rendtorff in his sermons often mentioned
economic pressures, though also warning of overemphasizing the
ultimate importance of economic issues.[48] But in 1934, after
Hitler was in power, Heinrich Rendtorff was still attacking the
economic ills of the 1920's. Luther, he said, had already in
the 16th century seen the pitfalls of a money economy not based
on real value. "His thoughts have a wonderful relevance even
today in our struggle against stock exchange and interest slavery."[49] Often Marxists were identified as the archetypal ma-
terialists, but as noted in the previous chapter, they were
usually lumped together with other "materialistic" enemies--the
French, the Bolshevists, and sometimes the Jews.

The Weimar Republic was accused of being internationalis-
tic. That is to say, mankind was valued over Volk. For those
who saw the Volk as an order of God, there was no justification
for the humanist attempt at world government or world law or
world-wide concepts of morality. "Was it not the 19th century

that led in the tendency to put mankind higher than the Volk, that scorned that strong joy in one's own type and mores, when we opened the door to all sorts of foreign things?"[50] Rendtorff, in saying this, overlooked the fact that it was precisely the 19th century that established the value of national differences. Nevertheless, what he saw as a dangerous tendency in the 19th century found its crowning point in the Weimar Republic. His New Year's sermon for 1932 voiced the hope that the state would abandon its internationalist leanings and speak out more forcefully against the "war-guilt lies."[51]

The conservative German Christian did not like the Weimar Republic's apparently disinterested attitude toward religion. "Everyone has more or less his own private religion or his atheism or even his own religious disinterestedness. There are mystic and monistic, Volkish and international cults and gods...."[52] The church should not just be an administrative apparatus, thought the CDB, reflecting a feeling that was held by most German Protestants in the Weimar Republic era. Some CDB writers called for the restructuring of churches to eliminate their allegedly new democratic character, and for the maintenance of Protestant education in the public schools.[53] The formal disestablishment of religion and the apparent lack of partiality on the part of government toward Lutheran Christianity was just another reason for conservative Lutherans to lose faith in the Weimar Republic.

Finally, it is common to read of CDB despair over the lack of basic Christian morality in the decade of the 1920's. Pflugk complained of the society that had fostered murder, divorce, prostitution, free love, and trial marriage (the latter two he blamed on American and Soviet Russian influences). "For man today there is no hard and fast order of life. Everything has been placed in question. There is no sure moral judgment."[54]

The CDB ideologists could not recognize "natural law" as the basis of the state. The important role of the state was to provide firm rule--otherwise the state was not fulfilling its divine mandate. Two years after the Nazi revolution, Paul Althaus presented his justification for political revolution at times in the history of a people when the state operated contrary to the ways of the Volk. "A democracy that does not include truly responsible leadership means destruction of the divine order of the state."[55] Earthly law, Althaus also said, is based not on positivism but on faith.[56] The conservative German Christian consideration of Luther's teachings on state order were intrepreted in such a way that made it possible to deny respect for the Weimar state and by this disrespect help pave the way for Nazism.

How did the CDB members react to the new Nazi state? Although the conservative German Christians abandoned the Weimar Republic, it cannot be said that before January 30, 1933, the CDB generally supported Hitler or the Nazi movement. An individual member of the CDB, here and there, was a member of the Nazi Party (Friedrich Wieneke was the most important example), but for the most part, CDB members were only broadly nationalistic in their actual political affiliation. Hindenburg was more often mentioned as the example of German national stability than the firebrand Hitler. Even after the takeover by the Nazis, the editorial comments on the political scene were surprisingly calm and reserved. In an editorial in the February 15, 1933 issue of *Glaube und Volk*, Gerhard Günther noted the problems with which Hitler was faced—questions of reestablishing German honor and freedom before the world, national and constitutional reforms, and, "of greatest importance," the overcoming of the economic crisis by doing battle with unhealthy money powers. The author closed by sternly reminding his readers of the difficulties and responsibilities ahead.[57] But the CDB soon became used to the new regime and although there was a continued tenor of hesitation in all political pronouncements, there was, by the same token, no questioning of the correctness of the new state on religious-Reformation grounds. The people who were associated with the CDB believed generally that Germany was finding her way back to the values of the "good old days." After decrying the stagnation of fourteen years of liberalism, Rendtorff was happy to see familiar signs again. "...Now again the quest for faith is returning. Now awakens the yearning for that in which one can and ought to have faith. The visible sign of the old mentality was godlessness. The visible sign of the new must and will be the

92

complete turning toward new faith, new reliance on God."[58]
Even one or two years later conservative German Christians
were still claiming that the new regime had reestablished the
traditional values. Althaus enumerated the values that Nazism
had restored.

> The disintegration of the right to punish into social
> therapy and pedagogy that had already gone a long way,
> has come to an end; punishment must again be inflicted
> in earnest retaliation. The new state is again daring
> to wield the sword of right. It has repudiated the
> frightful lack of responsibility of the Parliament and
> showed us again what responsibility means. It has
> swept out the smut of corruption. It protects against
> the powers of destruction in literature and the thea-
> ter. It calls and educates our Volk to a new com-
> munity will....[59]

Bornkamm, for his part, was happy to see that, "the National
Socialistic thoughts prove their legitimacy for us Germans because they reach back to the deep sources of the Reformation."[60]

Conservative German Christian writers were happy with the
new order. Günther noted in April of 1933, that the picture of
the day at Potsdam (March 21, 1933, when Hitler and Hindenburg
reverently appeared together at Frederick the Great's tomb at
the Garrison Church) was the sign that, "the army, which was
homeless in the Weimar Republic, has again found its place in
the state."[61] Hirsch greeted the Nazi revolution as meaning,
"...a new historical age for evangelical theology and piety and
church...."[62] Some CDB writers indicated that Hitler had been
sent by God to reestablish order and authority in the state.
In a sermon in the autumn of 1933, Rendtorff, ironically already in trouble with local Mecklenburg German Christian groups
who were hoping to replace him with more radical church leadership, gave thanks for the Nazi revolution.

> God sent us in his mysterious way through the turning
> of German history, great tasks, great possibilities,
> an open door. The awakening of the German Volk became
> reality in the spring of 1933. We thank the Lord God
> in this hour that he has sent the German Volk in
> Adolf Hitler the man who led us out of brokenness,
> dullness, and decay to unity, lively struggle, and
> new service. We thank God the Master that we have
> again become a Volk, that we have again become a
> Reich.[63]

Others echoed these sentiments; Althaus said that God was
again calling the Germans to the law through the *Führer*, while
Hirsch believed that 1933 was the point at which the divine
will touched earthly developments and was thus an "hour of God"
(*Gottesstunde*).[64]   But usually, the belief that Hitler was sent
by God was not overdone as it was to be in other German Christian ideologies. A more characteristic comment after January
of 1933, was that the Church and the Third Reich needed each
other and belonged together because of similar inner dynamics.
As early as March of 1932, Pastor Gensichen of Halle hoped that
the church and Nazism could be of some service to each other,
although he was at that time clearly most interested in showing
the Nazis their "responsibility before the living God."[65]   Just
days before Hitler came to power, Rendtorff found himself clar-
ifying the CDB position toward Nazism apparently as an answer
to readers, some of whom had asked for clear rejection of
Nazism, others for affirmation. Rendtorff's analysis is a
classic example of the conservatism of the CDB and its lack of
decision.

> While some political movements today place themselves
> openly with the enemies of Christianity and faith in
> God, and others are undecided, uncertain, or indiffer-
> ent toward Christianity, the National Socialist move-
> ment has indicated its will to place itself on the
> basis of a positive Christianity. The church is duty
> bound by its calling to take seriously this declara-
> tion of the intentions of the National Socialist
> movement.[66]

On the other hand, Rendtorff noted, this did not constitute
political recognition of the Nazi movement, because the church
could not take a stand on day-to-day political issues. Rendtorff continued to note, however, that the church and Nazism
had in common their affirmation of Volk and *Volkstum*.[67]   Elsewhere, after the Nazi revolution, Rendtorff characterized the
church as "movement." Dogma, liturgy, church law, morality
(its reflection in the Volk life), the constitution, all of
these, he said, were characterized by movement even if it was
not always reflected in the "organized church." "The fact is:
the real church is movement, is *dynamis*, is happening."[68]   This
basic characteristic of the church made it imperative to

cooperate with the new regime which was also essentially characterized by movement.

> The church and the Third Reich! Movement belongs with
> movement....They belong together: in our jubilation
> over the breaking out of a movement that has raised
> up our rigidly oppressed Volk; in the readiness for
> service in which there is the recognition and affirma-
> tion of the final eternal goals; in a community that
> does not shirk from the truth and responsibility of
> struggle....[69]

The possibility that the totalitarian nature of the state
might conflict with the total demands of Christianity did not
cause much difficulty for the CDB. Heinrich Bornkamm, writing
in 1937, devoted his attention to explaining how the Lutheran
interpretation of the "total demand" of the Gospel was of a
complementary nature to the total political state.

> If there is a total claim of the Gospel on man, then
> this gives the Protestant (unlike the Catholic) the
> complete freedom to participate in political works
> and orders that are demanded of him. His only measure
> need be his God-given reason, instinct, objectivity,
> recognition of Volk necessity.

The total demands of the Gospel and of the Volk both have their
special place in creation.[70] Since the two "totalitarianisms"
were not mutually exclusive, but complementary, the church and
state had all the more reason for allowing each other their
correct realms. Cooperation might be called for in some areas,
but the danger also had to be guarded against that either the
state or church would overstep its grounds. Theoretically,
this careful stance could be the rationale for the unwillingness of the CDB at times to take a forceful stand on political
issues. By the same token, the CDB was concerned to have the
church's realm left to the churches. "The German freedom movement seems to be recognizing more and more clearly that the
full freedom of the preaching of the Gospel is at the same time
the best service to Volk and state," said one CDB writer in
mid-March, 1933, before the attempts of more radical German
Christians to blur the line between church and politics had become obvious to everyone.[71] A number of articles later in the
year voiced distrust of the *Glaubensbewegung Deutsche Christen*
for confusing the distinct boundaries between the two "total"
realms of Gospel and state affairs. One example of this was

that some GDC ideologists believed that ordination vows sometimes contained ideas that were high treason against military
oaths, while CDB writers denied this, saying that the issue did
not involve choosing between ordination vow and military oath.
"It is precisely our military oath that requires of us that at
all times we conceive of our ordination vow as holy."[72]   As
another example, the CDB supported Ludwig Müller for the office
of Reich bishop although many members were shocked by the rabid
unchristian politicking that characterized the activities of
the German Christians during the early summer of 1933. None of
this, however, diminished the CDB belief that the total state
was proper for giving freedom to the historic life of the Volk.
Gogarten supported the total state on the basis of its ability
to provide the all-important order requisite to keep man from
destroying himself. Paul Althaus, however, explicitly stated
that Gogarten had confused the total state with authoritarian-
ism, while really Nazism was not essentially authoritarian nor
even fascist! Rather, he said, the Nazi experience was a reflection of German Volk truth and freedom. "It is not a matter
of the totality of the state as a system, rather the education
to totality, i.e., the responsibility of all forms and areas of
life for the greater life, the history of the Volk. It is just
in this connectedness that...[we find] true freedom."[73] Regardless of the reason--whether for purposes of order or of the development of the Volk destiny--CDB ideologists found it natural
to support a politically totalitarian state.

The church's primary role with regard to the state was to
help the people understand their duties as Christians. There
was some difference of opinion as to the church's duty regarding ethical behavior. Gogarten, whose ideas sounded similar to
Wilhelm Stapel's, denied that earthly ethical behavior was
based on the autonomous individual's interpretation of Christian norms. Ethics was rather based on social-political bases
and on service within the state. But most CDB ideologists were
not thinking on such a theoretical basis, and simply saw their
duty to show the Germans how to act in a Christian way. Althaus, for instance, thought God demanded of Christians not only
that they render obedience to the state or Volk, but also that
they submit the civil law and morality to the test of divine

ethical commandments. In 1935, Althaus could say that the
Christian ethical position had the right to measure civil actions pertaining to such concrete issues as

> ...the sacredness of life, including that of the un-
> born; the holiness of a lifelong single marriage;
> the majesty of the Creator who alone sets the goal
> and borders of our life and denies us the right to
> suicide or euthanasia--the "elimination of unworthy
> life." ...[Reason] requires the critique that comes
> from the Word of God. Thus the Christian critique
> of [civil] orders is necessary and possible.[74]

Most other CDB writers agreed with Althaus, though they did not
always put their sentiments into the same terms. There was a
pervading belief among the CDB people that the Nazi regime offered the churches the opportunity to help reestablish an upright Christian moral outlook that would repudiate the ethical
relativity that had characterized the Weimar Republic.

Another goal of the church (as seen by the CDB) was to
bring the nationalists--especially the Nazi Party--to a reali-
zation of their dependence on God. This is a characteristic
intention voiced over and over in the pages of *Glaube und Volk*
both before and after the Nazi assumption of power. Thus the
CDB saw itself as a mediating guardian of correct German Christian ways both by teaching the citizen his duty to the state,
and by helping the government to fulfill its function as a divine order.

The above considerations determined the CDB concept of
correct church-state relations. There was to be no doctrinal
interdependence of the two--each had its own ideological basis.
Thus the concept of a national church in the sense of a non-
denominational religion based on peculiarly German religious
concepts was rejected as pagan syncretism.[75] But although
church and state were two different realms, they worked within
the same Volk community and therefore could not be neutral toward each other--their concurrent history, said the conservative German Christians, made that impossible.[76] Without theoretically taking a stand on the ideological merits of Nazism,
the CDB nevertheless contributed a valuable aid to the Nazi
state's efforts to obtain an obedient German citizenry.

The World War and Pacifism

The CDB provided religious bases for the maintenance of order within the state, and thus found the Hitlerian state a more suitable government, according to the CDB interpretation of Lutheran principles, than the Weimar Republic had been. It seems ironic now that the Nazi regime was welcomed and support- ed as being responsive to Christian ideas. After all, one af- ter another of the conservative German Christian values on the basis of which the Weimar Republic was condemned were also sub- verted between 1933 and 1945. Surface order was maintained in the state, but only by acts of terror; a kind of public moral- ity in Puritanic terms returned to Germany, but new and more thorough ethical degeneracy became policy in the acts of anti- Semitism, genocide, and euthanasia; economic rebuilding was based on the speedy and necessarily continuing development of massive rearmaments; the Party's declaration of its "Positive Christian" outlook in its Program exhibited itself in the same kind of neo-paganism and Aryanism based on blood that the CDB had rejected before 1933. Not all of these paradoxes were ob- vious to members of the CDB, but by the same token, much could be excused or overlooked by the CDB as long as the Third Reich continued to satisfy patriotic urges and apparently adhered to the basic requirements of the correctly conceived state as an order of God. In addition to the domestic order of the state, the CDB had ideas concerning the relationships of Germany to other nations--specifically in war. For almost all of the Ger- man Christian groups, World War I had been an experience of much more than normal importance. It had taken on, in their minds, a quasi-religious significance. In the following pages, ideas are presented which reflect the spiritual and patriotic importance that the Great War had on large numbers of German Protestants. The conservative Lutheran's characteristic anti- pacifistic sentiment is put in conjunction with the discussion of CDB reactions to the war in order to show the continuing in- terest in militarism and the justifications that were made for war and war-service on Christian grounds.

Most of the writers who were associated with the CDB be- lieved that God had been somehow at work in the World War, or, at least, that the war had been a religious experience. Paul

Althaus, writing in 1934, mentioned how even non-Christians had undergone religious experiences in the war. Lutheran theologians and pastors need not scoff at this, he said. "We know from the Holy Scriptures and the theological traditions of our church that the testimony of the living God [appears] in the reality of the world and men."[77] Althaus compared the war experience in this respect to the Nazi movement.

> It is a simple fact that in August of 1914, and then again in the years of the nationalist movement, men who did not wish to know anything about the God of the Bible and of the Church, by living through [the events of] history felt seized by the power that called for unconditional sacrifice and gave their lives, for the first time, its meaning and joy. It is a simple fact that German men who no longer knew anything about faith and devotion in life experienced a reality in their relationship to the *Führer*, in their willingness for sacrifice, in the heeding of the call of the hour, in their response to obedience to this call, which can only be called "religious." The call of the unknown soldier of the World War who was struck by the emergency and shame of the nation, driven and held by the certainty of an unconditional mandate...this call was accepted by uncounted many as the bidding voice of German history itself.[78]

The god who was at the center of this religious experience seems to have been, in Althaus' mind, equivalent to the movement of history itself. Emanuel Hirsch also believed that the World War (and war in general) was a spiritual experience. Writing in 1934, he introduced his comments on the meaning of the war by apologizing for the fact that his duties as pastor during the war were exercised on the home front and not on the battlefield.

> But it appears to me, and I had many friends on the front for whom the unsettling sense of reality was also an experience, that there is no deeper earthly preparation than war for the comprehension of the paradoxical situation of life, which leads to a relationship with God. There, daily, is experienced the consciousness of the instability of all natural bases of our earlier untested ideas which were buffered by Volk and state, of the ability of God to break to pieces the Volk and state despite all their good human law, [and] of the actual divine destruction of countless human fates. There was, on the other hand, daily reborn the consciousness, despite the way in which the immediacy of life is bound up with and ought to be bound up with uncertainty, that it is just in this uncertainty that it is possible to continue to exist

> humanly and ethically. In the contradictions of this
> experience, we were prepared as Germans to pierce
> through the connection of the earthly and the eternal.
> It often seems to me that the hatred against the war
> is in great measure simply the defensive reaction of
> men against this uncovering of the ultimate paradox
> of our existence....[79]

These were comments made after the Nazi revolution, but similar
sentiments had been voiced by conservative German Christians
before 1933 also. In an early article of *Glaube und Volk*, H.
W. Beyer devoted several pages to a commemoration of the sacrificial death of German soldiers. "We men of today cannot talk
of sacrificial death [*Opfertod*] without seeing directed toward
us the inquiring eyes of those who fell in the World War."
There is no greater reality of our times, he continued, than
those fields with their uncounted thousands of crosses. "Sacrifice is the true creative power in all development. That we
do not live and die for our own sake, but rather in service to
something higher that asks this of us." Only from this willingness to sacrifice could real community arise. It was in the
"front-experience" that such concepts as "comradeship," "Volk
community" (*Volksgemeinschaft*), and "Fatherland" obtained their
deepest meaning.[80] Interestingly, the conservative nature of
the CDB shows through in the same article. Without really taking away from the sacrificial accomplishments of the soldier,
Beyer nevertheless found himself called upon to note, as did
Hirsch above, the paradoxical nature of the soldier's action.
The soldier was called upon to kill out of love and faith.
"And it is the most fearful reality of our life that even the
best, the purest, the most sacred of actions is tainted by
sin."[81]

The war brought to the Germans a renewed appreciation for
this Volkishness. Bruno Doehring, who was one of the founders
of the CDB, had only lived through three months of the First
World War when he noticed the effect that it was having on the
German awareness. In a sermon, clearly presented as war propaganda but preached in 1914 in his capacity as court preacher
in Berlin, Doehring recalled how pre-war Germans let events go
by without really "experiencing" them. But the war, he noted,
had begun to change that. "What we experience today, we can
call...the rebirth of our Volk life...[or] what we call

faith."[82] Althaus, writing fourteen years later, came to the
same conclusions. New love of Volk, a new sense of one's responsibility to others, the will to see the Volk renewed--
these were beliefs that by and large gained their impetus in
August of 1914, with perhaps some foreshadowing in the pre-war
German youth movement. The awareness was based on the traditional values of family, calling, work, soil, and country.[83]
Heinz Pflugk noted that the war experience had hastened the
German yearning for the Third Reich (this was written in 1931,
two years before the Nazi revolution!), not only in the political sphere but also in the areas of law, the press, literature, the economy, family affairs and marriage.[84]

The war, it was thought, had put materialism below other
more lasting values. Doehring complained that in pre-war times
Germans had worshipped material things in too high a degree.
Already in 1914, he was talking about the dangers of man's
self-reliance and his slavery to "quantity rather than quality...form over right." The war, he said, had effectively
shown the Germans the relative unimportance of material concerns when placed against sacrifice and patriotism.[85] Gogarten
was saying much the same when he noted years later that the
World War was a new kind of war in that it marked the beginning
of the end of the "dream of humanism."[86]

Another reason that conservatives were not appalled by the
war was that it was their opinion that in very real ways the
war had justified the existence of the church after decades in
which Germans had been turning to other interests. Doehring
noted this development, when people were indifferent to the
church or accused it of ignoring progress. With the effect of
the way, however, who could fail to see that this was Germany's
fateful hour? The existence of two great powers in Germany--
the standing army and the church--was justified by the war.
The former provided outer protection, the latter the complementary inner strength.[87]

War was seen by CDB writers as something that could be
blessed by the Divine. Doehring quoted a poem by Gottlieb von
Schenkendorf, the theme of which was the storm of war sent by
God.[88] Hirsch noted that war is always horrible, but that on
the other hand, it can be the highest form of piety to rely on

the conscience and place one's life before God.[89] Heinrich
Bornkamm quoted Luther to the effect that the soldier was like
a surgeon who must amputate a hand or leg to save the rest of
the body. "One must view [the soldier's work] as an office
[*Amt*], that is in itself godly."[90]

The conservative German Christians were convinced that the
World War had some religious meaning. At the very least, it
had given Germans cause to reconsider their value systems and
had thereby prepared the way for the rebirth of the Volk community and reestablishment of old spiritual values. The war
was not remembered, however, as an experience that was to be
condemned nor one that should be prevented from happening
again. In their corollary stance against pacifism--especially
against pacifism allegedly based on Christian principles--the
CDB ideologists continued a positive evaluation of militarism.

The following analysis of the CDB position against pacifism is taken from a variety of sources, but is especially reliant on the analysis of war and Christianity made by Paul
Althaus for the Protestant encyclopedia, *Die Religion in Geschichte und Gegenwart*--a widely-read and authoritatively accepted evangelical reference work.[91] In a few short pages,
Althaus summarized the conservative Lutheran position on war
and pacifism.

The attitude of the conservative German Christians was
that pacifism might weaken the political order and was, furthermore, not necessarily Christian in and of itself. Althaus
described the question of war and Christianity as both a theological and ethical issue.[92] But an analysis of either aspect
of the question revealed, for Althaus, that war and Christian
beliefs were not antithetical. Of course, to the insufficient-
ly informed person, the Biblical message often might seem to be
the hope for a peaceful kingdom. It has also been pointed out
that Jesus' disciples, while engaging in struggle to spread the
Word, did not countenance war. Althaus found this view to be a
misinterpretation.

> In spite of this radicalism that apparently was sin-
> cere among Jesus' disciples, it should not be over-
> looked that according to Jesus' teachings of the
> Kingdom of God not only war (this is nowhere in the
> New Testament especially rejected!) but also any kind

> of state leadership (Luke 22:25), or legal forms or
> rule by law (Matthew 5:39ff and I Corinthians 6:1ff)
> are impossible. But still Jesus did not reject law
> and state generally; he passed by the issue with no
> special yes or no.[93]

What Althaus was saying was that, given the connectedness of
war and statecraft and the lack of pronouncements by Jesus concerning earthly statecraft, the pacifist was not on firm ground
when he claimed to base his opposition to war on Christian
principles. Althaus proceeded in his argument to pass to the
Lutheran theological interpretation. One cannot, he said, base
questions of law and the meaning of law and the state on the
Gospel's commandment of love. The same goes for one's discussion of war. One must remember, "Luther's teachings about the
Christian's citizenship in two kingdoms--the Kingdom of God and
the earthly state....The life order of the Gospel is different
from that of the law and the state." One cannot rule the world
with the Gospel. The world, however, must be ruled, according
to the church's interpretation, with a view to maintaining
order--which is the state's God-given office.[94] The primary
question is not war or peace, but the maintenance of the
state's *raison d'être*. In a definition that is in between
Friedrich Gogarten's order maintenance rationale and Hirsch's
organic concept of Volkish values in the state, Althaus says,
"The state is called upon to ensure for the Volk the freedom of
the unfolding of its own life. In the form of the state the
Volk surrounds itself concretely in its own being and in its
historical responsibility." But in the world even today there
is continual flux. One Volk-state is just developing, another
is living out its last years; the races are wandering and inevitably clash with each other. "The Volk-nations living amongst
each other create difficult Volkish and state questions. Thus
the nations are inevitably forced into conflicts with each
other." This sometimes results in war. International fora
(Althaus disparagingly noted Wilson's Point 14 on this) are not
necessarily the best ways to settle these disputes of historical significance. What had to be understood was that, "power
and law [*Recht*] are not opposites...." Althaus was not convinced that the days of the nation-state were numbered in favor
of international adjudication of disputes. "The world of the

state is the sphere of the powerful formation of history....The
call for 'peace through law' instead of a peace decided upon
through struggle, stems from the pacifistic-doctrinaire opposition of law and power."[95] Other CDB members accepted Althaus'
interpretation. Heinz Pflugk, in his pamphlet setting forth
the principles of the CDB, mentioned Althaus' article as authoritative on the topic of war and pacifism, and added, "Pacifism at any price simply cannot be made into a Christian
duty."[96] For Pflugk and others, however, the pacifism issue
always was intertwined with the memory of the hated Versailles
Treaty. This was undoubtedly in Pflugk's mind when he wrote
the following.

> World peace is something completely different from
> the peace of God. World peace aims at ensuring human
> life as such, because men cling to life and do not
> want to sacrifice it for anything or anybody. But
> the peace of God is the certainty of faith that I be-
> long to the Lord God in sin and death, in life and
> struggle, even in war and the trenches, and that
> nothing can separate me from God's love....The world
> conscience is not the voice of God, but rather the
> whore of the press and of public opinion....We see in
> world reconciliation and world brotherhood disobedi-
> ence toward the creation order of God when and insofar
> as thereby the divine order of the creation of *Volk*
> and *Volkstum* and state are overcome or actually al-
> tered. Behind the call for world reconciliation and
> world brotherhood often hides the will of self-reliant
> men for emancipation who want to be free from all real
> bindings and seek to justify their moral emancipation
> through proclamations of general love of man that, in
> spite of their vague generalities, offer no service
> and no sacrifice.[97]

War could be a moral duty, according to CDB thinkers.
Althaus believed that such a war was not anarchism, but rather
a matter of justice when it concerned the need of peoples in
history for a place and room (*Raum*). "Whether any particular
war's results ever really help bring living justice to victory
or just result in more evil and brutality, is another question."[98]

The opinion of Althaus, expressed in various places, was
that passive opposition was no more Christian than active participation. "We are as much against a peace that forgets one's
calling as against unjust war, against lack of decisiveness as
much as against a decision light-mindedly and arbitrarily made."[99]

Althaus showed his conservative nature, however, in noting
that war is, as with other human activities, tainted by sin.
(Similar sentiments have already been noted above in an article
by H. W. Beyer on "sacrificial death").[100]   There is no such
thing as a completely just war, given the inevitable inclusion
of some who would profit from it for selfish reasons.[101]   But
it is possible for good to come of war. Not only had experience shown that the war may be a religious experience of a
deep sort even for those who have previously been indifferent
to spiritual matters, but "in the seriousness of conflict ori-
originates the high, majestic calling for the ultimate stake
and sacrifice for the cause of the fatherland. The terror of
one's having to die has on the other hand the *dulce et decorum*
of one's being allowed to die for the fatherland."[102]

Finally, Althaus indicated that the ability to decide for
war was in the highest tradition of Protestant strength. Bismarck's words of 1877 were quoted: "Without me there would not
have been three great wars, 80,000 men would not have perished,
and parents, brothers, sisters, and widows would not have sor-
rowed. Nevertheless, I arranged it with God." This, said
Althaus, "is Protestant virility."[103]

The evangelical church's duty on the topic of war and pacifism was to be mindful of the arguments set forth above. It
was not the Protestant church's position, said Althaus, to ape
the Catholic Church and place itself behind the peace movement
and the League of Nations. Rather, the CDB and the German
evangelical church were to "...keep the consciousness living,
that the difference between moral and immoral politics is never
based on whether one leads to peace and the other to war. To
wage war can be a sin for a Volk, but so can maintaining peace
when the struggle, as in the case of a struggle for freedom, is
a clear duty."[104]

1. Pflugk, *Die Christliche-deutsche Bewegung*, p. 14.

2. *Ibid.*

3. Rendtorff, *Das Wort Gottes über das Volk*, p. 9.

4. *Ibid.*

5. Pflugk, *Die Christliche-deutsche Bewegung*, p. 16.

6. Rendtorff, *Das Wort Gottes über das Volk*, p. 7.

7. Pflugk, *Die Christliche-deutsche Bewegung*, p. 8.

8. Friedrich Gogarten, *Die Schuld der Kirche gegen die Welt* (2d ed.; Jena: Eugen Diederichs, 1930), p. 18.

9. Hirsch, *Die Liebe zum Vaterlande*, pp. 19-20.

10. Althaus, *Evangelium und Leben*, pp. 93-94.

11. G[ünther, Gerhard], "Ruckblick und Vorschau der Schriftleitung," *GuV*, I, No. 12 (December 15, 1932), 195.

12. Gogarten, *Die Schuld der Kirche*, pp. 21, 24.

13. Friedrich Gogarten, *Politische Ethik* (Jena: Eugen Diederichs, 1932), p. 3.

14. *Ibid.*, p. 145.

15. Gustav Hartz, "Glaube und Arbeitertum," *GuV*, I, No. 1 (February, 1932), 10-11.

16. Tilgner, *Volksnomostheologie*, p. 183. Tilgner refers specifically to Althaus, whose ideas on this topic developed in the 1920's from emphasis on God's work in the soul (Kingdom of Heaven) in earlier years to God's involvement in earthly orders toward the end of the decade.

17. Klaus Scholder, "Neuere deutsche Geschichte und protestantische Theologie," *Evangelische Theologie*, XXIII, No. 10 (1963), 526.

18. Gogarten, *Politische Ethik*, p. 58.

19. *Ibid.*, p. 195.

20. *Ibid.*, pp. 109, 197.

21. *Ibid.*, p. 210.

22. Bornkamm, *Luther und der deutsche Geist*, p. 10.

23. Althaus, "Das Reich," *GuV*, I, No. 11 (November 15, 1932), 163.

24. Gogarten, *Die Schuld der Kirche*, p. 36.

25. Schomerus, "Thesen über Christentum und Deutschtum," *GuV*, II, No. 1 (January 15, 1933), 15-16.

26. *GuV*, I, No. 5 (May 15, 1932), 79.

27. Hirsch, *Die Liebe zum Vaterlande*, p. 9.

28. Hirsch, "Vom verborgenen Suverän," *GuV*, II, No. 1 (January 15, 1933), 5.

29. *Ibid.*, p. 7.

30. *Ibid.*, p. 12.

31. See the discussion of this point in Tilgner, *Volksnomostheologie*, pp. 140-142.

32. Neurohr, *Der Mythos vom dritten Reich*, p. 169, notes Gogarten's comments on this.

33. Rendtorff, "Furcht und Vertrauen," *GuV*, I, No. 2 (February, 1932), 17.

34. Althaus, *Evangelium und Leben*, p. 115.

35. Pflugk, *Die Christliche-deutsche Bewegung*, p. 4.

36. Rendtorff, *Kirche im Kampf*, p. 35.

37. Pflugk, *Die Christliche-deutsche Bewegung*, p. 4.

38. Rendtorff, "Die Nation vor der Kirche," *GuV*, II, No. 3 (March 15, 1933), pp. 43-44.

39. Gogarten, *Politische Ethik*, p. 143.

40. Hirsch, *Staat und Kirche*, p. 26.

41. G[ünther], "Aus der Zeit," *GuV*, I, No. 10 (October 15, 1932), 158-59.

42. G[ünther], "Aus der Zeit," *GuV*, I, No. 11 (November 15, 1932), 176-77.

43. Gerhard Günther, "Protestantismus und Demokratie," *GuV*, I, No. 4 (April 15, 1932), 59.

44. Gogarten, *Politische Ethik*, pp. 149-50.

45. Pflugk, *Die Christliche-deutsche Bewegung*, p. 3.

46. Gogarten, *Politische Ethik*, pp. 139, 164.

47. *Ibid.*, p. 140.

48. For example, see Rendtorff's sermon from August of 1931, entitled "Wirtschaft und Seele," *Kirche im Kampf*, pp. 83-86.

49. Bornkamm, *Luther und der deutsche Geist*, p. 13.

50. Rendtorff, "Die Nation vor der Kirche," *GuV*, II, No. 3 (March 15, 1933), 44.

51. Rendtorff, *Kirche im Kampf*, p. 124.

52. Pflugk, *Die Christliche-deutsche Bewegung*, p. 4.

53. Grell, "Neuer Most in neuen Schläuchen," *GuV*, I, No. 7 (July 15, 1932), 104.

54. Pflugk, *Die Christliche-deutsche Bewegung*, p. 4.

55. Paul Althaus, "Thesen zum gegenwärtigen lutherischen Staatsverständnis," *Kirche und Welt: Studien und Dokumenten*, No. 2 of *Die Kirche und das Staatsproblem in der Gegenwart* (Berlin: Furche-Verlag, 1935), p. 7.

56. Paul Althaus, *Theologie der Ordnungen* (2d ed.; Gütersloh: Verlag C. Bertelsmann, 1935), p. 39.

57. G[ünther], "Die neue Regierung," *GuV*, II, No. 2 (February 15, 1933), 38.

58. Rendtorff, "Die Nation vor der Kirche," *GuV*, II, No. 3 (March 15, 1933), 45-46.

59. Althaus, *Die deutsche Stunde*, p. 7.

60. Bornkamm, *Luther und der deutsche Geist*, p. 13.

61. G[ünther], "Aus der Zeit," *GuV*, II, No. 4 (April 15, 1933), 78.

62. Hirsch, *Deutsches Volkstum*, p. 8.

63. Rendtorff, *Kirche im Kampf*, pp. 215-16.

64. Hirsch, *Die gegenwärtige geistige Lage*, p. 27.

65. Pfarrer Gensichen, "Evangelische Kirche und National-sozialismus," *GuV*, I, No. 3 (March 15, 1932), 39.

66. Rendtorff, "Unsere Stellung zum Nationalsozialismus," *GuV*, II, No. 1 (January 15, 1933), 14.

67. *Ibid.*

68. Rendtorff, "Die Kirche und das dritte Reich," *Kirche im Kampf*, p. 183.

69. *Ibid.*, p. 189.

70. Heinrich Bornkamm, *Der Totalitätsanspruch*, pp. 7, 11.

71. Werner Wilm, "Evangelium, Kirche, Freiheitsbewegung," *GuV*, II, No. 3 (March 15, 1933), 50.

72. Superintendent Neumann, "Ordinationsgelübde und Fahneneid," *GuV*, II, No. 5 (May 15, 1933), 96-97.

73. Paul Althaus, "Totaler Staat?" *Luthertum*, XLV, No. 5 (1934), 131, 134.

74. Althaus, *Theologie der Ordnungen*, p. 39.

75. Pflugk, *Die Christliche-deutsche Bewegung*, pp. 18-19.

76. Paul Althaus, "Thesen zum gegenwärtigen lutherischen Staatsverstandnis," *Kirche und Welt*, p. 8.

77. Althaus, *Die deutsche Stunde*, p. 10.

78. *Ibid.*

79. Hirsch, *Die gegenwärtige geistige Lage*, pp. 164-65.

80. Hermann Wolfgang Beyer, "Opfertod," *GuV*, I, No. 1 (January, 1932), 4, 6.

81. *Ibid.*, p. 6.

82. Bruno Doehring, *Gott, das Leben und der Tod: Drei Kriegsvorträge...gehalten im Dom zu Berlin* (Berlin: Verlag von Reuther & Reichard, 1914), pp. 9, 23.

83. Althaus, *Evangelium und Leben*, pp. 113, 116.

84. Pflugk, *Die Christliche-deutsche Bewegung*, p. 5.

85. Doehring, *Gott, das Leben und der Tod*, pp. 32-33.

86. Gogarten, *Politische Ethik*, p. 1.

87. Doehring, *Gott, das Leben und der Tod*, pp. 33-36.

88. *Ibid.*, p. 34.

89. Hirsch, *Die Liebe zum Vaterlande*, p. 27.

90. Bornkamm, *Luther und der deutsche Geist*, p. 12.

91. Paul Althaus, "Krieg und Christentum," *Die Religion in Geschichte und Gegenwart* (hereinafter referred to as *RGG*), (2d ed.; Tübingen: Verlag von J. C. B. Mohr, 1927-1932), III, 1306-12.

92. *Ibid.*, p. 1306.

93. *Ibid.*, pp. 1306-07.

94. *Ibid.*, p. 1307.

95. *Ibid.*, pp. 1307-08.

96. Pflugk, *Die Christliche-deutsche Bewegung*, p. 17.

97. *Ibid.*, p. 14.

98. Althaus, "Krieg und Christentum," *RGG*, p. 1308.

99. Quoted from a review of Althaus' book *Staatsgedanke und Reich Gottes* in *Deutsches Volkstum*, No. 1 (1929), p. 86. Also see similar comments in Althaus, "Krieg und Christentum," *RGG*, p. 1308.

100. Hermann Wolfgang Beyer, "Opfertod," *GuV*, I, No. 1 (January, 1932), pp. 4-7.

101. Althaus, "Krieg und Christentum," *RGG*, p. 1309.

102. *Ibid.*, p. 1310.

103. Althaus, *Evangelium und Leben*, p. 103.

104. Althaus, "Krieg und Christentum," *RGG*, p. 1311.

PART III

THE *GLAUBENSBEWEGUNG DEUTSCHE CHRISTEN*

CHAPTER V: "POSITIVE CHRISTIANITY"

As one turns to the ideas of the *Glaubensbewegung Deutsche
Christen* (GDC), he must remember that this was a movement with
a double identity, being both an organizational and an ideological center. It was not always possible to separate the two
aspects, and church-political needs were constantly intruding
upon the independent life and integrity of GDC ideas. This in
itself was partly why the ideas of the GDC were characteristically opportunistic. But it was also true that the founders of
the movement and the people who were attracted to it were often
motivated by thoughts of personal or party welfare.

"Positive Christianity," as used by the GDC, was an idea
that reflected the movement's opportunistic nature. The term
"positive" had a pre-Nazi history in the German Protestant
church, having been associated in the 19th century with a certain traditionalist anti-liberal theological position. There
was little, if any, relationship, however, between this interpretation of "positive Christianity" and the use of it in article 24 of the National Socialist Party program (see the discussion of this in Chapter II). The GDC platform reaffirmed
the party phrase saying, "We stand on the basis of positive
Christianity. We confess ourselves to be for an affirmative
Christ-faith, appropriate to our type, corresponding to the
German Luther-spirit and heroic piety."[1]

GDC writers believed, or claimed to believe, that the affirmation of "positive Christianity" by the Nazi movement meant
that Hitler and the party based their actions on Christian
principles. One after another of the GDC members assured each
other that this was the case. Denying that Hitler's spiritual
beliefs were in any way influenced by Rosenberg's anti-Christian religion (which was probably true), a member of the GDC in
Frankfort picked a passage from *Mein Kampf* to make his point:
"Typical for Hitler is a sentence such as this one: 'Eternal
nature avenges itself without bitterness against the

transgression of its commandments. Thus, I believe myself to be acting in the meaning of the Almighty Creator; when I go against the Jews, I am fighting for the work of the Master.'"[2] Another GDC pastor had a mental picture of the piety of Hitler that now seems difficult to imagine. "He, the most German man, is also the most pious, a believing Christian. We know that he begins and ends his daily tasks with prayer and that he has found the deepest source of his power in the Gospel."[3] Julius Kuptsch wrote several books all designed to prove the parallel nature of Christianity and Nazism. He believed that the similarity of Christ and Hitler was striking. The following statement is typical of Kuptsch.

> Whether Hitler consciously or unconsciously has taken
> Christ as the model and teacher for his work of polit-
> ical salvation of the German volk, that I do not know.
> But it is an undeniable fact that world history has
> never known two appearances, living in different
> arenas of life, that nevertheless have such great
> similarity and essential kindredness as Christ, the
> divine *Führer* and saviour of mankind who called into
> life the Christian movement of the first century,
> and Hitler, the German political Führer and liberator
> who called into life the National Socialist freedom
> movement of our time. National Socialism and its
> leader are striving for the realization of Christian
> principles.[4]

This was all wishful thinking. Many German Protestants were taken in by the Party's claim of adherence to "positive Christianity." The most important thing about the use of the term in the Party platform was its lack of definition. GDC ideologists often felt called upon to elaborate on the con- cept, setting forth their own interpretations of what it meant. These attempts were furthered by the fact that the GDC platform (i.e., the *"Hossenfelder Richtlinien"* of May 26, 1932) gave only a slightly more enlightening explanation of "positive Christianity" than the Nazi platform. What follows is a pre- sentation of various GDC definitions of "positive Christianity" and their ramifications for the German Protestant church. The fact is, it is impossible to find one single clear definition of the term. At best one can only speak of an ideological trend. Just as the word "Socialism" in the term "National So- cialism" was vague and open to various interpretations, so

"positive Christianity" was a useful term for the Nazis because
it allowed the faithful to indulge in wishful thinking without
having any concrete meaning.

For some GDC members, "positive Christianity" could mean
something very traditional and reserved. Friedrich Wieneke, at
one point, found its meaning in the theme "back to the Bible."

> Positive Christianity is and will always remain Biblical
> Christianity. "Positive" simply means "fundamental."
> It has to do with the spiritual freeing of the nation
> from liberalism and Marxism, and this freeing is only
> possible through the book that "presents Christ."[5]

Although there was a surprisingly large degree of conservative
and orthodox ideology in Wieneke, he ranged himself as a follower of Joachim Hossenfelder, who was a disruptive figure in
church-political life and, at times, very unorthodox in his
thinking. But Hossenfelder too could claim a Biblicist position. "Even though the seeking of God is different among the
nations of the earth, God's answer is once and for all and absolute. God answers all peoples in the Gospel."[6] One cannot
take Hossenfelder too seriously however. His affirmation of
the Bible as the repository of once-and-for-all revelation
seems to have been simply a denial of modern theological speculation of a systematic sort, and was, in any case, contradicted
in numerous places in his own writings. As will be shown in
various examples below, Hossenfelder did not believe that there
had been only one revelation of God for all times, but saw
God's handiwork especially in contemporary events. The same
observation applied to the position held by Pastor Kuptsch, who
explicitly condemned modern liberal and systematic theology,
claiming that the new church must get back to Christ as its
only basis. He specifically condemned the Protestant historical and textual "theoreticians" and Catholic scholastic nit-
pickers who, he said, could add nothing to the basic authority
of the Bible. All church traditions which had accrued since
New Testament times were to be thrown out. But Kuptsch too destroyed his argument for the authority of the Bible by himself
denying the usefulness of the Old Testament.[7]

The preceding examples are from the "left-wing" of the
GDC. There were also those in the GDC whose "Bible Christianity" was completely sincere. In some cases, the definition

of "positive Christianity" as "Bible Christianity" came after
the debacle of the *Sportpalast* meeting of November of 1933.
The German Christian Saxon *Landesbischof* Otto Coch, for instance, chose to withdraw his state's German Christian movement
from GDC control because he felt Hossenfelder and his colleagues had based their politics too much on liberal values of
human self-sufficiency. Countering them, Coch noted,

> the Bible remains for us the unequivocal basis for the
> Christian message. The confession also has, to our
> thinking, an obligatory meaning despite its time-bound
> form....With Luther we say: I believe that Jesus Christ
> is my Master. This Christ is for us the decisive rev-
> elation of the eternal God. He is for us the only way
> to God. We bow to him as German men who believe in
> him. This Christ is positive Christianity.[8]

One of the best-known spokesmen of the Biblicist position was
Christian Kinder, head of the *Reichsbewegung Deutsche Christen*.
In his efforts to keep a national German Christian movement
alive after 1933, he found it necessary to affirm the Biblical
and confessional foundations of the German Christian movement.
Although he noted the German Christian belief in the divine
creation orders of blood, race, and Volk, he was careful to
give the impression of orthodoxy. "We 'German Christians' are
very clear that any church is only a church if it derives its
life from the Gospel and Confession."[9]

Another rather uncontroversial definition of "positive
Christianity" was said to have been formulated by Hossenfelder
during a discussion with Gregor Strasser:

> Positive Christianity signifies that the Gospel is
> the objective life power that is given from God, not
> from men. This short precise sentence is a clear
> rejection of the charge that is often unjustly
> leveled against the NSDAP for its [alleged] racial
> paganization and a clear testimony to Hitler's sense
> of the "fact of the Almighty."[10]

This seems to have been the definition that Friedrich Wieneke
had in mind as a basis for his discussion of a German Christian
theological systematics. He distinguished the new "organic
systematics" from both liberal and orthodox positions.

> It [the new systematics] will renounce a theology
> "from below" as is the case in liberalism, as well
> as orthodoxy. But it will also move away from a
> theology "from above" as has resulted in dialectical

systematics. Thus originates a truly positive systematics that recognizes the God-sent life basis as the
starting point of faith, thought, and action. The
theologian knows himself as a creature of the God that
he meets in the Holy Scriptures, but also in his own
life. He feels himself set down in God's workshop
and wants to explain in a scientific way [*wissenschaft-
lich*] only that part of God's will as put forth in the
Holy Scriptures that is still of value today. The
faith confession will be locked together with the life
confession in an inseparable unity.[11]

What on the surface appears to be a restrained presentation of
one man's intentions to order his life according to divine
guidance is really an example of one of the basic German Christian ideas--that the German Christian could feel called upon to
interpret contemporary events in their spiritual meanings.
Wieneke's insistence on the inseparable unity of faith and life
activities was an implied acceptance of the historical revelation of divine will in mundane human affairs.

Hossenfelder's GDC platform, as noted above, associated
"positive Christianity" in vague terms with two concepts--
first, that Christianity reflected itself in forms that were
appropriate to one's type [*artgemäss*], and second, that the
German type of piety was the Luther-spirit and heroism. Koppel
Pinson, in his work on the interrelatedness of pietism and German nationalism, has commented on the fact that such late 18th
century German thinkers as Johann Hamann, Johann Lavater, J. G.
Herder, and Friedrich Schleiermacher already believed in the
multiplicity of the religious impulse and even in the multiplicity of Christian types of piety.[12] Numerous GDC writers
also noted the peculiarities of Volkish religiosities. One New
Testament scholar put it this way:

The Volkish peculiar type, a [commonly] experienced
history, and certainly other reasons (such as the
special holdings of religious leaders) form the
piety of a community....The fact of the matter is
that different peoples are pious in very different
ways.[13]

Hans Michael Müller, professor of systematic theology at Jena
and the Reich Bishop's theological "Referent," recommended a
similar observation.

The history of religion is a history of the question
of men about ultimate things, and is indeed the history of the nations [*Völkergeschichte*]. Types of

116

> piety are, in addition, racially connected. Every
> Volk has its own type of spiritual basic feeling.
> This colors all of its utterances about life....The
> calling for and wrestling with God is not monotonous--
> despite the mystics. The quest of God is always mani-
> fold. In the history of religions and confessions it
> has always been put in different ways.[14]

The German type of Christianity was said to be characterized by
a peculiar Lutheran heroic piety. A GDC pastor identified
Luther as the "greatest Germanizer of Christianity" and set him
apart from other interpreters of Christianity.

> He among us who understands the voice of the blood knows
> that repentance and the love of freedom--the will to
> self-determination, to free sovereign decisiveness,
> and self-reliant responsibility, together with attach-
> ment and affirmative fidelity--belong together as the
> basic structure of the German. If we name two other
> essential characteristics, unconditional truthfulness
> and unflinching courage, then we have named the four
> pillars of German, Nordic life. Naturally, one can
> find these virtues and the results of these virtues
> among other peoples. The peculiarity of the structure
> of the German, Nordic religiosity is their primacy
> and the way they work together, so that one charac-
> teristic relies on, and is contained by, the other.
> And this spirituality is incorporated in a wonderful
> way in Luther the German.[15]

The state bishop of Saxony, Coch, specifically defined "positive Christianity" as the interpretation of piety best suited
to the German type. The Gospel, itself, he said, is never
"*artgemäss*," but the German Christians needed to interpret it
in such a way to make it understandable to the Volk. "There
has scarcely ever been a people in history that has understood
Christianity and with it the Gospel of Jesus Christ so deeply
as the German Volk, as the German, the Nordic man with his
strong will to freedom."[16]

Not only was the German piety seen as characterized by
strength and love of freedom, but some GDC writers asserted
that Christ himself was correctly seen as a heroic type. Pastor Martin Wagner, leader of the Düsseldorf GDC, assured the
readers of *Evangelium im dritten Reich* that, "Jesus possessed
an heroic piety. He bore no similarity at all to the soft,
weakly sentimental pictures of Jesus that the painters have
shown us for centuries. As with all heroes, he demanded the
most from existence. He who does not will the greatest does

not belong in his discipleship."[17] Professor Leipoldt believed
that, "the manly kind of piety may be put not only in war-like
images [*kriegerischen Bildern*]. Similar are the images that
compare piety to an athletic struggle."[18] Leipoldt devoted an
entire chapter in one of his books to the topic, "Jesus as
Kämpfer." Referring to Jesus throwing the money lenders out
of the temple, he observed, "In the language of today one can
say: here Jesus had the look and skill of a general."[19] The
German Christian desire to see Christ and Christianity in terms
that denoted strength and struggle was common. Speaking of the
traditional pictures of Christ, one GDC pastor called for more
realism.

> We all know these pictures of the master with the
> gentle oval shape of head, the mild look, the womanly
> weak mouth, the cleanly-parted hair and cultivated
> beard, for which the expression "temperamentless" is
> still too complimentary, and which has little or
> nothing to do with true art.
>   In truth, the Savior as we know him in the Gos-
> pel is rich in manly harsh characteristics. He had,
> as all great men do, a strong choleric touch. He
> also did not shy away from the harsh word, the gruff
> action. To follow him means to follow his whole
> essence--not simply his mildness, his placidness,
> his compassion that is presented in the customary
> one-sided picture of Jesus! Just as important are
> the other characteristics: his anger, his inexorable
> nature, his decisiveness, his strong will, his heroic
> courage.[20]

What these people were calling for, as consonant with the
heroic interpretation of "positive Christianity," was the
"*Kämpfer* Church." Struggle (*Kampf*) was a very important part
of GDC terminology. One can trace the development of a positive valuation of the concept of struggle in all areas of life
to, finally, its transference into the religious sphere. H. M.
Müller spoke of struggle in general as the only way to triumph
over evil. After deprecating the motives of pacifists as he
saw them, he asked, "Who will still deny today that intractable
arbitrariness and injustice can only be broken through *Kampf*
and organized, disciplining power?"[21] Pastor Kuptsch found
human struggle to be in line with the wise ways of nature.

> As in the world of nature, so in the world of nations,
> there is a struggle for life, both to maintain life
> and to annihilate it. National Socialism intends and

works for only the former. In the already noted
example of the world of nature this can be explained
the best. The various trees in the forest only grow
so high, so straight, so beautiful and useful because
they engage in struggle with each other for life and
for the certainty of having a place with sufficient
nourishment and sunshine. Trees that do not struggle
this way lose their power of life and die. And even
if a few do live among others without struggling,
they remain bowed, crippled, and suitable only for
firewood. It is the same in the world of nations.
Only where and if the peoples wage the struggle with
each other for self-assertion and their place [*Raum*]
on earth, their country, do they maintain healthy
life powers and develop into true culture-nations
that make progress in all areas of life and are useful
to each other.[22]

Hossenfelder also found struggle to be the basis of all
life. "Struggle is the father of life. That is the law of God
that our day carries in its mind." Agreeing with H. M. Müller,
he contended that life of men and nations dies when it ceases
to struggle.[23] Hossenfelder transferred the concept of struggle to matters of faith. "But when we talk about struggle as
Christians, we know that all struggle is ultimately a wrestling
between day and night, light and darkness, faith and lack of
faith, Christ and antiChrist."[24] Pastor Martin Thom, the GDC
authority on Germans outside the Reich, repeated the familiar
comments about Christ being the greatest of all examples of
heroic struggle, adding that the combination of Christian
struggle and love found its most poignant expression in the
"law of life": "Be willing to lay down your life for your
brothers."[25] Kuptsch said further that because it was a natural fact that only he who struggles can alter the world, the new
German Christian church would also have to be made up of those
willing to engage in *Kampf*. Christ could be called the "Prince
of Peace," he said, only because peace comes through struggle.[26]
The Reich Bishop, Ludwig Müller, reflected his happy former
career as a military chaplain when he asserted that, "Christ
was a *Kämpfer* who was the greatest of all times, a *Kämpfer* loyal until death....To be a Christian means to be a *Kämpfer*,
filled with trust in God, in the strong consciousness of personal responsibility before God."[27]

The call for an heroic and *kämpferisch* Christianity reflected militaristic virtues, fears of national weakness, and

the continuing influence of the popular Darwinian virtues of
claw and fang in some members of the GDC. In addition, in its
extreme presentation, this interpretation was on the borderline
between Christian and pagan. Part of the speech by Reinhold
Krause, which broke up the GDC organization in November of
1933, called for a return "to an heroic Jesus whose life pos-
sesses exemplary meaning for us and whose death is the seal on
his life, the end of an heroic and struggling life conferred on
him as his task by his Father."[28]

"Positive Christianity" often had the additional meaning
that the church was not going to be neutral toward the state
and Volk. In point one of the Twenty-eight Theses of the Saxon
Volk Church, the possibility of a strict separation of church
and state was denied as unwise.

> The German Evangelical Church stands in the state. It
> cannot lead its own subterfuge course next to the state
> as the anti-Christian types would like. It cannot
> persist in a neutral attitude toward the state as
> those circles would do who view the National Socialist
> state with mistrust. It cannot be a church over the
> state, which reflects the Catholic position. Further,
> it cannot be a church under the state as it was in the
> old system of *Staatskirchentum*. Only as a church in
> the state is it a Volk church. Thus Luther's original
> thoughts about state and church will become reality.[29]

Hossenfelder voiced the same view of the Volk church, but he
had a social sense that showed up in his comments. He was concerned, for instance, that the Inner Mission--the Protestant
social concerns organization--would work hand-in-glove with the
total church, and together they would affirm the "social mira-
cle of the Volk growth in the National Socialist revolution; it
[the church] wants to fill the newly awakened and growing German Volk with the spirit of the word of God, so that a new
Volkish and social Christ-will might come to fruition in the
whole Volk community." This, Hossenfelder did not view as in-
consonant with the work of the church.

> In service to our Volk and its political, economic,
> social and cultural life, we will not be surpassed by
> anyone. Here already we are doers of the Word and
> not listeners alone. A Christian social teaching
> that teaches the "neutrality of the church" and dares
> to make no social decisions, we reject as erroneous
> and faithless.[30]

Hossenfelder was willing to offer up the church to the unre-
served service of the Nazi state. His accusations of "church
neutrality" were probably directed against Barthian dialectical
theology. Emanuel Hirsch, who by 1933 had moved from the conservative German Christians into the GDC camp, also countered
Barth by saying that the church was not a timeless *ordo* that
could not essentially change with, and react toward, historical
circumstances. "That is the life-destroying lack of a sense of
history that characterizes all legal religion, including a
Christianity that makes the Gospel into a new law." The German
Christians, he said, believed that the Gospel could help to
bind the church and Volk together in new ways.[31] The rationale
for the church's close cooperation with the Volk-state was that
the revival of the Volk had been willed by God. One of the
contemporary GDC historians quoted Hossenfelder as saying, "God
said, let there be Volk, and there was Volk."[32] It was the
logical result to demand the German Christian's participation
in the Volk renewal. Hirsch believed that the new construction
of the Volk ethos in 1933 needed the deepening and clarifica-
tion that belief in justification by faith could provide,
"...and that we are shirking the service God has laid before us
if we do not participate [in Volk renewal] with new thoughts
and wisdom from the Gospel."[33] The radical individualism in
matters of faith that is associated with Reformation Protestantism was largely denied by GDC writers faced with the phenomenon of Volkish ideology. "The German Christian knows in
faith that not only the individual man stands before God, but
that also the German *Volkstum*, as every *Volkstum* of the earth,
gets its meaning by serving the eternal." To flee from this
Volkish faith responsibility was seen as sin.[34] Both the Volk-
state and the church would, in addition, benefit from the defeat of Marxism and Bolshevistic godlessness. Wieneke, whose
definitions of "positive Christianity" were manifold, believed
that "positive Christianity" meant partly to help "...spiritu-
ally free the German nation from liberalism and Marxism...."[35]
In the GDC call to vote for the Nazi Party in the March 5, 1933
elections, the editors associated the church's interest in com-
batting the "internal front of the godless" with the desires of
the state. "Remember that in Russia, churches have been made

into movie theaters, granaries, cattle stalls, that majestic
old church buildings have been blown up because of hate-filled
mad fury."[36]   The anti-Marxist and anti-Bolshevist utterances
were common in GDC writings and, of course, characterized pro-
Nazi ideology of all sorts. The use of these references by the
GDC ideologists was a way of asserting the need that the state
and the "positive Christian" church had for each other.

Similar to the rejection of church neutrality in regard to
the Volk-state was another Wieneke definition of "positive
Christianity," as "organic Christianity." One is not always
certain what Wieneke meant by "organic Christianity" because it
was used in different ways. At one point, he said "positive
Christianity" was the affirmation of "the organic values of
life" which included freedom of the race, the spirit of heroism, and leadership.[37] Elsewhere, he favorably quoted the action of the first Reich convention of the GDC (April 3-5, 1933)
which in part declared that, "God created the 'organic' German
man. Sin is separating oneself from the organic life process,
whose whole truth was revealed to us by Christ who was also the
Savior of the Germans."[38] Apparently "organic Christianity"
meant not compartmentalizing one's religious activities away
from political and racial involvements. Wieneke discussed this
use of the term "positive Christianity" in an interesting passage that compares Hitler to Kant.

> National Socialism was nothing but the cry of the
> Volk for its lost soul. Its Führer, however, recog-
> nized instinctively wherein this spiritual value ex-
> isted, and in point 24 of his program named "positive
> Christianity" clearly and in certain terms as the
> religious basis of the Party. On this point, one
> could compare Hitler to Kant. The great philosopher
> brought together the whole of human knowledge into a
> single system of thought. In one place, however, he
> opened a window into this system, when he spoke of
> the categorical imperative and felt spoken to by the
> divine voice that then was able to permeate the en-
> tire system with eternal values. The greatest German
> politician [Hitler] also put down his powerful system
> in a classic program. He also opened the window at
> one point to the eternal. He refused, as a politi-
> cian, to come closer to the essence of the eternal,
> leaving that to the Reformers. He was just satis-
> fied with the word "positive Christianity." --But
> therein the creator of the National Socialist move-
> ment says simply that German-Volkish culture as well

> as all knowledge is bound up in its inner essence
> not simply with the Volkish type, but also with the
> power of Christianity. Here is now the call to
> German theology....To it belongs above all a positive
> stance toward Volk and race, i.e., an organic
> Christianity.[39]

Elsewhere in the same work Wieneke compares the goals of a
"positive Christianity" in theology to those of Richard Wagner
in striving for the organic unity of art.[40] When Hossenfelder
was faced with pressures to resign his church offices after the
excesses of the November, 1933 *Sportpalast* speeches, he clari-
fied his position in a series of programatic points. One of
them seems to follow the definition of the goal of "positive
Christianity" and the German Christian church as establishing
an "organic" connection between church and Volk. "Our goal remains that Volk and church be made one. The *Reichskirche* established the outer framework for the coming Volk church.
Their inner fulfillment can only result from the basis of the
oneness [*Einheit*] of Gospel and Volkstum."[41] Or, put another
way: "God and nation--the two ultimate issues of our day are
perhaps one and the same: God and nation."[42] What the interpretation of "positive Christianity" as something "organic" and
unity-bringing really meant was the handling of the Nazi revolution in religious terms. This GDC viewpoint gave a meaning
to the activities of the Third Reich's leaders that more orthodox and definitive positions could avoid.

"Positive Christianity" might be construed also as the
protection of traditional Christian ethics. Actually, "positive Christianity" was never explicitly defined as such, but
certain GDC ideologists did have the reestablishment of "ethical behavior" in the front of their minds. Reich Bishop
Müller, for instance, believed that the new Reich Church would
be a watchdog for maintenance of "...churchly and German morals
and discipline in city and village, keeping of the sabbath,
Christian schooling and cultivation of the type that is anchored in our racial and Volkish good, pious German mores."[43]
One can find the same desire for moral uprightness exhibited at
various places in GDC writings. An article in an early edition
of *Evangelium im dritten Reich* complained of the desecrations
of Sundays (this was in 1932--still in the Weimar era). The

writer noted that all too often the pious thoughts of Sunday worship were disrupted by the loud sounds coming from a theater or "dance palace" or the "shrill Gramophone tones of Negro music...." The author asked, "Does that really reflect a God-willed kind of culture?"[44] However, these concerns reflected more the author's complaints about modern culture than any very deep interpretation of ethics. There was really not very much importance attached to Christian ethics by the GDC writers, except in the already mentioned shallow sense, or in the question of one's political obligations to the state or Volk. The fact is, what normally passes for Christian ethics, e.g., the Sermon on the Mount, was embarrassing to GDC ideologists. In many cases, the view taken toward the Sermon on the Mount, is very similar to the position elaborated on by Wilhelm Stapel (see Chapter I above). The Sermon was not to be taken as a general Christian moral teaching, but something limited to a particular time and place, or to one's spiritual activities only. Professor Leipoldt, referring to the passage in Matthew concerning "turning the other cheek," denied that this had practical meaning for daily affairs.

> But I see in this comment of Jesus' no law about which the whole life can be formed....One gets the meaning of the words of Jesus in the most sure way when he compares his comments with his deeds. Jesus threw out the merchants in the temple with force and similarly opposed the Pharisees....Jesus had a very fine conception of the relative value of things. It is just because he let the insignificant daily things go by that he established room for the important, the eternal things.[45]

What bothered GDC writers most were the strong pacifistic overtones of the Sermon, and it was this aspect that was most denied. Wieneke disgustedly noted that the Sermon on the Mount was often quoted incorrectly by pacifists and those who simply wanted to shirk their duty in the army.[46] As were the members of the conservative wing of the German Christians, the GDC ideologists were sensitive to moral injunctions against war. Again referring to Christ's command to turn the other cheeck, another GDC writer warned against a "mechanical" Tolstoyan misuse of the Sermon. "This comment [of Christ's] is a so-called 'paradox,' i.e., an apparently contradictory statement

124

such as is frequently encountered in the Gospel of Jesus."[47]
When faced with contradictions between Christian ethics and the
alleged German type of piety and character, the GDC ideologists
inevitably opted for the latter.

In an article showing the social message of the GDC,
Hossenfelder presented another angle of "positive Christianity."
"The message of Christ binds us to a life in obedience to God,
in service to our neighbor, who is in the first instance our
German Volk comrade, and in a selfless, fighting Christianity
of the deed [Tatchristentum]."[48] Hossenfelder elaborated by
saying that just as the evangelical Christian church needed
strong authority to achieve its acts of love, so the Volk needed the creation of a church of German Christians to help build
the Third Reich.[49] Hossenfelder represented an aspect of the
GDC that, unlike the traditional Lutheran position, stressed
social work, at least claiming involvement in social areas that
were normally of concern to the state. Elsewhere, although
Christianity of the deed was affirmed, there was little definition of its meaning. The Twenty-eight Theses of the Saxon
Church, which were taken over by the moderate *Reichsbewegung
Deutsche Christen* as its program, touched on this definition of
"positive Christianity" but followed it up with a very orthodox
statement.

> Christ-faith that does not become deed is worth-
> less in a Volk-church. The deed of Christ-faith is
> decisive struggle against everything evil, and coura-
> geous resoluteness for service and sacrifice.
> Therefore, the Volk-church understands under
> positive Christianity (point 24 of the Party program):
> faith in Christ, salvation through Christ, acting in
> Christ.[50]

Tatchristentum seems to have meant two things. Those who
followed Hossenfelder felt some need to emphasize social work.
Hossenfelder, as already mentioned, was very interested in a
renewed Inner Mission, purging it of political and churchly reaction. "The spirit of national and Christian socialism must
also break through in it."[51] Wieneke, a follower of Hossenfelder, dealt with the topic, comparing Christian social activity with Nazi "Winter Help," welfare concerns, and the saying
"*Gemeinnutz geht vor Eigennutz*" (the public good goes before
individual good).[52] But others seemed to have used the concept

of "Christianity of the deed" as a corrective to an allegedly
overly-theological Christianity. Many GDC writers displayed
anti-intellectualism. The German Christian bishop of Magdeburg, Friedrich Peter, played down the importance of theology
in the movement. Talking about the first year of the GDC, he
commented:

> The distinctive thing about such an hour...when we
> worked together was the fact that again and again the
> objective triumphed over all subjective. We never
> had thoughts about whether we were theologically in
> agreement. We never dissected each other theological-
> ly. The one thing that kept us together inseparably
> was the goal toward which we were striving. It gave
> us a powerful bond in action [zur Tat]. All endless
> theological sifting was to us a crime against the com-
> monly felt task.[53]

Professor Cajus Fabricius, writing several years later, also
emphasized action and vague feelings rather than study in his
analysis of his own allegiance to both Christianity and National Socialism.[54]

During the first several issues of *Evangelium im dritten
Reich*, each of the individual points of Hossenfelder's GDC
platform was given elaboration for the benefit of new readers.
The explanation of "positive Christianity" emphasized the heeding of God in history and in the present.

> Here is found the dynamic power of our faith movement
> that we refer to as positive Christianity, as the
> historical act that goes back to Christ and his good
> news, as the historical testimony of God by which,
> through God's powerful words and deeds, the "fullness
> of time" was prepared, which since the fulfillment in
> Christ continued to be positively set forth and pushed
> ahead, and which even in our day speaks and works,
> saves and blesses, among us...as the unequivocal testi-
> mony of the permanent presentness of Christ and our
> God of reality in the midst of existence, in his
> church, in our Volk.[55]

Again it was Friedrich Wieneke who had something to say to this
interpretation. He was a Troeltsch-scholar in his early academic days, and he admired the theologian because Ernst
Troeltsch "superseded 'historicism,' that view which interpreted world history only out of the objective according to the
laws of natural causality." Troeltsch, he said, glimpsed the
Absolute as the inner active power of history.[56] Wieneke believed that Hitler had much the same insight and had been able

126

to restore the nation's faith in its historical mission. The
new German Christian form of German theology would include the
practical ministry of awakening historical understanding,
"...so that to all of us the call of God is great and powerful,
so that we sense how here also the destiny of our own life is
hidden."[57] One of the contemporary German Christian historians accused the pre-1933 German church of saying that anything
beside the once-and-for-all revelation was the "world" as opposed to "God." The author spoke of "the freedom of God" to
reveal himself in all times and circumstances, and asked that
those in the church keep their eyes and ears open for what happened in the world in order to hear the voice of God.[58] It was
characteristic of the GDC, however, unlike the conservatives,
that although history in general was often referred to, it was
always the here-and-now that was emphasized. History, for the
GDC ideologists, usually was remembered only as far back as
1914. It was the war experience, said one writer, that shat-
tered the 19th century belief in progress and faced one with
the question: "God or nothing? Meaning or lack of meaning?"[59]
Most often, Hitler and Nazism were interpreted as a religious
experience sent by God for the salvation of the German Volk.
Hossenfelder was enthusiastic about the "fulness of time" that
was represented by the Nazi revolution.

> We German men can again understand what a time
> of fulfillment is. With such blessed days as the
> 30th of January and the 5th of March, 1933, we know
> that through God's intercession, the primeval will
> of the best of the German Volk has been lifted from
> the realm of wish to reality....One person whose
> home was in heaven walked on our earth: Jesus Christ.
> His words, "Go and tell John what you have seen and
> heard: the blind see and the lame walk, the lepers
> are cleansed and the deaf hear, the dead rise up
> and the poor are preached the Gospel," say everything
> that can be said over such a time of fulfillment.[60]

God had chosen a man out of the millions in the World War and
had given him "the greatest mission of our history: to pull the
German people out of their doubt and reestablish in them their
faith in life."[61]

It is difficult to imagine more joyful responses to anything than what GDC writers had to say about the coming of

Hitler after decades of alleged spiritual decay. The Germans, one pastor said, had forgotten how to believe.

> And today we again know. The German Volk has found itself again. In an unforgettable majestic hour, under the waving banners of the Third Reich, the banners with the swastika, and under the words of the *Führer*--God bless him!--he happened, that millions of hearts beat as one, lighted and glowed with one spirit, one will, one thought: We will be what in our innermost being God created us for: to be German to the marrow--German and pious!
> And he who has not simply experienced this on the surface, but has felt it innerly, knows: Behind this experience God stood in his omnipotence and his goodness! He sent us the *Führer* whom we needed to again become a Volk.[62]

H. M. Müller denied that Hitler's Catholicism was of any concern to German Protestants. God was perfectly capable of using him to do his work. After all, according to the Old Testament, Cyrus the Persian did God's work even though he was of a "foreign faith."[63] Some GDC writers interpreted God's intervention in 1933 as a call for the completion of Luther's reforming work.

> But it is not enough for us only to call on Luther, rather we must complete Luther's work; we must create a German evangelical church out of his spirit. He who correctly understands the signs of the times knows that we could do it today if we only wanted to: our relationship to Luther is the same as the relationship of the Bismarckian Reich to the National Socialist idea of the state....On the basis of the Gospel, we must so build the church with German Spirit and German ways that it becomes one with the German Volk, that it becomes flesh and blood in us.[64]

Often the call to continue the Reformation was put in such vague terms that it is impossible to determine what the concrete program might be. Still, there was always the sense that, faced with God's obvious intervention in German history, the church was called upon to present something new. To some ideologists of the GDC it was the correct interpretation of the Gospel to recognize the movement of God in the world of observable reality.[65]

Finally, strange as it may now seem, "positive Christianity" was seen by some members of the GDC as the "middle way."

The German Christian movement, said the GDC historian Andreas
Duhm, chose the middle way between revisionless orthodoxy and
the pagan German faith movement.[66] Pastor Grossmann rejected
those who praised "Nordic piety" based on unchristian interpretations of blood and race. On the other hand, he criticized
dialectical theology for not being understandable to most lay-
men.[67] With these sentiments, one is almost full circle to the
first interpretation above of "positive Christianity" as a traditional and orthodox belief. Against neo-paganism, against
dialectical theology, against church reaction and confessionalism, "positive Christianity" could be seen as the "golden
mean," guarding against subversion of the kernel of Christian
truth, yet changing its outer form to be able to speak to
changing Volk needs. The new German Christian church would
have to be progressive and flexible.

The hope was established at the beginning of this discussion of "positive Christianity" that some kind of general con-
sensus could be charted as to the meaning of the term. But it
is impossible to do so. The fact is, the definitions of "positive Christianity" varied greatly not only between one GDC
writer and another, but even within the ideas of individuals
(Wieneke is a good example of this). There was no commonly-
held interpretation of "positive Christianity," but rather a
series of definitions to suit particular occasions and sectors
of the Protestant public. Definitions at various times claimed
orthodoxy, neo-paganism, heroic faith, anti-intellectualism and
moderation.

But "positive Christianity" had a political and proga-
gandistic value. The term "positive Christianity" was compared
at the outset with the word "socialism" in "National Socialism."
David Schoenbaum says the following about "socialism": it was
"...difficult, if not impossible, to locate in Nazi practice.
But as an effective concept it had a very real meaning in Nazi
attitudes. It was hortatory and defined a state of mind."[68]
One could say similar things about the GDC use of "positive
Christianity." Wieneke admitted that even Hitler's use of the
term stemmed from "instinct."[69] One's real intentions could
be hidden behind the phrase. GDC churchmen could interpret

"positive Christianity" ingenuously or otherwise to mean almost anything.

The ideological result of the vagueness of "positive Christianity" was a high degree of theological uncertainty, flexibility, and opportunism, to the point where any action of the Nazi state could be interpreted as Christian. It is not surprising therefore that "*Gemeinnutz geht vor Eigennutz*" and "you are nothing, your Volk is everything" were compared to the Christian spirit of brotherly love.[70]

1.   Beckmann, *Kirchliches Jahrbuch*, p. 5.

2.   Walter Franke, *Deutsches Christentum und deutsche Reichskirche als Forderung der Gegenwart* (Frankfurt am Main: Verlag Moritz Diesterweg, 1933), p. 12.

3.   Constantin Grossman, *Deutsche Christen. Ein Volks-buch: Wegweiser durch die Glaubensbewegung unserer Zeit* (Dresden: Verlag E. am Ende, 1934), p. 9.

4.   Julius Kuptsch, *Im dritten Reich zur dritten Kirche* (Leipzig: Adolf Klein Verlag, 1933), pp. 30-31.

5.   Friedrich Wieneke, *Deutsche Theologie im Umriss* [No. 5 of *Schriftenreihe der "Deutschen Christen"*] (Soldin: Druck und Verlag H. Madrasch, 1933), p. 44.

6.   Hossenfelder, *Unser Kampf*, p. 18.

7.   Kuptsch, *Im dritten Reich*, pp. 17-20.

8.   Duhm, *Kampf*, p. 120.

9.   Christian Kinder, ed., *Der Deutschen Christen Reichs-Kalender, 1935* (Meissen: Schlimpert & Püschel Verlag, 1935), p. 39.

10.   Wieneke, *Glaubensbewegung*, p. 18. The same definition is given, without attributing it to Hossenfelder, in an article by Martin Wagner in Franke, *Deutsches Christentum*, p. 15.

11.   Wieneke, *Deutsche Theologie*, p. 88.

12.   Pinson, *Pietism*, pp. 92-93.

13.   Johannes Leipoldt, *Gegenwartsfragen in der neutesta-mentlichen Wissenschaft* (Leipzig: A. Deichertsche Verlag, 1935), p. 21.

14.   Hans Michael Müller, *Der innere Weg der deutschen Kirche* (Tübingen: Verlag von J. C. B. Mohr, 1933), p. 34.

15.   Grossmann, *Deutsche Christen*, p. 126.

16.   Coch, "Der deutsche Christ und das Evangelium," in Kinder, ed., *Der Deutschen Christen Reichs-Kalender, 1935*, p. 47.

17.   Martin Wagner, "Heldische Frömmigkeit," *Das Evangelium im dritten Reich* (hereinafter shortened in foot-notes to *EDR*), II, No. 6 (February 5, 1933), 45.

132

18. Leipoldt, *Gegenwartsfragen*, p. 16.

19. *Ibid.*, p. 3.

20. H. M. Müller, *Der innere Weg*, p. 8.

21. *Ibid.*

22. Julius Kuptsch, *Christentum im Nationalsozialismus* (Münich: Verlag F. Eher, 1932), pp. 16-17.

23. Hossenfelder, *Unser Kampf*, p. 8.

24. *Ibid.*

25. Martin Thom, *Christenkreuz und Hakenkreuz* (Berlin: Kranzverlag, 1933), p. 28.

26. Julius Kuptsch, *Mit Hitler zur Volksgemeinschaft und zum dritten Reich, mit Christus zur Glaubensgemeinschaft und zur dritten Kirche* (Heiligenbeil: Ostpreussischer Heimatverlag, 1934), pp. 38-40.

27. Ludwig Müller and Christian Kinder, *Die Deutschen Christen: Die Reden des Reichsbischofs und des Reichsleiters der deutschen Christen, Dr. jur. Kinder, im Berliner Sportpalast am 28. Februar 1934* (Berlin: Gesellschaft für Zeitungsdienst G. m. b. H., 1934), p. 14.

28. Quoted in Duhm, *Kampf*, p. 85.

29. Beckmann, *Kirchliches Jahrbuch*, p. 30.

30. Hossenfelder, *Unser Kampf*, pp. 26, 30.

31. Emanuel Hirsch, *Das kirchliche Wollen der deutschen Christen* (Berlin-Steglitz: Evangelischer Pressverband für Deutschland, 1933), pp. 7-8. Also see similar anti-Barthian comments in H. M. Müller, *Der innere Weg*, pp. 19-23.

32. Dannenmann, *Geschichte*, p. 44.

33. Hirsch, *Das kirchliche Wollen*, p. 10.

34. Wilm, "Der deutsche Christ, das Volkstum und das Brauchtum," in Kinder, ed., *Der Deutschen Christen Reichs-Kalender, 1935*, p. 73.

35. Wieneke, *Deutsche Theologie*, p. 44.

36. *EDR*, II, No. 10 (March 5, 1933), 1.

37. From an article by Wieneke in Joachim Hossenfelder, ed., *Volk und Kirche*, No. 4 of *Schriftenreihe der "Deutschen Christen"* (Berlin: M. Grevemeyer, 1933), p. 11.

38. Wieneke, *Glaubensbewegung*, p. 13.

133

39. Wieneke, *Deutsche Theologie*, p. 10.

40. *Ibid.*, pp. 11-12.

41. *EDR*, II, No. 50 (December 10, 1933), 523.

42. Grundmann, *Gott und Nation*, p. 13.

43. Buchheim, *Glaubenskrise*, p. 93.

44. Alfred Bierschwale, "Kirche und Kultur," *EDR*, I, No. 3 (October 30, 1932), 5.

45. Leipoldt, *Gegenwartsfragen*, p. 8.

46. Wieneke, *Deutsche Theologie*, p. 56.

47. Grossmann, *Deutsche Christen*, pp. 62-63.

48. Hossenfelder, *Unser Kampf*, p. 25.

49. *Ibid.*, p. 26.

50. Beckmann, *Kirchliches Jahrbuch*, p. 32.

51. Hossenfelder, *Unser Kampf*, pp. 29-30.

52. Friedrich Wieneke, "Der deutsche Christ als Sozialist," in Kinder, ed., *Der Deutschen Christen Reichs-Kalender*, *1935*, pp. 63-64.

53. Dannenmann, *Geschichte*, pp. 26-27.

54. Cajus Fabricius, *Positive Christianity in the Third Reich* [English edition of *Positives Christentum im neuen Staat*] (Dresden: Hermann Püschel, 1937), p. 10.

55. Pastor Petri on "Positive Christianity," *EDR*, I, No. 8 (December 4, 1932), 5.

56. Wieneke, *Deutsche Theologie*, p. 66.

57. *Ibid.*, p. 64.

58. Duhm, *Kampf*, pp. 9, 11.

59. Grundmann, *Gott und Nation*, pp. 12-13.

60. Joachim Hossenfelder, "Deutschland und der Leidensweg des Heilandes," *EDR*, II, No. 14 (April 2, 1933), 114.

61. Hossenfelder, *Unser Kampf*, p. 22.

62. Grossmann, *Deutsche Christen*, p. 8.

63. H. M. Müller, *Der innere Weg*, pp. 26-27.

134

64. Pastor Wiesner, "Deutsches Christentum," *EDR*, II, No. 29 (July 16, 1933), 266-67. Also see very similar statements concerning the completion of Luther's work in Grossmann, *Deutsche Christen*, p. 136, and Duhm, *Kampf*, pp. 55ff.

65. This sentiment is put into similar terms in Grundmann, *Gott und Nation*, p. 43, and Fabricius, *Positive Christianity*, p. 23.

66. Duhm, *Kampf*, p. 78.

67. Grossmann, *Deutsche Christen*, p. 3.

68. Schoenbaum, *Hitler's Social Revolution*, p. 52.

69. Wieneke, *Deutsche Theologie*, p. 10.

70. Grossmann, *Deutsche Christen*, p. 9.

CHAPTER VI: THE *FÜHRERPRINZIP* AND CHURCH UNITY

During 1933, the *Glaubensbewegung Deutsche Christen* played
a major role in the transformation of the twenty-eight distinct
Protestant state churches into a unified quasi-national church.
Desires for such a union can be traced back into the 19th century, at least, but the immediate impetus was the institution
of the Nazi Volk state which seemed to many German Protestants
to call for a similar renewal of the church administrative
structure on solid Volkish principles of governance. What follows is a study of the GDC interpretation of the *Führerprinzip*
as it applied to the church, and the GDC concept of church
unity.

All GDC ideologists found problems that needed to be overcome in the already existing church (or churches). The 1920's
had seen what the GDC thinkers viewed as a wild growth of
"private" religions. Not only did non-Christian *ersatz* religions of neo-nationalism flourish, but even within the Christian context itself there was thought to be too much individual
initiative. GDC writers blamed the development on the liberal
or socialistic "Volk-destroying" belief in "religion as a private affair" which was voiced in the Weimar Constitution.[1] Too
much differentiation within the church and unhealthy denomina-
tionalism could not be allowed in a correctly-conceived Volk
state. Another unfortunate result of the Weimar Republic, according to GDC ideas, was that many of the churches had been
infected by parliamentary rule. One after another of the various GDC programs stressed the end of church parliamentarism
and politics. Hossenfelder's GDC program stated that the German Christian movement "does not want to be a church political
party in the earlier usual sense....The time of parliamentarism
has outlived itself, also in the church."[2] Professor Fezer's
GDC platform of a year later noted that the goal of a Volk
church could be reached only by adopting a new church constitution, "which does not put the organs of church life on the
basis of a democratic system of election...."[3] Other GDC

theorists similarly rejected parliamentary church government.
Looking back after the institution of bishops in 1933, one
pastor noted how much more efficient the new church was bound
to be. Under the older system, he said, it had been impossible
to get work done quickly or to respond to new ideas, and church
leaders had often mixed theology and jurisprudence in unpro-
ductive ways.[4] Friedrich Wieneke, also looking back, admitted
that Reformed theologians would have more difficulty than
Lutherans adjusting to the "aristocracy of *Führertum*" instead
of parliamentary democracy, but gave his reasons why the old
system was wrong.

> Parliaments and parties put the right of the masses
> over that of personality and contradict the facts of
> sacred history and also the wonderful life work of
> Dr. M. Luther, that it is out of one's aloneness with
> God that gives the strength to make evangelical church
> leaders in the most real sense.[5]

The old conservative church governments were accused of
lacking life and vigor. Hossenfelder accused the existing
church (in 1932) of being a "class and caste" church.

> As an example: of the twenty-one elected members of
> the church senate [of Prussia?] there are seven own-
> ers of large estates, seven theologians, three aca-
> demicians, one manufacturer, and the "Volk" consists
> of a business secretary and a rector. The only rea-
> son this has not had even worse results than it has
> is due to the good sense of a number of ministers
> and faithful members of the congregations.[6]

Hossenfelder blasted the existing church government from two
sides. On the one hand, he accused it of playing politics by
making a pact (the Concordat), in the Prussian case, with a
"Marxist-ultramontane" government, while at the same time he
complained that the church was so reactionary it could not respond to the new Nazi circumstances.

> [The church reactionary] sees only the past, and where
> he knows something about the present he considers it
> only in conjunction with the past. He rejects every
> new idea in the church just because he thinks it un-
> necessary, and because to him church life as it used
> to be appears beautiful and great.[7]

GDC thinkers objected to the old church's neutrality when faced
with Volk renewal.[8] For the last decade, one GDC member recalled scornfully, the church leadership had displayed an

appalling "lack of instinct" (*Instinktlosigkeit*).[9] There is a
strong overtone here of generational conflict. *Evangelium im
dritten Reich* often stressed the needs of youth and the "youth-
fulness" of the GDC movement.[10] Hossenfelder believed that the
existing church reaction was doomed. "The reaction will experience over and over that the power of youth is against it,
and with the youth as such is also the youth of a Volk."[11]
Along with the appeal to, and emphasis on, youth, Hossenfelder
especially hoped to appeal to the workers. "If we want to
create a true evangelical Volk church, then we must not maintain our present stance, but rather win over the army of millions of German educated people and workers."[12] The writers
for the GDC were convinced that the outer structure of the
church would have to change with the new form of the Volk.

In their desire to bring the church into an up-to-date
relationship with, at first, the nationalist undercurrent and,
later, the Nazi state, GDC writers accepted the principle of
the leader (*Führerprinzip*) rather than a democratic or even
traditional synodical form for church government. It is not
necessary here to discuss the general value of the *Führerprinzip* in German nationalist circles, except to say that it was
tied up with what was thought to be a peculiarly German concept
of "true freedom," i.e., one's responsibility to authority (as
opposed to Western parliamentarism which many Germans viewed as
chaotic, falsely individualistic, and community-destroying).
What GDC writers added to the *Führerprinzip* were additional
connections to religious ideas and the application of the principle to Protestant church governance.

The *Führer* somehow rose above the human. One German
Christian writer, whose comments appeared in 1937, made the
divine nature of *Führertum* explicit. "A true leader of the
people, one occupying the highest position of all and at any
moment prepared to pronounce momentous decisions undertaking
thereby responsibility for millions of his followers, knows he
is united with the superhuman, and bends his will to God."[13]
The author was talking about Hitler, of course, but the statement was a religious one based on the conviction held by earlier GDC writers that the *Führerprinzip* was not only wise but
also somehow more in tune with divine will. One view presented

by GDC ideologists was that the Godhead, whether represented by God the Father or Christ, was the supreme example of *Führertum*. Hossenfelder, as might be expected, connected this view with his picture of German Christianity as heroic and *kämpferisch*.

> The picture of the good shepherd that the Savior has given to us has no connection with a pastoral idyll. ...Christianity is a thing of struggle and has to deal with the continuing contradiction of this world. The good shepherd is the *Führer* who stands the test in this struggle....No one can clarify the depths of a *Führer* personality better than the Savior himself. He who could say: "I am the way, the truth and the life," is the *Führer* of the redeemed man in the Kingdom of God.

Hossenfelder also pointed out that the "good shepherd as *Führer* was always closely bound up with his Volk.[14] Pastor Nobiling, who was considered the GDC authority on *Führertum* in the Church, also thought of the divinity as the best example of "leadership." Emphasizing God's words to mankind in history, he declared that, "He is the *Führer*. He is the unbounded Master and *Führer* of the fate and history of the nations in the past, present, and future."[15] In order to be of service in the new Volk-state, GDC writers demanded the spirit of *Führertum* in the church--a spirit that could be recalled by heeding Christ's example. "It is precisely Christianity that has brought *Führer* concepts to their clearer expression....In [Christ's] spirit Christian *Führer* personalities must show our Volk its god-willed way in the difficult future."[16] The glorification of the *Führerprinzip* began with political nationalism, and German Christian ideologists picked it up from there. The imputing of *Führertum* to Christ was an accommodation to the Nazi movement, and very often the rationalization of the "Christian" *Führerprinzip* was made by comparing it to the Nazi phenomenon. Pastor Kuptsch, for instance, said that just as Nazi party members disavowed other party dogmas and leaders and followed only Hitler and his direction, so should good Christians follow the divine *Führer*--Christ. "For a Christianity in which Christ and his good news are not all in all, is no Christianity but only a pseudo-Christianity, just as a National Socialism in which Hitler is not all in all is only a pseudo-National

Socialism."[17] It was very natural for the GDC writer to compare Hitler to Christ, or Nazism with Christianity, on the basis of this common concept of the *Führerprinzip*. Such, for example, was the theme of all of Pastor Kuptsch's books, which it must be admitted, however, never quite succeeded in presenting an internal ideological connection. It was only by association that Kuptsch was still pointing out in 1939 the compatibility of Nazism and Christianity. "Never before has a *Führer* of the post-Christian age led his people so unifiedly and consciously in the way of Christ as Hitler has. The similarity between the spirit and struggle of Christ and that of Hitler is in my opinion completely undeniable."[18]

In addition to the similarities on the surface, however, some writers went further in imputing spiritual strength to Hitler. Walter Grundmann, who strangely enough presented his analysis of *Führertum* in the conservative journal *Glaube und Volk*, spoke of the "magical power of the personality of Adolf Hitler."[19] One of the best examples of the confusion of Hitler and Christ was presented in an article by a member of Ludwig Müller's staff. The enthusiasm for Hitler that he presented spilled over sometimes explicitly, sometimes implicitly, into a view of Hitler as divine, and a glorification of

>...our Führer Adolf Hitler of whom everyone on first meeting him shockingly recognizes: that is a completely pure man! All of us see it thus. In this man there is nothing disunited [*zwiespaltig*]. He is in himself completely one, completely simple, clear and true [*ganz einig, ganz einfach, klar und wahr*]. We also know that the power of such a clear and truthful man does not derive from the earth, but rather out of that higher world that the Master, Christ, called the Kingdom of Heaven. We also know from [the accounts of] men who are close to the *Führer* that he knows of his inner connection [*Verbundenheit*] with God. He knows himself to be the instrument of God and has the clear, simple trust in God of a man who--as the Bible puts it--is reconciled with God. Some people have said of Adolf Hitler that a magic power radiates from him. I do not know whether one ought to put it that way. When one experiences this man for the first time, he certainly feels one thing: the deep humility of the man which is at the same time completely consistent with his higher commission. This oneness [*Einssein*] of man with his God is a symbol of what the old church teachers intended to say with the Three-in-one [*Drei-Einigkeit*].[20]

Some GDC writers said that the *Führerprinzip*, as it applied to the church, was reflected in the writings of the Reformation fathers. One German Christian author (actually a member of the *Reichsbewegung Deutsche Christen*) hoped for a new formation of a church that would synthesize the two concepts (which, he said, were only "apparently contradictory") of the *Führerprinzip* and the general priesthood of all believers. However, the author was referring to the organizational use of the two concepts and not to their ideological consistency.[21]

In practical terms, the *Führerprinzip* in the church was realized in the institution of Bishops--and particularly a Reich Bishop--in the evangelical churches. Comments by GDC writers on the question of the office of bishop in the Protestant church were almost always coldly political and practical. The GDC demanded, for instance, that one of its own members be chosen Reich Bishop since without the GDC impetus the concept would have remained wishful thinking.[22] When Pastor Friedrich von Bodelschwingh was elected to the position, the official GDC position was that the choice was unacceptable even though Bodelschwingh, it could be agreed, was a good and honorable man. Bodelschwingh did not satisfy the GDC requirements for a *Führer*. "That which the German Evangelical Church needs and which the church people long for is a *Führer* who will say 'yes' not only to service but also to the very often bitterly difficult duty of governance."[23] The GDC wanted a bishop, not a "deacon." Pastor Nobiling set down the requirements of church *Führertum* to which any Reich Bishop or bishop would have to conform. First, the church could only have leaders who took a "positive position toward the political situation in Germany created by the national revolution." Old leaders who were ambivalent would be replaced. In addition, church leaders must have outstanding "*Führer* qualities." "Every *Führer* must have a churchly charisma for leadership." The real church *Führer* would derive his character from the blood and race of his Volk. The personal qualities of church leaders were "authority, discipline, and trust."[24] The proposals that Pastor Kuptsch made concerning the bishops and church constitution were even more mechanical, establishing a direct and hierarchical chain of command down from the *Führer* (*Reichsbischof*) through the *Gau-führer* and *Kreisführer* to the *Gemeindeführer*.[25]

The *Führerprinzip*, as used for church interests by the GDC, was taken over from the political usages of National Socialism. To a large extent, therefore, the use of the concept in the Protestant church was an opportunistic accommodation to the new times. But the principle of the *Führer* played an additional role in the theological and moral ideology of the GDC. It was popular as a religious concept because it provided stability, authority, and the possibility of abdicating from personal responsibility. As Paul F. Douglass, an outside observer, noted as early as 1935, relativity in religion and ethics was overcome by the introduction of the *Führer* as an "absolute."[26] Koppel Pinson has also shown how man's feeling of helplessness and weakness without God can be directed toward dependence on the nation in secular times.[27] A similar psychology worked with reference to the *Führerprinzip*. One need only look at the overall theme of H. M. Müller's book on the ideas of the German Church to see that he was predominately presenting a jeremiad against the relativity of all things modern--especially in spiritual concerns. The salvation of Germany, according to Müller, came when Hitler assumed power (and responsibility) and resolved complex issues into black and white.[28] Müller was not the only GDC ideologist to interpret the *Führer* this way. One pastor described Hitler's assumption of power as an act of faith because it silenced incessant debate.[29] Pastor Kuptsch asserted that in the case of both National Socialism and Christianity there need not be complexity. The only essential thing that one needed to remember was that in each there were only single authorities--Hitler and Christ.[30]

The other aspect of the form of the new church governance, in addition to the bishops, was the unification of the twenty-eight *Landeskirchen* into one greater German Evangelical Church. This was perhaps the most important goal of the GDC. In fact, in his "Call to German Christians" in the first edition of *Evangelium im dritten Reich*, Hossenfelder significantly noted the single task of the paper was to "lay the groundwork for a Reich church that would include all German state churches."[31] Hossenfelder's GDC platform voiced the same goal, as did

Professor Fezer's 1933 program. The latter was written after the political revolution and claimed that the "new state wants the church...because it knows where a Volk's foundation lies. With the tasks of the state, the tasks of the church have also grown enormously. In the form that the German churches have today, they are not able to fulfill this task." Unification of the evangelical state churches would follow with recognition of their historically-developed peculiarities.[32]

It is important that most GDC members saw the coming church as only Protestant, because the *Kirchenbewegung Deutsche Christen*, for instance, did not make such a limitation. For the GDC the two great denominations--Evangelical Lutheran and Roman Catholic--would remain separate. But the Reich Protestant church was coterminous with all German Protestants. It would include all German Protestants, as the GDC legal adviser Friedrich Werner put it, "...from Riga to Strassburg, from the Maas [*Meuse*] to the Memel, from the Etsch [Adige River in northern Italy] to the Belt."[33] But it proved more difficult to erase the intra-Protestant differences than GDC writers had hoped, and Christian Kinder, writing in 1935, was scornful of the denominational differences still in evidence. He denied that the average German churchman really knew the differences between the "Evangelical," "Lutheran," "United," or "Reformed" branches of German Protestantism.[34] In general terms, however, the GDC paid lip-service to the Reformation confessions. At the first national convention of the GDC in April of 1933, a proposal was adopted that, "the Reich Church must be constructed in the Luther spirit, in friendly cooperation with the Reformed."[35]

The GDC called for the elimination of church parties, not only because of their reliance on the hated parliamentary and democratic system of government, but also for purely practical reasons. Friedrich Wieneke noted somewhat shame-facedly that the post-war era and its Marxism had been withstood more successfully by the Catholic Church with its united powers than by the "countless evangelical insulated churches [*Inselkirchen*]."[36] When the GDC was attacked as being itself a political creature, Hossenfelder retorted by saying that it was a faith movement and not a church-political party.[37] On the other hand, when

the official Nazi position, as formulated in October of 1933 by
Rudolf Hess, announced that no National Socialist was to be
discriminated against for holding to a certain faith confession
or to none at all, the GDC position was still to deny that
"religion is a private concern."[38] One GDC ideologist noted
that freedom of belief (which he said was self-evident to every
Protestant Christian) must nevertheless conform to Hitler's
broad yet responsible interpretation of Christianity.[39] The
limitation of freedom of belief to the two great Christian
churches remained a demand of the German Christians long after
the Nazi leaders displayed indifference and even enmity toward
Christianity. In 1937, Professor Fabricius was still warning
of the incompatibility of National Socialism and rampant denom-
inationalism.[40] What Fabricius and the other GDC members wanted was a single evangelical Volk church--a Volk church because
the GDC could not conceive of a new church that was not bound
up with the fate of the nation. Hossenfelder said that "Jesus
Christ is the cornerstone and head of the church, but still
there can be no church without the fatherland."[41] The Protestant church and Volk were seen as necessarily growing together.
The end result of GDC comments on the unification of the
churches was not very profound and not very complicated. It
seems that there was little comprehension of exactly what the
new Protestant church would be like after unity was achieved
except a willing instrument of the new political regime.

The real goal of church unity for the GDC was to live up
to Nazism's call. The resolution adopted at the GDC convention
on April 5, 1933, concluded that:

> the church is, for the German, the congregation of
> the faithful who are duty-bound to struggle for a
> Christian Germany. The goal of the Faith Movement
> of German Christians is an Evangelical German Reich
> Church. Adolf Hitler's state calls to the church,
> the church must heed the call.[42]

Alfred Bierschwale, GDC authority on "cultural affairs," found
it abhorrent that there should still be, in late 1933, church
groups that found it possible in any way to oppose the Nazi
regime.[43] Speaking in Berlin in February of 1934, Reich Bishop
Müller devoted his attention to how the Evangelical Church
could help bring the Nazi goals to fruition.[44] In almost every

case, GDC pronouncements about the new Protestant Reich Church reflected the desire to follow the Nazi political example, rather than to lead the new regime in the Christian direction, as the conservative German Christian ideologists had hoped to do. But this could follow from the belief claimed by the GDC that it was the essence of Nazism to rely on spiritual bases and to protect Christian principle. In his Good Friday sermon of 1934, Reich Bishop Müller stated that God had sent Hitler to the German Volk party to help bring unity to the church.[45] The role that the GDC would play in helping to unify the church and place it behind Nazism made it the "spiritual S. A. [*Sturmabteilung*=Storm-troops]" or the "S. A. of Jesus Christ."[46] The GDC was therefore not at all against the *Gleichschaltung* of the churches with the Nazi Volk state. Pastor Bierschwale claimed that "the masses stand behind our faith movement and hope for the more and more energetic *Gleichschaltung* between state and church..."[47] Friedrich Wieneke pointed to *Gleichschaltung* of the theological faculties as the first step. "Not in the sense that one could ever command knowledge. But in the sense that the necessary transformation of the teaching profession (e.g., the introduction of religious Volk studies, etc.) as well as the education of our theological young people can indeed only be undertaken in completely positive conditions." Wieneke asked that all empty professorial chairs be filled in the foreseeable future with German Christians.[48] The GDC ideologist knew that in the totalitarian state there had to be a coordinated Volk culture which included the church. Emanuel Hirsch pointed out that the soul cannot be divided between the state on the one hand and the church on the other. The church had to be innerly bound up with the stormy will characteristic of the hour to build again. "A church that closes itself against the spirit of movement is dead."[49] Ludwig Müller located the place of the Volk church as follows: "We stand not next to nor against the state, but rather in the middle of the state as its truest helper and its most solid support."[50]

In all of the striving of the GDC for a Reich-wide Evangelical Church there was a pervasive opportunism. The call for the elimination of church politics and church parties did not hide the blatantly political emphasis of the GDC. The shallowness or lack of real content in the GDC ideas on the role of the new national church reflected its lack of interest in church affairs beyond the purely structural one of outer unity. With the call for *Gleichschaltung*, the GDC members were willing to abdicate any moral, cultural, or religious authority to the desires of the political power in exchange for attaining a GDC predominance in church offices. The fact that the GDC could not survive the crisis at the end of 1933 reflected its lack of sure ideological footings.

NOTES

1. Gerhard Kittel, *Die Judenfrage* (Stuttgart: W. Kohl-hammer Verlag, 1933), p. 67.

2. *EDR*, I, No. 2 (October 23, 1932), 3.

3. *Ibid.*, II, No. 21 (May 21, 1933), 188.

4. Pastor Otto Eckert, "Evangelische Bischöfe," *EDR*, II, No. 40 (October 1, 1933), 399.

5. Wieneke, *Deutsche Theologie*, p. 115.

6. Hossenfelder, "Partei, Politik, Kirche und 'Deutsche Christen,'" *EDR*, I, No. 2 (October 23, 1932), 5.

7. Hossenfelder, *Unser Kampf*, pp. 14, 32.

8. Kuptsch, *Im dritten Reich*, p. 10.

9. Pastor Nobiling, "Kirchliche Führertum," in Hossen-felder, ed., *Volk und Kirche*, p. 44.

10. See especially *EDR*, I, No. 9 (December 11, 1932), which is entirely devoted to the topic "youth."

11. Hossenfelder, *Unser Kampf*, p. 15.

12. Hossenfelder, "Die Kirche und die Reaktion," *EDR*, I, No. 5 (November 13, 1932), 3.

13. Fabricius, *Positive Christianity*, p. 35.

14. Hossenfelder, "Der Heiland und der Führergedanke," *EDR*, I, No. 1 (October 16, 1932), 2.

15. Pastor Nobiling, "Christus--der Führer der Kirche," *EDR*, II, No. 28 (July 9, 1933), 255.

16. Heinrich Meyer, *Wie stellst Du Dich, deutscher Christ, zum Nationalsozialismus?* No. 1 of *Schriftenreihe der nationalsozialistischer evangelischer Geistlicher* (2d ed.; Leipzig: Adolf Klein Verlag, 1933), pp. 35-36.

17. Kuptsch, *Mit Hitler zur Volksgemeinschaft*, pp. 26-27.

18. Julius Kuptsch, *Nationalsozialismus und positives Christentum* (2d ed.; Weimar: Verlag Deutsche Christen, 1939), p. 14. Also see his similar comments in *Im dritten Reich*, p. 21, and *Mit Hitler zur Volksgemeinschaft*, p. 12, where he says: "You German Christians, if you want to reach the high divine goal of the faith community of your Volk and make a new history in the area of its faith life, then you must behave toward your divine *Führer* Christ as the first Christians once behaved

148

toward him and as the National Socialists in our time have behaved and continue to behave toward their political *Führer*, Hitler.

19. Walter Grundmann, "Führer-Erlebnis und Priestertum," *GuV*, II, No. 8 (August 15, 1933), 147.

20. Horst Schirrmacher, "Drei-Einigkeit," *EDR*, II, No. 24 (June 11, 1933), 214-15.

21. Pastor Hellmuth Gerlich, "Wesen und Aufbau der Deutschen Evangelischen Kirche," in Kinder, ed., *Der Deutschen Christen Reichs-Kalender, 1935*, pp. 34-35.

22. *EDR*, II, No. 23 (June 4, 1933), 207-08.

23. Pastor Lux, "Reichsbischof oder Reichsdiakon?" *EDR*, II, No. 25 (June 18, 1933), 228.

24. Pastor Nobiling, "Kirchliches Führertum," in Hossenfelder, ed., *Volk und Kirche*, pp. 44-46.

25. Kuptsch, *Im dritten Reich*, p. 67.

26. Douglass, *God Among the Germans*, p. 29.

27. Pinson, *Pietism*, pp. 61-62.

28. H. M. Müller, *Der innere Weg*, p. 24.

29. Pastor Wiesner, "Deutsches Christentum," *EDR*, II, No. 29 (July 16, 1933), 267.

30. Kuptsch, *Im dritten Reich*, p. 21.

31. *EDR*, I, No. 1 (October 16, 1932), 1.

32. *Ibid.*, II, No. 21 (May 21, 1933), 188.

33. Friedrich Werner, "Die Rechtsgrundlage der Kommende Reichskirche," in Hossenfelder, ed., *Volk und Kirche*, p. 30.

34. Kinder, *Volk vor Gott*, p. 28.

35. Wieneke, *Glaubensbewegung*, p. 13.

36. Wieneke, "Richtlinien der Glaubensbewegung," *EDR*, I, No. 6 (November 20, 1932), 4.

37. *EDR*, II, No. 50 (December 10, 1933), 523.

38. Fritz Lörzer, "Deutsche Gewissensfreiheit," *EDR*, II, No. 44 (October 29, 1933), 448.

39. *Ibid.*, p. 447.

40. Fabricius, *Positive Christianity*, pp. 13-14.

149

41. Hossenfelder, "Advent in der Kirche," *EDR*, I, No. 10 (December 18, 1932), 1.

42. Beckmann, *Kirchliches Jahrbuch*, p. 14.

43. Duhm, *Kampf*, p. 18.

44. Müller and Kinder, *Die Deutschen Christen*, p. 7.

45. Duhm, *Kampf*, p. 302.

46. References to the GDC as the "spiritual S. A." can be found in numerous sources, including *EDR*, II, No. 49 (December 3, 1933), 516, Hossenfelder, *Unser Kampf*, p. 25, and Franke, *Deutsches Christentum*, p. 20.

47. Duhm, *Kampf*, p. 18. See similar statements by Pastor Nobiling, "Kirchliches Führertum," in Hossenfelder, ed., *Volk und Kirche*, p. 44.

48. Wieneke, "Gleichschaltung der theologischen Fakultäten," *EDR*, II, No. 19 (May 7, 1933), 171.

49. *Völkischer Beobachter*, (May 28/29, 1933), p. 1.

50. Müller and Kinder, *Die Deutschen Christen*, p. 11.

CHAPTER VII: ANTI-SEMITISM AND THE OLD TESTAMENT

"Positive Christianity" meant many things to many people, and the *Führerprinzip* and ideas about church unity simply covered over the *Glaubensbewegung Deutsche Christen* desire to further Nazi political influence in the church. A third element of GDC ideology was also irrational and opportunistic. Anti-Semitism provided a focus for the ills that the GDC hoped to overcome. With only a few exceptions, anti-Semitism was absolutely central to GDC ideology. Much of it was borrowed from the increasingly common holdings of racial and cultural pseudo-science. But the GDC contributed an additional input of what one might have thought the modern secular age would have long before laid to rest--that is, religious anti-Semitism. Religious and cultural anti-Semitism made such a strong impression on German Christians that it basically affected the way in which one of the pillars of Christian faith--the Old Testament of the Bible--was viewed. It is a sad comment on the GDC that a major idea that united the movement--the hatred of the Jews-- contributed to the destruction of the integrity of its own claimed religion.

Racial and cultural anti-Semitism were the common property of GDC writers. Differentiation of race, blood, and *Volkstum* were viewed as God-given. Hossenfelder approvingly noted that the renewed appreciation for race was a healthy antidote to the "utopian," "anti-Godly" concept of "humanity in itself."

> The creative will of God is being newly recognized that God wants race and nations [*Völker*] and intends that men remain, grow, and become more valuable in their type [*Art*]. God speaks a more powerful language in blood and Volk than in the mankind concept. God has laid greater beauty and greater value in differentiation and manifoldness than in monotony and similarity. Certainly we know that our Volk is not racially pure, as it is not without sin. But we know that it is God's will that we point out and struggle for the maintenance of race and type.[1]

H. M. Müller spoke of his desire for the new Volk state to deny citizenship to those who were "foreign" (by which he meant

Jews) and create a special category of law for them (*Gastrecht*). He too justified this on religious principles. "God's will for creation is manifoldness, not sameness....The Gospel does not point out the equality of men among each other, but rather their equality before God."[2] A GDC pastor explained this position as a "law of manifoldness." "Thus there is no such thing as uniform men; nor is there a uniform Volk [*Einheitsvolk*] in this world."[3] Wieneke identified German Christian theology with the racial differentiation viewpoint. "The theology of the German Christians is in its nature the work of the everlasting Father. The differences of the races were willed by him. Man ought never to place constructions over the outlines set up by the Almighty."[4] Even a writer for the *Reichsbewegung Deutsche Christen* could in 1935 claim that, "race is not an accidental construction, but rather 'kairogenesis' [*Kairiogenese*], i.e., a progress of organic nature that makes its appearance in the right place and at the right time."[5]

God's law required, for the GDC ideologists, that the true Christian strive to keep the races as pure as possible. In Hossenfelder's GDC program of 1932, the maintenance of the "life order" of races was presented as "God's law." The corollary was a denial of racial mixing, especially represented by the "Jewish Mission" which was referred to as the "entrance gate" by which foreign blood came into the Volk body.[6] The program of the Twenty-eight Theses taken over by the *Reichsbewegung Deutsche Christen* a year and a half later was more specific in prohibiting interracial marriage as an "offence against God's will."[7] Walter Grundmann said that being created as a German meant, "at the same time: we have received from God the tasks of keeping the Volk pure and helping the Volk to unfold and live according to the possibilities given it by the Creator."[8] One pastor noted that God was already punishing those who had transgressed the healthy laws of the racial Volk and dared to speak of such things as the "world conscience."[9] Racial health, said an ideologist of the *Reichsbewegung Deutsche Christen*, was intimately connected with the spiritual health of a people. "I must confess," he said, "that my decade-long ongoing study of the race question has led me to a deeper and deeper understanding of the secrets of God's work of creation."[10]

In addition to being "God's law" to keep races distinct, the GDC would make it a law of the church. To bolster their argument, Christ was sometimes presented as the "*Volksmann*." Pastor Julius Kuptsch presented in various of his writings the thesis that Christ directed his attention to racial and national units.

> Some people endeavor to present Christ and Christianity as international and maintain that this contradicts the great cultivation of the Volkish, racial, and patriotic consciousness in Christ and his teachings. That is not true! Christ is not an internationalist and a witness against the reality and creation order of God nor an opponent of the latter, rather the best witness of it and its defender....Nowhere in the New Testament do we come across the thought that Christ had had the intention of changing the given reality of the world of the nations and of making out of the different Volks and races a Volkless and raceless international brew of humanity. Just the opposite! He always speaks only of different nations and never, nowhere, of a mankind.[11]

His call to the disciples to go out and preach to all the nations was evidence, said Kuptsch, of Christ's emphasis. "According to this, the true Christianity has also never been an anti-Volkish international appearance, and will also never be that."[12]

For some German Christians, there were limits to this command. Wieneke warned that, "the German Volk must understand and learn to perceive that race neither blesses [*selig macht*] nor protects from sin."[13] Some GDC writers could at times see the dangers of the paganization of race and blood, remembering that the *Bund für Deutsche Kirche* with such ideas had been falsely based on theological liberalism. After the embarrassing statements by Dr. Reinhold Krause in his *Sportpalast* speech of November, 1933, Wieneke explained it as the carryover of ideas from the *Bund für Deutsche Kirche*.[14] But except in times of crisis, there was no limitation on the excesses of GDC ideas concerning race. From the basic view among GDC members that races were the creatures of God, racial anti-Semitism was a logical conclusion.

154

GDC writers also reflected the usual cultural anti-Semitism. The elements of cultural anti-Semitism included attacks against alleged Jewish internationalism and materialism. Gerhard Kittel, Professor at Tübingen, attacked Jewish internationalism of Karl Marx and Rosa Luxemburg. The Jew, he said, generally owes no allegiance to a Volk or nation, but to a humanity ideal--"*Menschentum*." A good example, he continued, was Heinrich Heine and his ideals of world citizenship and a humanity-wide literature, art, and culture.[15] Kittel claimed to be giving an unimpassioned objective analysis of the Jewish question, and thus he corrected, or so he claimed, the centuries-long myth of Jewish "child-murder" and "ritual murder." But his method of absolving Jews from guilt was double-edged.

> Certainly there have been Jewish murderers and sadists; but the idea that they did this [ritual murder] because of their religion is really just a medieval fairy tale and superstition. It is not ritual Judaism that kills men, but rather the impious liberal Judaism that does not work with poison and dagger, but corrupts the nations with other weapons of death.[16]

The issue of the internationalism of Jews was a common point of attack. It was alleged in various places that Jews, because of their inability to think or feel in national German terms, were therefore unwilling to defend the country, made poor soldiers, and were unwilling to be martyrs for any cause--especially a patriotic one. It was alleged further that Jews were willing to cooperate in unpatriotic ways with foreign powers. Pastor Kuptsch said that "those who receive their [orders and ideas about what is right] from Jerusalem, ought to go back to Jerusalem as quickly as possible....In Germany everything must be German."[17] Another professor, Johannes Leipoldt, presented his view that at least in ancient times the political goal of Judaism was Jewish world domination under a messiah-king, and that, "as a rule, the Jew sees only his own *Volkstum* as worthy of notice." In addition, he said, unlike Christ and his disciples, the Jew has never seen the inconsistency between piety and economics. Leipoldt also disparaged the "chosen people" concept.[18] Jews were presented as enemies of European ideals of statecraft. Emanuel Hirsch commented that even after the baptism of Jews or intermarriage with Christian Germans, it

took generations before their progeny could fit into the whole
Nomos of Christian German Volkishness and appreciation of the
European state form.[19] A Pastor Kessel noted to a Berlin au-
dience that Jews were to be found especially in revolutionary
organizations and that after the collapse in 1918, the new
German government was "at least 80 per cent Jews...."[20]

GDC members agreed that Jewish assimilation was a dangerous course to follow. Gerhard Kittel noted that assimilation
was a result of the "liberal age" firmly anchored in the whole
outlook of the 19th century.

> There were always opponents of assimilation and, to
> be sure, on both sides. [In] orthodox Judaism...[and]
> on the Christian side it was never absent in such men
> as Adolf Stoecker and movements such as the Pan German
> Union and the Union of German Students. But because
> they swam against the current, they always were scolded
> as "reactionaries" and made laughable: which hatred
> Adolf Hitler and his movement erased, because they
> dared to put the Jewish question in the midpoint of
> their political program...[21]

Usually GDC writers tried to claim their anti-Semitism was
not a matter of individuals, but of the Jewish people and their
influence in general. Professor Kittel admitted that the Jewish shortcomings he had just finished cataloging were sometimes
found even among members of the German Volk. But that did not
erase the fact, he said, that assimilationist Judaism was in
a special way the "mother earth" for the growth of decadence in
the German Volk. The last fourteen years, with a series of
celebrated "incidents" (*Fällen*), had shown in coarse ways that
not all was in order.[22] Another GDC writer, who was later the
Bishop of Hamburg, was less radical in his disparagement of the
Jewish assimilationism. Dissociating himself from racial anti-
Semitism because he said it was unscientific, he noted, "it is
not the blood, but rather the spirit of Judaism that is the
great danger!"[23] To the question of whether there were not
some outstanding Jews that the GDC could especially note, the
answer was: "Yes. There are those Jews who only want to be
Jews and do not push themselves as 'Germans'....Unfortunately
there are only a few of them."[24]

Jewish assimilation was seen as a cause of cultural decadence. Pastor Kuptsch said as much in an open letter to

American church organizations justifying Hitler's efforts against the Jews. Again it was Gerhard Kittel who had well-developed theories on the problem. Speaking only of the "intellectual facts" of the matter (he would leave the biological results of race-mixing to a biologist), Kittel pinpointed the fundamental fact that the assimilationist Jew was uprooted from his own Volk. The tragedy was that he had lost his home in Judaism without becoming rooted in German *Volkstum*. "That is his tragedy and that is his curse: for out of that arises his decadence...the real basic problem of the present Jewish question."[25] What happened to the Jew who was uprooted from any national or Volkish connectedness? Kittel said it could be reflected in several ways.

> It can be a tired, insensitive, and yet, because it debilitates and infects, a dangerous resignation that eats away at the mark of a Volk; it can be cold, reckoning, perhaps even a self-tormenting and lacerating relativism; it can be wild agitation and demagoguery to which nothing is sacred. Always it is spiritual homelessness, and therefore poison and dissolution.[26]

Jewish emancipation and assimilation were tied up with all the ills of the 19th century. If the situation were allowed to continue as it had the past one hundred years, the German Volk blood could be destroyed by being mixed with the decadent Jewish. Fifty more years of assimilation and intermarriage, said Emanuel Hirsch, and "the bearers of good, old, and pure German blood" would be in a minority.[27] Hirsch also said that when historians of the future look back to the 19th century, they will see that Marxism was the result of German-Jewish mixed marriages.[28] With the undermining of the German Volk, the GDC ideologist believed there was also a danger of Christianity being undermined. One after another of the GDC spokesmen warned against the Jewish Mission, "as long as the Jews enjoy civil rights in the state and therefore the danger of transgression of racial lines and bastardization continues."[29] The GDC hoped to deny the pastorate in German Protestant churches to non-Aryans, or, at least, to limit Jews to their own "Jewish-Christian" churches with their own liturgies, prayers, and religious songs.[30]

In all of the above examples, one can see that many Protestant pastors in Germany were not immune from stereotyped racial and cultural anti-Semitism. Already one can notice, however, that their anti-Semitism did not ignore religious or churchly justification. Cultural and racial anti-Semitism led GDC ideologists to an anti-Jewish position in their Christianity that, as will be shown below, was even further bolstered by blatant religious anti-Semitism.

GDC religious anti-Semitism was based on the premise that Christianity was and is characteristically and basically anti-Jewish. The state Bishop of Saxony, Otto Coch, speaking in September of 1933, at the funeral of a well-known church scholar, revealed the extent to which anti-Semitism had become a central issue in GDC ideology.

> I have also noted how this man recognized the essence of Christianity in the struggle against Judaism, in the basic differences between Christianity and Judaism. Goethe coined the well-known words: the real meaning of world history is the struggle between belief and unbelief. It means basically the same when, from the experience of the last century, we define the words even more closely and say: the real meaning of world history is the struggle between Christianity and Judaism. Since that hour on Golgotha it has been and remains thus.[31]

GDC ideologists claimed that Jews had a basically different concept of God from Germanic or Aryan belief patterns, or, for that matter, from the general Christian concept. Emanuel Hirsch wanted to banish from Christian usage the Jewish legal-religious character of God as *deus absconditus*. The harsh and judging picture of God he found to be portrayed in such places in the Old Testament as the stories of Isaac's offering, David and Goliath, and Jonah.[32] Professor Leipoldt, in his study of the "non-Jewishness" of Jesus, concluded that the Jew knows only one way to approach God. "He reckons with God, as a merchant reckons with his suppliers or customers." Leipoldt was not certain how this attitude had come about, noting nevertheless that historical influences had led Jews into the way of industrialism, marketing, and banking. Overemphasis on these pursuits, said Leipoldt, can further the danger that, "one sees everything, including spiritual life, including piety, only from the viewpoint of economics."[33] Leipoldt noted that Jews

referred to God as "King," while Christ preferred "our Father."
"Jesus lived among a people for whom the belief in a distant
God was especially important, but he himself preached the
benevolent nearness of God."[34] In an article written in 1940
for the "Institute for the Study of Jewish Influences on German
Church Life," Leipoldt continued the same arguments, adding
that the reason there could be no Jewish idea similar to the
parables' teachings about the Kingdom of God nor to the Good
Samaritan, was that the Jews had a philosophy that bad luck
was somehow a punishment for a special sin.[35] Professor
Kittel's suggestion of separate Jewish-Christian churches and
church usages was based on a similar opinion that Jews could
only hope to think of God in "Jewish" terms.[36] Pastor Grundmann noted that at one time in history there had been a pure
Aryan piety, free of all Semitic influences. He distinguished
between the two types of faith--the Semitic and Aryan interpretations of the experience of God.

> The religion of the Semites is history-faith, a
> religion of outer revelation, a foreign-God teaching.
> *Fremdgottlehre*! That means...that God and man
> confront each other essentially as strangers....
> Against this is the similarly racially charac-
> teristic...counterview of Aryan piety....Religion is
> a fact of human nature unconnected with any special
> historical arrangements, something assumed as prior
> and overall.
> On the one hand faith in history, understandable
> recognition and trustful self-contained, insulated
> sacred facts of the past....On the other hand "con-
> temporary religion"; God is always and everywhere the
> same and close....[37]

GDC writers found other aspects of Judaism to be incom-
patible with Christian beliefs. Leipoldt noted how Christianity no longer followed Jewish-style ceremonial law. "Jesus
himself set aside the commandment of the Sabbath when it was
necessary to do so." Similarly, Christ and Christians had
broken through adherence to useless laws of cleanliness [*Rein-
heitsordnungen*].

> The ultimate basis for this is the new relationship
> to God that Jesus established. For the Jews, God is
> first of all the King. The pious man is God's slave,
> must therefore live according to the paragraphs and
> always be ready to settle accounts with God. The
> Christian is God's child; paragraphs can never crowd
> in between God and him.[38]

159

Leipoldt later claimed that this Jewish relationship to God resulted in the unfortunate view that one does charitable works to receive rewards from God. Not unnaturally, he concluded, there is thus among Jewish groups a prevalent feeling that can only be called hatred.[39] Emanuel Hirsch said that Judaism was a religion of national or personal egoism, retaliation thoughts, and slavish observances.[40]

Among GDC writers, there was often an obvious feeling of wounded pride that the Jews seemed not to "know their place." Wieneke ironically noted that the Jew was "the most radical advocate of racial egoism that one could think of...."[41] Gerhard Kittel, speaking about 19th century Jewish emancipation and rejection of the ghetto, was highly critical of the "liberal Jew" who, he said, saw himself as something better than the Christians with their "backward dogma-beliefs."[42] Professor Leipoldt pinpointed hatred of Jews throughout the ages as a reaction to the Jewish belief in being the chosen people. In an argument that contradicts other GDC ideologists' distrust of Jewish assimilation, he deprecated the idea that, as he said, the Jew somehow thinks he is too good to mix with the pagan.[43]

In addition to their alleged incorrect religious practices and relationship to God, Jews, according to GDC ideologists, actually continued to bear the wrath of God. Not only had the Jews abandoned a healthy view of God, but they had not even recognized him when he walked among them. The GDC writers thus resurrected the condemnation of the Jews for crucifying Jesus. The Twenty-eight Theses included one point that summarized the GDC (and the *Reichsbewegung Deutsche Christen*) view of Jewish guilt.

> We see thus in the Old Testament the desertion of the Jews from God and therein their sin. This sin was revealed before the entire world in the crucifixion of Jesus. From then on the curse of God has weighed on this Volk to the present day.[44]

Since the infant murders in Bethlehem, since Golgotha, the struggle of the faithful to confess the "God in the flesh" concept has been going on against the Jews, said another GDC writer. "There is no more tenacious enemy of God, represented by Jesus, than the Jews. They are still today simply the Anti-Christ, and everything that has made a pact with them

spiritually or even in formal church usages, has taken on
their poison."[45] Pastor Grossmann was just one of the GDC
writers who elaborated on Paul de Lagarde's comment that "'No
Volk nails its ideal to a cross.'...The Jews crucified Christ
because he was foreign and repugnant to them, and they have
pursued him down to the present day with their most enraged of
hatreds."[46] The Saxon state bishop Otto Coch contrasted the
Jews to the Germans.

> I once heard someone say: if Christ had come to our
> forebears, to the Germans--they would have understood
> him, welcomed him with open arms, opened up their
> hearts to him, and not nailed him to a cross....I am
> of the opinion: it is precisely in the deep meaning
> of world and sacred history that Christ had to come
> into the world just at that point where hearts were
> the most obdurate, where darkness, where sin was at
> its greatest....The Jews could not understand the
> Gospel of Jesus Christ, but the Germans have under-
> stood it as scarcely any other Volk has.[47]

Another argument that GDC writers offered was that German
thinkers have always pointed out that Judaism and Christianity
have no connection. Pastor Grossmann went into great detail on
this point, quoting Kant, Schopenhauer, Fichte, Paul de Lagarde,
and Houston Stewart Chamberlain, as well as a large number of
German theologians, to show that Germanism was just as compati-
ble with Christianity or even more so than the Jewish context
had been. It is ironic, said Hossenfelder, that we immerse our
children and people in the foreign ways and faith of the Jews
from our church pulpits, and then wonder why Germans do not
understand the voice of God and do not take the Gospel seriously. Judaized Christianity that includes the Volk religion and
history of the Jews does not belong in the German evangelical
churches, nor in the schools.[48]

The degree of anti-Semitism in GDC beliefs could not help
but have an important effect on the view taken of the Old Testament. Most members of the GDC, excluding those who had come
from the *Bund für Deutsche Kirche*, could find some way of keeping the Old Testament intact and an integral part of the Bible.
Regardless of the logical results of their rabid anti-Semitism,
for most the complete rejection of the familiar stories was
just too radical. Wieneke stated this position by saying that
the Bible did not really deal with individuals but with a

"total meaning that must speak to us in the individual stories and allows individuals and actions to appear to us in a new light....Out of the whole alone, God's spirit speaks to him who seeks Him with his whole heart."[49] Even Hossenfelder, whose anti-Semitism was always vicious, could distinguish between the Volk history and the prophecy in the Old Testament.[50] Theologians such as Emanuel Hirsch emphasized the pedagogical or paradigmatic character of the Old Testament--the way in which God intervened directly in the history of a Volk.[51] Franz Tügel, state bishop of Hamburg, took anti-Semitism seriously but claimed not to let it affect his judgment about the Old Testament, the retention of which he called a basic Christian dogma. "The Christian valuation of the Old Testament ought in no way be dragged into the struggle over the Jewish question." Both the Old and New Testaments were the Word of God. Christ was the mid-point of the Bible and connected it all together. Tügel even concluded that the Old Testament itself was really an "anti-Semitic book" telling the struggle of the prophets against the same spirit that must be fought in modern times. "Isaiah 53:6 ["All we like sheep have gone astray; we have turned every one to his own way; and the Lord hath laid on him the iniquity of us all."] and the central point of the NSDAP program are one!"[52] But where the Old Testament was retained by GDC members, it was not nearly of the same value as the New Testament.[53] One example of this can suffice. Friedrich Wieneke, who fancied himself the "theologian" of the GDC, believed, as already mentioned, that the Old Testament would have to be retained by looking at the whole rather than the shameful parts (he specifically identified the stories of Jacob and Joseph among the latter). There are two themes that run through the Bible (including the Old Testament) according to Wieneke. First is the "black thread of sin" that became darker and darker the more the legal mores of Israel unfolded until it reached the depths in the Pharisees and Sadducees who made sin into religion itself. The second "golden thread," which was never completely lost, started with the prophets and ended with Christ and the disciples. Countering the call of Pastor Julius Kuptsch for an all-out struggle against the Old Testament, Wieneke asked only that the Old

162

Testament be read with a new viewpoint.[54] This did not mean
that Wieneke was a moderate among German Christians and really
saw no basic difference between the two parts of the Bible. In
his explanation of what the "new way" of reading the Old Testament would be, he showed the extent to which the revelatory
value of the book had been destroyed for the GDC.

> ...We read and study the Old Testament because with
> all its mistakes and weaknesses, it was still the
> religious book put before the Master Jesus Christ.
> A young National Socialist once said to another in
> a youthful debate over this theme: if you want to
> understand Hitler, you must know Marxism; if you
> want to come to Christ, you must previously study
> the Old Testament. In this formulation there is an
> undeniable truth.[55]

Later in the same book, Wieneke noted how "painful" it was for
Volkish-minded youth to come together in a church and sing
religious songs containing such statements as "...that God
'will make his Israel free,' that the 'God of Jacob' and the
'daughter of Zion' would fulfill this or that."[56]

When Walter Grundmann wrote the "Twenty-eight Theses of
the Saxon Volk Church" (soon adopted by the *Reichsbewegung
Deutsche Christen*), he included one point that summarized the
viewpoint of even the moderate GDC member. The New Testament
was, he said, of primary value.

> The Old Testament does not have the same value.
> The specifically Jewish Volk morality and Volk reli-
> gion has been superceded. The Old Testament remains
> important because it presents the history and fall
> of a Volk who despite God's revelation again and
> again separated from him. The God-fearing prophets
> show us, in this Volk, everything: the way in which
> a nation places itself before God is important for
> its fate in history.[57]

Other GDC writers also viewed the Old Testament as the story of
the fall of a people away from God, and the more radical among
them concluded that it could be canonical only for the Jews.
Pastor Julius Kuptsch called for the removal of the Old Testament from German church usage. Despite some few undoubtedly
good and beautiful things in it, "the Old Testament, the
canonical writings of Judaism, can no longer be the canonical
holy scripture of Christianity....For God only made the Old
Testament with the Volk of Israel, but the New, predicted in

the Old, he perfected with all peoples."[58] German Christians
believed that God had undoubtedly led the Germans in their history too and at times came close to proposing a "German Old
Testament" reminiscent of Wilhelm Stapel's concept of the
Krypta or pre-Christian national *Nomos*.[59]

   Another issue connected with the GDC view of the Old Testament was the question of whether or not Jesus was a Jew.
Some GDC members (excluding those who came from the *Bund für
Deutsche Kirche* and had no doubts about Jesus not being a Jew),
claimed that although the problems of research about the question were difficult, there was some indication that Jesus was
not racially a Jew. Johannes Leipoldt noted that Jesus was a
Galilean and that Galilee was not an "old Jewish land." At the
time of the Maccabees, neighboring peoples were forced to become legally and religiously Jewish, he continued. But most of
Leipoldt's arguments were circumstantial, based on an analysis
of the Jewish "mental type." For example, said Leipoldt, Jesus
rejected the title "son of David"--why, we do not know. Another indication that Jesus had a different Volk soul was that he
could be humorous. "I have the impression," said Leipoldt,
"that the Jew does not recognize humor, but only irony." Other
differences in outlook, somehow related to one's Volk background, were given by the professor with the conclusion that
Jesus was closer to Greek than to Jewish piety.[60] Elsewhere,
Leipoldt admitted that he found it difficult to give the final
answers on Jesus' background, but that in many cases, "men can
appear to be Jews who are not racially Jews but simply claim
the Jewish faith."[61]

   The more common GDC position was to say that although
Jesus may have been racially Jewish, he was intellectually and
religiously "the greatest anti-Semite of all time." In the
Twenty-eight Theses, it was said that the divinity of Christ
made the argument of his Jewishness immaterial. "The strife
over whether Jesus was a Jew or Aryan does not reach to the
essence of Jesus. Jesus was not the bearer of human ways, but
rather encapsulized for us in his person the being of God."[62]
It was the divine role of Jesus as the warrior against Satan
that Kuptsch identified as the proof for Christ's essential
non-Jewishness. The traditional church teaching of the Jews

164

as the elect, and of the Old Testament as sacred, came from the
mistaken view that Christ's proximity to the Jews meant somehow
that he had picked up something from them, said Kuptsch. The
truth was quite different:

> ...the father of lies, the devil, erected the strongest
> bulwark of his dominion among the Jews. Now, if Christ
> wanted to establish his divine dominion for the salva-
> tion of mankind in place of Satan's rule, and to over-
> throw the latter, then he certainly had to begin here.
> For if one wants to conquer a dominion, he must begin
> to conquer at its strongest point. And that the devil
> at all times, but especially in our times, has used
> the Jews as his tools and advocates for the erection
> of his dominion of darkness, corruption, vulgarity, and
> uncleanliness of earth, that is something that everyone
> recognizes today, except for our [reactionary] church
> advocates and our Marxists.[63]

Kuptsch was not above using the additional racial basis for
claiming that Jesus was not a Jew. Pastor Grossmann, for his
part, said he put very little value on attempts to prove Jesus
as Aryan.

> It is sufficient for me to see that the religion of
> Jesus is not an offshoot [Abwandlung] of Judaism...
> but rather a basically different and essentially
> foreign type of faith from Judaism.
>   A man to whom the "tax collectors and sinners,"
> as well as children of the world and heretics were
> more bearable than the Jewish models of piety...he
> was--no matter how his ancestry appears--in no way
> the "classical Jewish man," but much more the "great-
> est of anti-Jews."[64]

Most GDC ideologists limited the Old Testament to what had
a bearing on Christ, or used it in a paradigmatic way to say
something about the way God worked in a Volk's history. But
the Old Testament message was said to be basically different
from the New Testament's. Grundmann said, regarding the Old
Testament, one must make a distinction between what Jesus affirms and completes and what he denies.[65] Pastor Grossmann
counselled that German Christians be "conservative."

> Everything in the Old Testament that "puts forth
> Christ" [Christum treibet], "witnesses to him," or
> leads to the way of "eternal life," is and remains
> God's Word. And they [German Christians] distance
> themselves neither from Jesus nor Luther when they
> ...separate this from what in the Old Testament is
> pre- or sub-Christian. That is what they mean when
> they say: the Old Testament "does not have the same

value" as the New--and even in itself [the Old
Testament] not everything has the same value.[66]

Emanuel Hirsch said that one element alone of the Old Testament
that made it different from the New Testament was that the former never had anything like the Christian hope or certainty of
an eternal life distinct from earthly life.[67] It was most
characteristic of *Reichsbewegung Deutsche Christen* ideologists
to see the Old Testament as the place where one could see the
first glimpses of God's love that finally was revealed in
Jesus.[68] Specifically, some GDC writers denied, as did Pastor
Grossmann, that any "trace of the spirit of Jesus was in the
Jewish hope for a Messiah to erect a Jewish world empire!"[69]
Another attack was that the Old Testament was basically a religion of law while the New Testament was a message of freedom
from the law. Hirsch was one who referred to the Old Testament
as a *Gesetzreligion* and the New Testament as *Evangeliumsreli-
gion*.[70] Leipoldt denied any Old Testament legalistic basis in
Christ's belief and said that: "More strongly than is the case
in Judaism, Jesus emphasized: all doing of good must arise out
of a correct attitude; one ought not fulfill the will of God
unwillingly, but with joy."[71] Wieneke brought the issue up-to-
date by saying that the Old Testament legalistic "argument"
still could be seen in some "dogmatic explanations over the
satisfaction teaching [*Satisfaktionslehre*], as well as in certain attempts of dialectical theology..."[72]

To the question of whether or not the German Evangelical
Church would eliminate the Old Testament, there were two GDC
viewpoints. On the one hand, there was the radical position of
Dr. Reinhold Krause and Pastor Julius Kuptsch, reflected in the
resolution adopted by the Greater Berlin GDC on November 13,
1933: "We expect that our state church as a German Volk church
will free itself from all unGerman things in the holy service
and creed, especially from the Old Testament and its Jewish re-
ward morality."[73] Kuptsch summed up his viewpoint in one sentence: "The Old Testament 'puts forth' [*treibt*] as little of
the meaning of the true Christ as the November system [Weimar
Constitution] did for Hitler."[74] On the other hand, the general German Christian position was that although the Old Testament had little or no doctrinal meaning for Germans, it would

be retained at least in part. It had some churchly value as example.

The results of GDC anti-Semitism were deleterious on several counts. It prevented Jews from the possibility of having any positive relationship to the German Evangelical Church. Even for those few Jews who wanted to convert to Christianity, the way was made almost impossible. In his complaints against the heresy of Reinhold Krause, State Bishop Coch of Saxony continued to support the Aryan paragraph in the church and warned against misuse of Christian baptism. "The Jew becomes a Jewish-Christian through baptism, but he does not become a German."[75] This viewpoint also made it impossible for Jews to seek any kind of protective affiliation with the church as was possible, for example, in a limited way in the Confessional wing. An additional result of even moderate anti-Semitism was that it was a very easy and logical short step to the complete elimination of the Old Testament and "de-Judaizing" of the New Testament. Until the shock of Reinhold Krause's speech in November of 1933, this was, in fact, the direction in which GDC thinking was rapidly heading. Finally, and most importantly, GDC religious anti-Semitism reinforced existing racial and cultural anti-Semitism and thereby eliminated a potentially major stumbling block to Nazi hatred of Jews. The easy results that the Catholic Church had obtained by its intransigence against Nazi euthanasia practices, proves what power the churches could have exerted to ameliorate persecution of the Jews had they wanted to. Instead, GDC anti-Semitism allowed for, and willingly supported, all efforts against the Jews. An article in *Evangelium im dritten Reich* as early as September of 1933, called for strong new laws concerning eugenics and racial expertise that would result in euthanasia, sterilization, and prohibition of mixed marriages.[76] It was in the opportunistic nature of the GDC ideologists that they did not believe in the integrity of their ideas enough to judge Nazi actions by sincere Christian principles.

NOTES

1. Hossenfelder, "Unser Kampf," *EDR*, I, No. 2 (October 23, 1932), 3.

2. H. M. Müller, *Der innere Weg*, pp. 28-29.

3. Meyer, *Wie stellst Du Dich*?, p. 23.

4. Dannenmann, *Geschichte*, p. 14.

5. Pastor O. Kleinschmidt, "Der deutsche Christ und die Rassenfrage," in Kinder, ed., *Der Deutschen Christen Reichs-Kalender*, *1935*, p. 43.

6. *EDR*, I, No. 2 (October 23, 1932), 3.

7. *EDR*, II, No. 53 (December 31, 1933), 562, and Beckmann, *Kirchliches Jahrbuch*, pp. 30-31.

8. Grundmann, *Gott und Nation*, p. 65.

9. Meyer, *Wie stellst Du Dich*?, p. 24.

10. Kleinschmidt, "Der deutsche Christ und die Rassenfrage," in Kinder, ed., *Der Deutschen Christen Reichs-Kalender*, *1935*, pp. 44-45.

11. Kuptsch, *Christentum im Nationalsozialismus*, p. 14.

12. Kuptsch, *Im dritten Reich*, p. 33.

13. "Zur Lage," *EDR*, II, No. 45 (November 5, 1933), 465.

14. *EDR*, II, No. 49 (December 3, 1933), 514.

15. Kittel, *Die Judenfrage*, pp. 27-29.

16. *Ibid.*, pp. 41-42.

17. Kuptsch, *Christentum im Nationalsozialismus*, p. 13.

18. Johannes Leipoldt, *Antisemitismus in der alten Welt* (Leipzig: Verlag von Dörffling & Franke, 1933), pp. 52-53, 20.

19. Hirsch, *Die gegenwärtige geistige Lage*, p. 22.

20. Pastor F. Kessel, "Sind die deutschen Christen Antisemiten?" *EDR* für Gross-Berlin, supplement to *EDR*, I, No. 10 (December 18, 1932).

21. Kittel, *Die Judenfrage*, p. 31.

22. *Ibid.*, p. 26.

23. Franz Tügel, *Wer bist Du? Fragen der Kirche an den Nationalsozialismus* (Hamburg: Agentur des Rauhen Hauses G. m. b. H., 1932), p. 51.

24. "Fragekasten," *EDR*, I, No. 6 (November 20, 1932), 7.

25. G. Kittel, *Die Judenfrage*, p. 24.

26. *Ibid.*, p. 25.

27. Hirsch, *Das kirchliche Wollen*, p. 11.

28. Hirsch, *Die gegenwärtige geistige Lage*, p. 24.

29. "Richtlinien der GDC," *EDR*, I, No. 2 (October 23, 1932), 3. Also see in I, No. 1 (October 16, 1932), 7.

30. Hossenfelder, ed., *Volk und Kirche*, p. 48, and Gerhard Kittel, *Kirche und Judenchristen* (Stuttgart: W. Kohlhammer Verlag, 1933), pp. 1ff.

31. Poliakov and Wulf, *Das Dritte Reich*, p. 252.

32. From Hirsch's book *The Old Testament and the Preaching of the Gospel* (Tübingen, 1936), quoted in Nicolaisen, *Auseinandersetzungen*, pp. 92-93.

33. Leipoldt, *Gegenwartsfragen*, pp. 45-46.

34. *Ibid.*, p. 53.

35. Johannes Leipoldt, "Jesus und das Judentum," in Grundmann, ed., *Christentum und Judentum*, pp. 40-41.

36. G. Kittel, *Kirche und Judenchristen*, pp. 10ff.

37. Grossmann, *Deutsche Christen*, pp. 122-23.

38. Leipoldt, *Antisemitismus*, p. 52.

39. Leipoldt, "Jesus und das Judentum," in Grundmann, ed., *Christentum und Judentum*, p. 51.

40. Nicolaisen, *Auseinandersetzungen*, p. 92.

41. Wieneke, "Die Weisen aus dem Morgenlände," *EDR*, II, No. 2 (January 8, 1933), 12.

42. G. Kittel, *Die Judenfrage*, p. 21.

43. Leipoldt, *Antisemitismus*, p. 20.

44. Beckmann, *Kirchliches Jahrbuch*, p. 31, and *EDR*, II, No. 53 (December 31, 1933), 562-63.

45. Friedrich Peter, "Wahl aus Glauben," *EDR*, II, No. 10 (March 5, 1933), 76.

46. Grossmann, *Deutsche Christen*, p. 58.

47. Coch, "Der deutsche Christ und das Evangelium Jesu Christi," in Kinder, ed., *Der Deutschen Christen Reichs-Kalender, 1935*, p. 48.

48. Hossenfelder, *Unser Kampf*, p. 18.

49. Wieneke, *Deutsche Theologie*, p. 48. The same general view that the Old Testament must be retained in order to understand the "old Bible" as well as the "new," may be found in Wieneke, *Glaubensbewegung*, p. 16.

50. Hossenfelder, *Unser Kampf*, p. 18.

51. Nicolaisen, *Auseinandersetzungen*, p. 74.

52. Tügel, *Wer bist Du?*, pp. 54-57.

53. For a discussion of certain central German Christians on this, see Nicolaisen, *Auseinandersetzungen*, pp. 64ff.

54. Wieneke, *Deutsche Theologie*, pp. 44-49.

55. *Ibid.*, pp. 52-53.

56. *Ibid.*, p. 156.

57. Beckmann, *Kirchliches Jahrbuch*, p. 31, and *EDR*, II, No. 53 (December 31, 1933), 562.

58. Julius Kuptsch, sections on the Old Testament from his book *Der Lebendige Christ* (Eisenach: Neuland-Verlag, 1932), excerpted in Franke, *Deutsches Christentum*, p. 17.

59. See, for example, the discussion of German spirituality of pre-Christian days and of the *Heliand* poem in Grossmann, *Deutsche Christen*, pp. 101ff., and the account of the *Heliand* and the Icelandic Sagas in Grundmann, *Gott und Nation*, p. 75. In the latter case, Grundmann was specifically asking that the German past be substituted in youth education for the Jewish past presented in the Old Testament, although, it should be noted in all fairness, Grundmann pointed out the fears, barbarisms, and insufficiencies of the spiritualism of pre-Christian Germany corrected by the coming of Christianity.

60. *Gegenwartsfragen*, pp. 17-19, 54.

61. Leipoldt, "Jesus und das Judentum," in Grundmann, *Christentum und Judentum*, pp. 31-32.

62. *EDR*, II, No. 53 (December 31, 1933), 562, and Beckmann, *Kirchliches Jahrbuch*, p. 31. Wieneke said almost exactly the same thing in *EDR*, II, No. 49 (December 3, 1933), 514, although he was obviously mending GDC fences after the Krause affair.

63. Kuptsch, *Im dritten Reich*, p. 41.

64. Grossmann, *Deutsche Christen*, p. 58.

65. Grundmann, *Gott und Nation*, p. 73.

66. Grossmann, *Deutsche Christen*, pp. 39-40.

67. From a book review article by Wilhelm Stapel, "Das alte Testament," *Deutsches Volkstum*, December, 1936, p. 944.

68. Nicolaisen, *Auseinandersetzungen*, p. 75. Note also the 1936 "Theological Declaration" of the RDC which the Reich Church Committee found to be orthodox, and which included the statement, "We see in the Old Testament the documentation of divine revelation preparing for the coming of Christ, but we also view the revelatory authority of the Old Testament for the Church of Jesus to be limited to those statements that 'put forth Christ.'" *Die Christliche Welt*, L, No. 14 (July 18, 1936), 651.

69. Grossmann, *Deutsche Christen*, p. 39.

70. Nicolaisen, *Auseinandersetzungen*, p. 92.

71. Leipoldt, *Gegenwartsfragen*, p. 53.

72. Wieneke, *Deutsche Theologie*, pp. 74-75.

73. Beckmann, *Kirchliches Jahrbuch*, p. 29.

74. Kuptsch, *Im dritten Reich*, p. 43.

75. Duhm, *Kampf*, p. 120.

76. Annette Ramoser, "Der deutsche Christ und die Bevölkerungspolitik," *EDR*, II, No. 39 (September 24, 1933), 284-86.

PART IV

THE *KIRCHENBEWEGUNG DEUTSCHE CHRISTEN*

CHAPTER VIII: GOD'S REVELATION IN THE NINETEENTH
AND TWENTIETH CENTURIES

> New perceptions have been sent today to our Volk
> through its Führer, its seers, and heroes. These
> new perceptions knock at the gates of the church,
> asking the theologians whether they have an answer
> for the day and its profundity, or whether we can
> only sing the melodies of yesterday, remaining
> blind and deaf to the passage of God through our
> time.[1]
>
> > --Siegfried Leffler, Julius Leutheuser,
> > and Wolf Meyer-Erlach, November 23,
> > 1933.

The ideological framework of the *Kirchenbewegung Deutsche Christen* made it the most revolutionary of German Christian movements. The excesses of the KDC showed the danger that libertarianism or lack of firm foundations could have even in the realm of ideas. Yet, one must also observe the sincerity of most members of the KDC, their independent nature, their optimism, their willingness to endure ridicule and persecution even at the hands of other German Christians. They were, in addition, quite distinct from the other two German Christian movements already discussed. The *Christlich-Deutsche Bewegung* revealed the dangers that come, ironically, from too much reliance on an orthodoxy or a legalism that does not allow for rapid independent thinking. The *Glaubensbewegung Deutsche Christen* was more insidious with its political and ideological opportunism, and rabid anti-Semitism. The KDC attracted those people whose theology was emotional, fluid, and enthusiastic. Because they were easily affected by surface impressions, the KDC members never doubted the rightness, or even sacred nature, of Hitler's National Socialism, even when the regime looked askance at the KDC propensity to strike out into embarrassing radical directions. Elements of all the KDC ideas could be found in the other German Christian groups, but the KDC

172

ideologists had a way of enthusiastically overstepping the bounds of religious propriety.

One of the common ideas of KDC ideologists was that God had revealed himself in obvious ways in German history during the past 150 years. "History stands under the will of God, i.e., an historical happening is, in its ultimate base, not the working out of worldly powers of an economic or political nature, but rather leads out of the eternal will of God."[2] God revealed his movement in earthly happenings for definite reasons. "God does not suspend us in an empty somewhere separated from all earthliness; he lives and reveals himself to us as the creator in the creation of this our Germanness, and to seek him in his creation is obedience to him, service to the moral callings of the Volk body."[3] The KDC ideologists definitely believed that God had a mission for the Germans. At times it might seem that the content of the mission had not yet become clear. One KDC writer spoke of the "Gethsemane hours" through which Germany had already come. "And we can only come to the end if we see before us and over us God's sight that places before us the way and the sacrifice."[4] Siegfried Leffler, Julius Leutheuser, and the Thuringian State Bishop Martin Sasse vaguely defined their God-given mission as to aid the nation's rebirth, which had meaning for the whole world.

> We believe that in our fatherland's rebirth the power of God reveals itself, that in its fearful suffering the crucified Christ has come to us, and that in his healing announcements Germany's mission to the whole world finds its promise. We accept the faith bases of the old church. But the new times, the powerful experiences of our day, the spiritual immersion of the Third Reich in the all-embracing idea of Adolf Hitler, brings a new interpretation with it--the necessity of a new standpoint from which old truths obtain new meaning and new content. Only one thing is changed in the positive confession: we see the revelation of God not completed in ancient times, but rather we see God living among us and in our Führer Adolf Hitler, his instrument for our day.[5]

Julius Leutheuser tied up Germany's fate with the salvation of the world after giving his view that the meaning of history was God saying, "Become a Volk. As a Volk my Holy Spirit shall be your temple. Become my Volk."

> He who does not love Germany also cannot love the
> world. He who betrays Germany betrays the world.
> He who despairs in Germany despairs of the meaning
> of the world. He who cannot die for Germany does
> not know God's way of the cross through the world.
> He who does not believe in Germany's resurrection
> does not believe in the resurrection of God in spite
> of the darkness and power of this world.[6]

God chose the Germans as his special people, said Leutheuser. "God's kingdom and the German Empire have concluded a compact [Bund]: 'I will be your God and you shall be my people' is said to the hearts of those who heed the little word 'Germany.'"[7]

Walter Grundmann, who by the mid-1930's was affiliated ideologically with the Thuringian German Christian (KDC) movement, believed that Germans could seek God in the turning points of their recent history. Germans were said to be thrown into the "rhythm of historical events" and felt God's wrestling and shaping there. Grundmann valued this decision-demanding religion as a personal, unmediated type of relationship to God.[8] Other KDC writers also believed that Germans had the right actually to see God and his handiwork in their own recent history as earlier people (i.e., the Jewish people) did in theirs. Answering the attacks from the Confessional Bavarian State Bishop Hans Meiser, who claimed that the KDC had placed Volk-history as a second source of revelation next to the Bible, a KDC professor at Jena retorted:

> Is God only then the Jewish God and not the God of
> the Germans? Has God been mute since the conclusion
> of the Biblical canon and abdicated his world domin-
> ion in favor of the theologians? Are all those who
> since these days have spoken of being driven by him
> heretics?...For this God of these theologians is
> only a God of the dead and not of the living, is
> only a God for Jews, but not for Germans.[9]

The following is an analysis of the revelatory value that KDC members gave to German history since the beginning of the 19th century.

The German war of liberation against Napoleon was seen by the KDC writers as the birth of German Volk self-identification and the beginning of the compact made between God and the German people. It was indicative of the KDC lack of Lutheran orthodoxy, and at the same time their almost complete but sincere substitution of national affairs for religious, that the

KDC writers seldom considered earlier German history--e.g.,
Luther. "And we as children of the 20th century are the direct
descendants of the 19th century, not of the 16th, as some theologians would like to believe."[10] The liberation period, said
Wilhelm Bauer, was a time not only for men of action, but also
for men of faith--a quality that had too much been lost sight
of since then.

> We, the children of a technical century, the heirs of
> a "free" mentality, of a science separated from God...
> we men of the great cities and dead asphalt, we look
> yearningly back to the times when men lived enveloped
> in original nature, we grope troublesomely back for
> the secrets of a life based on the Volk.[11]

But the time of German innocence was a time of great spiritual
struggle between the sinless, simple German heart and soul, on
the one hand, and the French underworld (or antiChrist, as
Pastor Julius Leutheuser called Napoleon) on the other. Leutheuser said that the yet disunited German people at the beginning of the 19th century heard the clear word of God: "Germany,
you have I called. Build a likeness of my eternal Kingdom in
this world in which Hell seems [to have triumphed and] there is
no longer any heaven." Leutheuser reeled off the names of
those who heard God's call--General Scharnhorst, General
Gneisenau, Friedrich Jahn, Friedrich Schiller, Baron von Stein,
General Blücher, Theodor Körner, Johann Fichte, E. M. Arndt,
Heinrich von Kleist, Gottlieb von Schenkendorf, and Queen
Louisa.[12] Wilhelm Bauer believed that the liberators' readiness for sacrifice was only understandable as "the stand of the
German heart against a foreign spirituality, against the anni-
hilation of its own most sacred qualities."[13] The struggle was
directed against the French deification of reason which originated in the principles of 1789.

> In Paris at that time they placed a prostitute on the
> altar where the saints had once been enthroned. That
> was blasphemy. They called it reason. But this rea-
> son gave men the freedom to tear off all restraints
> and to be more animal-like than any animal. In pros-
> titution "love" became a life-destroying power; for
> [where there is] unbounded pleasure, where men seek
> pleasure for its own sake, and the fruit of love, the
> child, is set aside as the unwanted result, this
> devastates the bodily health of man and destroys
> reverence that lives in the soul. The Napoleonic

Empire was the attempt to build a world empire out of the Western spirit of intellectualism and imperialism, in which Volkish ways are rejected and their differences are erased.[14]

In the *Heilsgeschichte* view of KDC writers, the Germans of the early 19th century were somehow the chosen people among whom there were those who already saw the French deification of reason as the fall of man from God--original sin. Leutheuser was quite explicit about this interpretation.

What the world came to see again in the French Revolution, that men put reason on the altar and thereby set a human abstraction in the place of the living God, was the old original sin of humanity. This pestilence established itself strongly in the peoples of the Mediterranean basin and found finally its most consequential carrier in Judaism.[15]

Napoleon was seen simply as the logical end result of godless reason. The revelatory meaning of the liberation period was interpreted as, first, the struggle against the power of darkness (which because of the original sin of 1789 was actually victorious beyond 1815), and, second, as the origin of God's compact with the Germans in which God said: "Become a Volk."[16]

The 19th century was the age of false liberalism. Original sin had not yet been set aside. Community spirit disintegrated, said Wilhelm Bauer, and class struggle was set up in its place. Men became specialists; intellectual knowledge which once was an aid to the strengthening of one against dangers now began its tyranny over man. Technology and industry put man in their own service and sapped his soul by encouraging his haughtiness about personal knowledge, education, and possessions. "This haughtiness, however, produced hatred by those who did not have these possessions and drove them into the arms of a world outlook that made hate into a system--class-struggling Marxism--which separated the working comrades into workers and owners, the Volk community into proletariat, bourgeoisie, and barons, ripped apart brothers living in common spiritual feelings and intellectual values into classes of the educated and the despised uneducated."[17] It was in the 19th century, said Walter Grundmann, that the organic working together of body, soul, and mind were torn apart by materialism.[18] Marxism was a result, again, of original sin. With the triumph

of technology, science, and unbridled individualism, there
were only a few who kept in mind the call of God to become a
Volk. These were the prophets--despised and laughed at even in
their own land.

> Therefore the truly educated [*Gebildeten*] of our Volk
> stood lonely and misunderstood. They were in all
> classes, the workers, the farmers, the schooled. They
> were the *Stillen im Lande*...those inconsonant with the
> times. And certainly they were the only twinkling
> stars in the German night who showed the way home.
> Lonely ones, individuals, such as Nietzsche, de Lagarde,
> Langbehn, Chamberlain. In the church, Wichern,
> Stoecker, Bodelschwingh, and many who were uncounted,
> unknown, who in their places, despised or laughed at,
> sang the song of their home, each in his own way.[19]

In the 19th century, however, Bismarck fashioned the German Empire. But KDC writers were ambivalent toward it, and
certainly did not believe that the Germans had completely fulfilled their destiny by 1870. Bauer noted:

> the restless spirit of the front fighters of 1813
> and 1815 found its fulfillment in the Bismarckian
> state building. But in this state the liberalistic
> ideas of 1789 continued their subterranean struggle
> against conservative, strong, duty-fulfilling Prus-
> sianism. The materialistic world continued in the
> garment of science, industry, and technology, and
> that here the ruling "reason" really became a prosti-
> tute was evidenced in moral destructions, be they of
> family and marriage, fidelity to one another or re-
> spect for the opposite sex, [despised] as unmodern
> and laughable conventions.[20]

Leutheuser also believed that the Bismarckian wars of German
unification were simply an interlude. After the achievement
of unification the period of peace (1870-1914) was increasingly
characterized by the bourgeois "adoration of the 'I'" and the
money-God continued its poisoning of Germany.[21]

The 19th century was thus seen in *Heilsgeschichte* terms by
KDC writers. The comparisons of Germany's way to Biblical examples are obvious and, in fact, sometimes explicit. The Germans in the 19th century were like the Old Testament Jews, cast
out of Eden after the original sin, working out their history
in its relationship to God, increasingly bowing to the golden
calf of materialism, repeatedly being warned by a few despised
prophets, experiencing a few bright spots (e.g., German unification), but generally bearing the overriding mark of damnation

From their sacred-historical viewpoint, it only remained to
identify the coming of Christ to the Germans.

The period from 1914 to 1933 represented, to the KDC
ideologists, the "New Testament" of the German people. Other
German Christian writers had noted the effect that the war experience had on their outlook, though, in the case of the
Christlich-Deutsche Bewegung ideologists, for example, they
were not always certain of the war's true religious significance. KDC writers, however, were not reluctant to define the
war as the beginning of German's most significant dealing with
God. Wolf Meyer-Erlach put it this way:

> Truly the experience of the front let us see the
> background of life not just from books but rather in
> the hell of battle. We know something of the borders
> of death, not because of cleverness, but because of
> horrible experience. We know something of the abyss
> of the fact of man which Nietzsche talked about.
> That we know something about the grace of God in
> Christ, of the power of his word, that in itself is
> grace.[22]

Elsewhere Meyer-Erlach identified the war as the point at which
he and many of his friends had become "passionate Christians,
with unbowing and strong faith, and passionate Germans." He
told of times of "sacred quiet" in the trenches. "Thousands
had hours of silence, these sacred hours of decision, of meeting with Christ. And never again would they leave that which
had touched their soul to the innermost." This was how, said
the author, we became German Christians.

> Our whole life since those hours and years has been
> suspended between two poles: eternity and time, be-
> tween Christ and Germany, God and country, and as
> long as we live it will remain so....The trenches,
> the boundless distress of our Volk, the death strug-
> gle of our fatherland was the birthplace of new, yet
> very old, faith, of a new attitude that was yet only
> the old of the great German Christian times, the
> times in which, according to prophetic men, the af-
> fairs of God and our Volk became one.[23]

The war helped the Volk to become self-conscious. Leffler
spoke of the "quiet sacred hope" that asked: "When will you
finally appear, soul of the fatherland?"

> And see, there was a stirring in all corners and nooks
> of the earth. It was the step of the one who holds
> together the world at its innermost places. The world

was shaken by one of the most murderous wars that there has ever been. God sought it, God sought the German Volk home. Alone it would never have found itself, never found its way back to its original home. In the fearful material battle, on a sea of tears and blood, the German Volk experienced the meaning of its existence; it was shown what a Volk is.[24]

The German front soldier, said Walter Grundmann, discovered that men are not individual beings but essentially limbs of a body.[25] The war, said Meyer-Erlach, taught us to be a Volk by destroying the sense of class differences. "These upstanding martyrs for God teach us that which God has forged together with the bone hammer [Knochenhammer] of death, what God has united together with the blood, the deathly distress of millions, no man can rip apart. We experienced ourselves as a unique Volk."[26] The promise of the new arose out of the ashes of the old.

In the descent of millions, an entire Volk woke up for Germany. Now there were no longer individuals, no longer just a small vanguard; now it was the whole German Volk that travelled the way home--begrieved, wounded, afflicted to the very soul and full of yearning. An artist of the Great War movingly depicted this march of the silent columns--German troops wending their way back to their cities, towns, villages. Before them led the spiritual army of companies and battalions that had risen to the other world, homeward, always only homeward, in order to found the eternal Germany.[27]

Parallels of the war, especially the end of the war, with the experiences of Christ's life, were often made by KDC writers. Pastor Erich Fromm spoke of the loneliness of Germany's position. "For our way led certainly through Gethsemane hours in which the goal of our service appeared unattainable, where the whole horror of our lonesomeness suddenly struck us and made us timid." Only because Germans knew God was determining their fate, said Pastor Fromm, could they find strength to continue.[28] Even as early as 1933, Walter Grundmann, not then a member of the KDC, had observed that the moral of the World War had been that some die so that others live. This, he said, was a combination of God's judgment and grace, comparable to Christ's sacrifice on Golgotha.[29] The most striking examples of drawing the parallels between Germany's history and Christ's

life were achieved by Julius Leutheuser who likened Germany's
fate to Gethsemane.

> There while one slept, the others became the Judas
> of the holy Reich of Germans. Pieces of silver and
> peace at any price became their world outlook that
> they falsified as love of Volk, and thus Germany was
> delivered up to the knife of the Pharisees and Saddu-
> cees of the nations with the world kiss of Volk recon-
> ciliation. The traitor kiss in Gethsemane and the
> peace treaty of Versailles are the marks of the lie.
> "Yes, the devil was a liar from the beginning." This
> saying by Jesus applied 2000 years ago and it applies
> today.[30]

But Golgotha, Leutheuser knew, was not the end of the story.
"...We know that though a Golgotha once came to Germany, we
have a one who shows us that Golgotha is not the end, that
Gethsemane does not simply mean temptation, and that the ultimate result is not doubt, but rather that Golgotha leads to the
resurrection of the world."[31]

Between the end of the war and 1933, there was a hiatus in
which, said the KDC writers, as in the period between Good Friday and Easter, death seemed victorious. In the political
world of Germany in the 1920's, death was the antiChrist, Bolshevism. Wilhelm Bauer said:

> The smashing of Marxistic Bolshevism is to me not only
> an act of state, but also a struggle against devilish
> powers carried out on the political plane; the *Führer*
> is the instrument that God has chosen, and if we honor
> the *Führer* then we worship [*anbeten*] him not as a man,
> but recognize that through him God has spoken and
> worked.[32]

But in the early years of the Weimar Republic, Bauer said, the
outlook seemed dim. "The incomprehensible collapse of 1918,
despite the most brilliant victories, and the suffering that
broke in on us because of Versailles, meant the apparent victory of the opposite spirit [from what had been felt during the
war]."[33] The false spirits of parliamentarism, democracy, and
belief in the "decline of the West" insinuated themselves even
into the church, said Siegfried Leffler. The spirit of Karl
Barth and Weimar democracy "were one and the same mentality."[34]
Aside from a very few (perhaps the S. A. cells), most Germans
lost faith.

But Hitler came to power; the powers of darkness were overcome, and Germany had its "Easter experience." All of the KDC writers, to a greater or lesser degree, viewed 1933 as somehow comparable to the resurrection of Christ. Meyer-Erlach was relatively reserved for a KDC ideologist when he said he had seen faith reestablished in the new formation of state and Volk.[35] But Leutheuser and Leffler made no attempt to bridle their enthusiasm. Leutheuser's 1934 Advent message gave thanks for the turning away from "individualism and momentary demands," and for the way in which Germans had allowed for the triumph of the "eternally young, eternally new life of God in our Volk.... Let this be our Advent message: 'The Savior has come again to the Germans. He wishes to dwell with us.'"[36] Elsewhere, Leutheuser spoke in terms that made Hitler look as if he had assumed the sins and sorrows of the world on himself. It was typical of Leutheuser's parallelism that he pointed out the outstanding fact that God had chosen his instrument in the military hospital at Pasewalk--"the simple, unknown front soldier, Adolf Hitler."

> He allowed himself to be made an instrument for faith in Germany. Because of his love for Germany, he could not renounce his calling Volk, the sacred Reich of the Germans. "He who abides in love abides in God and God in him." Through the faith of Adolf Hitler, the road of suffering and death for the Germans could be changed to resurrection. Thus the Golgotha of the World War became the way of the resurrection of the German nation through the faith of Adolf Hitler. Around this bearer of faith now collected all those who, to be sure, had become weak, but who nevertheless never could leave the Reich, which constituted their happiness, the holy empire of the Germans. And there came the day of Whitsuntide [*Pfingsten*] also for the German nation. May we never forget the March days of 1933![37]

Later in the same book, Leutheuser referred to Hitler as "the young Siegfried of our day," out to do battle against "all enemies of life."

> Millions of German men who had lost all connections with the powers of eternity despite the churches, learned through Adolf Hitler to believe again in God and his Kingdom. Faith in the victory of good over evil again filled the heart of our Volk....Thus the spirit of Jesus walked through Germany, the faith in the victory of the Kingdom of God over the powers of Hell.

As Germany was saved, so was the world saved--from "Western
mammonism," from "Eastern anarchism," from being the plaything
of "Jewish high-finance" and the destructiveness of "Asiatic
bestiality."[38]

Leffler was only slightly less enthusiastic. Though
claiming that the KDC did not substitute Hitler for Christ, he
nevertheless pointed out that it was true that in the darkness
of recent Christian church history, Hitler was like a "miracu-
lous God-sent transparency, a window," through which the best
of German Christianity streamed like a light.[39] Hitler and the
Nazi revolution reestablished the whole man, said Leffler.

> Therewith, the disunity and brokenness between God and
> man, between brother and comrade, was overcome in a
> clear creative act. The experience of life binds to-
> gether heaven and earth for us German men and lends
> us the strength in all the most difficult hours to
> move any mountain that the world and all cosmic powers
> might set against us. From this vantage point, we
> recognize today as never before in history, how the
> real mystery of the Godhead in the form of Christ be-
> comes ever more revealed, how through the act of the
> *Führer*, Christianity was given freedom for its work-
> ings not only for the Germans but also perhaps for
> the entire remaining world.[40]

The theme of Germany's fate being pictured as world-fate was a
familiar one for Leffler.

> Had the German Volk died and fallen into the general
> world decay, then in Germany, in the whole world,
> there would have been no more history of Christianity.
> Then the spirit of the antiChrist in the form of Lenin
> and Bolshevist Russia would have celebrated its tri-
> umph. Therefore today all churches of Germany and
> all the Christians of our Volk must learn from the
> *Führer* and consider what the everlasting creator is
> trying to say through him to the German experience,
> the German soul, the German Volk. One could toss out
> the question: has Christianity anything to do with
> Germanness, in this case with political Germanness?
> To that may I let the Dane Sören Kierkegaard answer:
> "There will come a time when politics and political
> movements will speak, and lo, behind them stands
> Christianity."[41]

There was no difference for KDC members between one's political faith in Hitler and belief in God, or between the
teachings of the two. "What today has been put before us so
clearly and powerfully in the language of National Socialism is
as much Biblical truth as an Elijah or Amos. It is the truth

from the God that will not let transgressions of his orders go
unpunished."[42] Wilhelm Bauer called it a tragedy that National
Socialism spoke a different language than the church, because
"we speak out of the same spirit."[43] Again it was Leutheuser
and Leffler who voiced the most radical views. Leffler said:

> truly the *Führer*, driven on by God's holy spirit, has
> taken up the struggle against the antigod that in the
> guise of anti-Christian Bolshevism, in the political
> movement of communism, would suffocate life and love.
> Whether one looked at politics, the economy, yes, even
> religion, godlessness was everywhere entrenched.[44]

He later told of the effect of the coming of Hitler.

> Men who were tired and resigned because of nameless
> misery, lack of work, and hopelessness of outlook...
> looked with blank eyes and hateful hearts toward the
> future. [Then] they heard a new "Thou shalt" as if
> spoken out of eternity, as if a real word of God.
> Suddenly they saw the true creation orders as they
> had been given for the German men and German Volk.
> They heard these old words: "Do this, keep these com-
> mandments and laws and see, you will live." Thus
> have we Germans heard in reality God the Almighty
> speak through the acts and the voice of the *Führer*.[45]

The result of the radical KDC view of divine revelation in
history was the complete confusion of Christianity and Nazism.
Therefore, in November of 1933, the Thuringian German Christians could say that "National Socialism...is Volk community,
but it is also a community of faith; National Socialism is a
world outlook that is both political and religious..."[46] and
also, "No time was more filled with similes for his [Christ's]
eternal sacrifice than our generation, the Third Reich, that
was founded on the sacrifice of millions at the front, on the
death of almost four hundred S. A.--men in willing obedience,
on the blood of tens of thousands."[47] For Wilhelm Bauer, there
was to be no difference between the holy days of the church and
those of the nation. When he spoke of the latter--"the day of
the beginning of the war, the day of commemoration of the sacrifice of the World War and the day of the accession to power
[*Machtergreifung*]"--he was making a parallel to the Christian
days of Christmas, Good Friday, and Easter. By adding the
third element of the natural seasons, Bauer established very
tidy parallelisms. "...The natural course of creative life,
the fate and history of the nation, and the sacred history,

are, in our thinking and feeling, so bound up with one another,
that a day in the experience-sphere of one at the same time
calls for the commitment and trust that accrue to the other
two."[48]

To the KDC writers, the Germans took the place of the Jews
as God's chosen people.[49] Bauer had this in mind when he analyzed the derivation of the word "*deutsch*."

> People are puzzling a lot today over what the
> word *deutsch* really means. A respectable researcher,
> Hermann Wirth, now assures us that "*deutsch*" was a
> very old word and goes back to a people who swore to
> themselves always to live "from God" and in all things,
> actions, in life and striving as in death, only to
> seek after the will of God. *De-ut* or *Tu-at* translated
> means: "from God." The Teutons, the Germans were then
> the sons of God, and were thus the men that devoted
> themselves to God's will and lived and formed their
> life "from God."[50]

Leffler even more specifically put the impetus for the election
of the Germans on God's will, and noted how the "world now has
to choose between Israel or Germany," one living by the "law"
which stifled creative power, the other with the "will and
capability to bring heaven and earth to their mysterious creative connection and exercise the powers of destruction..."[51]

The KDC ideologists were optimistic that the Kingdom of
God could be established, and was being established, on earth.
There was absolutely no embarrassment or hesitation about this.
Even when replying to attacks on this point from other church
groups, the KDC held firm.

> Where the German men find peace for the soul and
> thereby become strong for faithfully carrying through
> the German struggle for life, there comes the Kingdom
> of God again and again to our German people that our
> Savior assured for us over 2000 years ago.[52]

KDC ideologists differed significantly from other German
churchmen, and even from some branches of the German Christians
(such as the *Christlich-Deutsche Bewegung*) because they had almost no sense of sin, and constantly exuded an optimism about
man's ability to be good. This is why the Kingdom-of-God-on-
earth concept was possible for the KDC. "God's Kingdom is certainly in heaven, but it reaches also right down into the
present."[53] Sometimes the Kingdom of God was called "the
eternal Germany."

> We German Christians believe, therefore, that God's
> Kingdom originates here among us. We are not looking
> for another world, one that is imagined or invented.
> We believe that God created this world in which we
> are permitted to live, out of his power and will.[54]

The KDC interpretation of history as the obvious and in-
terpretable revelation of God was indicative of the movement's
radicalism. Even other prominent German Christians were very
critical of the KDC interpretation. Paul Althaus, for instance, wrote a much-circulated pamphlet attacking the ideas
of the movement point by point.[55] And, of course, the Reich
Church Committee refused to put its *nihil obstat* on the ideas
of the KDC, though welcoming some other German Christian groups
with open arms. The KDC concept of divine revelation in history was a truly revolutionary idea, but represented the viewpoints of a certain temperament attracted to the German Christian movements.

1. "Aufruf der Landegemeinde Thüringen der Deutschen Christen zur Kirchlichen Lage," in Duhm, *Kampf*, p. 124.

2. A. Daum, "Der Weg der Deutschen zur Vollendung der Volkswerdung," *Briefe an Deutsche Christen* (hereinafter shortened in footnotes to *BDC*), III, No. 14 (December 1, 1934), 219.

3. Wilhelm Bauer, *Im Umbruch der Zeit* (Weimar: Verlag Deutsche Christen, 1935), p. 38.

4. Erich Fromm, "Nicht mein, sondern Dein Wille geschehe!" *BDC*, IV, No. 15 (August 1, 1935).

5. Reprinted from a Thuringian Nazi newspaper in Duhm, *Kampf*, p. 91.

6. Julius Leutheuser, *Die deutsche Christusgemeinde: Der Weg zur deutschen Nationalkirche* (2d ed.; Weimar: Verlag Deutsche Christen, 1935), pp. 3-4.

7. *Ibid.*, p. 4.

8. Walter Grundmann, *Völkische Theologie*, No. 1 of *Schriften zur Nationalkirche* (2d ed.; Weimar: Verlag Deutsche Christen, [1937]), p. 16, and the review of his book *Der Gott Jesu Christ* (1936), in *Zeitschrift für Theologie und Kirche*, XVIII, No. 2 (1937), 183.

9. Wolf Meyer-Erlach, *Kirche oder Sekte: Offener Brief an Herrn Landesbischof D. Meiser* (Weimar: Verlag Deutsche Christen, 1934), pp. 16-17.

10. Erich Fascher, *Grosse Deutsche begegnen der Bibel: Eine Wegweisung für Deutsche Christen* (Weimar: Verlag Deutsche Christen, 1935), p. 135.

11. Wilhelm Bauer, "Um das Geheimnis unserer Seele: Dem Gedächtnis der Gebrüder Grimm," *BDC*, V, No. 4 (February 15, 1936), 39-40.

12. Leutheuser, *Die deutsche Christusgemeinde*, p. 4.

13. Bauer, *Im Umbruch der Zeit*, p. 19.

14. *Ibid.*, p. 26.

15. Leutheuser, *Die deutsche Christungemeinde*, p. 25.

16. *Ibid.*, p. 3.

17. Bauer, *Im Umbruch der Zeit*, p. 21.

18. Grundmann, *Völkische Theologie*, p. 4.

186

19. Siegfried Leffler, *Christus im dritten Reich der Deutschen: Wesen, Weg und Ziel der Kirchenbewegung Deutsche Christen* (Weimar: Verlag Deutsche Christen, 1935), p. 18.

20. Bauer, *Im Umbruch der Zeit*, pp. 26-27.

21. Leutheuser, *Die deutsche Christusgemeinde*, p. 6.

22. Wolf Meyer-Erlach, "Deutsche Glaubensbewegungen und Deutsches Christentum," *BDC*, III, No. 7 (July, 1934), 125.

23. Wolf Meyer-Erlach, "Deutsche Christen," *BDC*, III, No. 8 (August, 1934), 138.

24. Leffler, *Christus im dritten Reich*, p. 20.

25. Grundmann, *Völkische Theologie*, pp. 4-5.

26. Wolf Meyer-Erlach, "Die Toten erwachen," *BDC*, IV, No. 6 (March 15, 1935), 61.

27. Leffler, *Christus im dritten Reich*, p. 22.

28. Fromm, "Nicht mein, sondern Dein Wille geschehe!" *BDC*, p. 171.

29. Grundmann, *Gott und Nation*, p. 50.

30. Leutheuser, *Die deutsche Christusgemeinde*, pp. 6-7.

31. From a speech by Julius Leutheuser, *BDC*, III, No. 12 (October, 1934), 199; special issue concerning the Reich KDC convention at Eisenach.

32. Bauer, *Im Umbruch der Zeit*, p. 25.

33. *Ibid.*, p. 27.

34. Leffler, *Christus im dritten Reich*, p. 117.

35. Wolf Meyer-Erlach, "Deutsch sein heisst Kämpfer sein," *BDC*, III, No. 12 (October, 1934), 192; special issue concerning the Reich KDC convention at Eisenach.

36. Leuthauser, "Advent: Macht hoch die Tür, die Tor macht weit," *BDC*, III, No. 14 (December 1, 1934), 214.

37. Leutheuser, *Die deutsche Christusgemeinde*, p. 7.

38. *Ibid.*, pp. 13-14.

39. Leffler, *Christus im dritten Reich*, p. 29.

40. Siegfried Leffler, *Unser Weg* [speech by Leffler at the *Sportpalast* in Berlin, May 28, 1938] (Weimar: Verlag Deutsche Christen, 1938), p. 16.

41. Leffler, *Christus im dritten Reich*, pp. 29-30. Another group of German Christians (from Braunschweig) expressed similar views of Hitler to those of the KDC. Their program included such statements as: "In Hitler is the time fulfilled for the German Volk. For through Hitler has Christ, God the helper and Savior, become powerful among us....Hitler (National Socialism) is now the way of the spirit and will of God for the Christ church of the German nation....Hitler wants the church. He waits for us. Achievement and success are decisive for him. Christ says: 'By their fruits shall you know them.'" Schmidt, *Bekenntnisse...1934*, pp. 178-79.

42. [Pastor?] Ende, "Wort Gottes," *BDC*, IV, No. 2 (January, 1935), 20.

43. Bauer, *Im Umbruch der Zeit*, p. 26.

44. Leffler, *Christus im dritten Reich*, p. 25.

45. Leffler, *Unser Weg*, pp. 12-13.

46. Reprinted from a Thuringian Nazi newspaper in Duhm, *Kampf*, p. 91.

47. "Aufruf der Landgemeinde Thüringen der Deutschen Christen zur Kirchlichen Lage," in Duhm, *Kampf*, p. 123.

48. Bauer, *Im Umbruch der Zeit*, p. 8.

49. A German religious view of themselves as the chosen people was not entirely new. For comments on this view as held by some early 19th century German thinkers, see Klaus Scholder, "Neuere deutsche Geschichte und protestantische Theologie," *Evangelische Theologie*, XXIII, No. 10 (1963), 527-28.

50. Bauer, *Im Umbruch der Zeit*, p. 51.

51. Leffler, "Ein Gott--ein Volk!" *BDC*, IV, No. 8 (April 15, 1935), 90.

52. *BDC*, III, No. 7 (July, 1934), 129.

53. Lehnert, "Das Reich Gottes steht nicht in Worten, sondern in Kraft," *BDC*, IV, No. 31 (November 5, 1935), 251.

54. Superintendent Spangenberg, "Das Reich," *BDC*, IV, No. 21 (November, 1935), 252-53.

55. Paul Althaus, *Politisches Christentum: Ein Wort über die Thüringer "Deutschen Christen"* (2d ed.; Leipzig: A. Deichertsche Verlag, 1935).

CHAPTER IX: NATURE AND THE FARMER IN KDC RELIGION

One of the differences between the *Kirchenbewegung Deutsche Christen* journal *Briefe an deutsche Christen* and the official papers of the *Glaubensbewegung Deutsche Christen* and the *Christlich-Deutsche Bewegung* was that in the former, one was always made aware, by poems, articles, and pictures, of the importance attached by the KDC to nature--the soil, the open air, the seasons--and to the man who has always been closest to nature, the farmer. In the cultural and social background of the KDC leaders--especially Leffler and Leutheuser--there were two obvious reasons for this. After the war, both were active in the *Wandervögel*--the youth movements which originated at the turn of the century and which emphasized in varying degrees, neo-pagan rites, love of nature, folk music, and, after 1913, anti-Semitism.[1] Leffler often referred to those years nostalgically:

> They wandered. The forest took them up and they engaged in dialogue with it. The mountains and valleys, the meadows and fields lived for them. The clouds and the wind, the stars of the night heavens, all was filled with soul, with pleasure, sorrow and love, filled with death and resurrection.[2]

The *Wandervögel* experience had also taught Leffler the importance of cultivating the whole man--not just the mind.

> Life consists not only of the mind but also of the body. Too much contempt for the body was often the mark of mark of the best German clergymen. A day ought never to pass without the first victory that is achieved being a victory of the will over the body ...in order to make it not only a willing, but also a beautiful instrument for the mind [*Geist*], for their common commission; body and soul must be brought to an attractive healthy harmony with each other. The comments about the body-soul [*Körperseele*], that was spoken of before the World War in the German *Wandervögel*, are not without meaning. That is unconditionally necessary for a profession of clerical soldiers and officers who must combine in one the shepherd, priest, and warrior.[3]

In addition, as mentioned above in the introductory chapter, when Leffler and Leutheuser came to Thuringia from Bavaria in 1927, they were assigned to two small contiguous church

189

districts in the Wiera Valley. The two districts--Flemmingen and Niederwiera--included thirteen small villages with seven churches, and were almost entirely made up of farmers. But surrounding areas were industrialized, and the worker movement and "free thought" were strong there. Leffler and Leutheuser, with tactics that they learned in the *Wandervögel* which included singing and study of Volkish writings in small groups, were able to attract farmers and some artisans, but not, as Kurt Meier, says, the "class-conscious workers."[4] So there were reasons in the backgrounds of Leffler and Leutheuser for emphasizing the natural environment and the farmer.

Modern civilization presented problems for KDC writers. Industrialization, said Leffler, was an unfortunate development. When the Germans went to the factories and mines, they were crippled by the loss of air, sun, and earth. There have been attempts, he continued, to bring the development of the machines, material things, selfishness, under control, but so far nothing had been accomplished. "The titanic will with which some great individuals have thrown themselves against the ruin, could not stop the distress." There was now only one last hope: "the day will come when the stream of life is again victorious over the stream of death."[5]

KDC ideologists concentrated their attacks against the city. Wilhelm Bauer introduced his book with the comment that he had made the order of his articles correspond with the course of the year or seasons so that the "whole man" could identify with the ideas in his "thought, feeling, and experience"--"insofar as he is not yet completely urbanized [*verstadtet*], i.e., lost all connection with nature and history..."[6] Some urbanized people knew they had lost health and a relationship to nature, Bauer continued. "Even in the large city one sees today the yearning for a healthy, sun-tanned complexion. Yet the faces in our cities become whiter and whiter, sickly with a light paleness, or nervously unravelled and tormented."[7] An article in *Briefe an deutsche Christen* in 1934 told the sad story of the death of a village, thriving in 1900, almost deserted in 1914. Everything was there to make the perfect farming village in 1900, said the author, who catalogued the characteristics of the village, from the orchards and fields, the country church, charming houses and cobble-stoned market place, to the noises of the animals in the barnyards. "Inside, the wife worked and the daughter helped if she was not working in the fields with father, brother, and hired man, where the plowshare glistened [pulled] behind the broad back of the horse, the golden grain ripened, and the scythes flashed." In 1900 it was still thus, but the money-fever gripped the young people who went off to industry. "Gold lured the farmers away, one after the other. And in 1914 when the first war alarms sounded, [the village] was almost completely depopulated."[8]

What happened in the city was that one lost his connectedness to the eternal soil and to nature. Leffler noted how Germans left the villages and farms for the cities where their memories became pale; they forgot "mother earth." Leffler had an idyllic view of village life:

> ...Such a sunny farm village, filled with rustling
> trees, surrounded by fields,...was once the original
> home of all of us. There a German mother rocked us,
> there was the soil of our fathers. There we heard
> the sounds of God, blood, and earth all together.
> Then the fields became too small and could no longer
> support us. Son tore himself from father, daughter
> from mother, brother from brother, and betook them-
> selves into the foreignness of the city. They had
> to establish and build a new outer home [*äussere
> Heimat*].[9]

Wilhelm Bauer told how, "we men in the cities frequently live far from the life of the soil, far from the ground of our being." This, he said, accounted for the lack of respect for the rule of a higher being and for the prevalent unfortunate view that the human mind could create and achieve all things. "What would have become of the German Volk and empire if the German man had not had in him the ancient power of the farmer to remain ready to give service, in spite of hard times and bad luck..."[10] Another writer could not understand how anyone could fail to see the absolutely basic position of the farm.

> The larger the cities become and the more they
> encroach on the village, the more they distance them-
> selves from *Bauerntum*. On the one hand the machine,
> on the other hand bread. It would be interesting to
> compare the machine with bread to analyze their value
> and meaning for the Volk....Without bread, no machine;
> without bread, no civilization. That is the fact of

it all....But I have often enough come across men
who saw in the machine the basis of their existence.
...Many have almost lost their regard for a ripening
field of grain....But for me today it is always a
pious thrill to my soul when I remember how my mother
made the sign of the cross over fresh bread before
she cut into it.[11]

The city was based on materialism and money which corrupt-
ed the soul. Money, said Leffler, became our homeland (*Heimat*).
It was the goal for which workers now went daily to their work
benches, for which farmers plowed their fields, and for which
the educated thought. It became the "calf to which we brought
holy sacrifices." "Gold tortures men, captures hearts and
minds, makes them homeless, murders them on the battlefields
of the economy."[12] Leffler drew the contrast between the
countryside and the city:

There are still farmers who, in the early hours
of the morning when very often the cities are still
sleeping, gather together their family, their workers.
They offer their common prayer. Then everyone goes
out to his work as a member of the family, bound
above all work, above all differences, by a common
ultimate feeling in their hearts. How flustered in
contrast are one family after another in the cities.
How they run and dash senselessly to their place of
work. Already at the beginning of the day the
family is separated by its struggle for its daily
bread, and seldom are they brought together anymore
in the evening. Tired, they return one after the
other to their "living quarters" [*Wohnhaus*].[13]

And what was it that was at the root of the destruction of the
village Runstedt and others like it? Economy, industry, and
trade had tumbled over themselves in making the "technologized"
19th century into the "over-technologized" 20th. "Sufficient
value was not the determining factor but surplus value."[14]

Man's spiritual life ought to be parallel to, or one with,
nature, thought the KDC writers. Wilhelm Bauer presented the
typical view when, as already mentioned, he chose as the theme
of his book the three concentric arenas of man's life--the natural, Volkish-historical, and religious. Leffler and Walter
Grundmann both stressed the yearning of man for wholeness and
connectedness not only with nature, but in all mental and phy-
sical activities of life.[15] Man was properly seen as himself
a part of nature. Leffler noted how for centuries the Germans
had been a part of the German soil:

> They went out to their fields when the morning sun
> rose. They worked by the sweat of their brows and
> struggled for the existence of their farms. The walks
> and the fields greened and bloomed when spring came
> to the land. How sparkling were the stars of the
> night. How near were the heavens. The earthly and
> the heavenly fatherland touched each other in the
> quiet of the heart and a deep beautiful longing built
> bridges over and around any kind of suffering in the
> homeland.[16]

"I know of hardly any one of worth in the world," said Leffler,
"who did not have a bond with nature and his homeland."
Leffler found God in every bit of nature. The sun and the
stars attested to God; the winds were God's angels; blades of
grass, flowing water, and trees were God's greetings to man.
All of this said to Leffler: "Be trusting! Be courageous! God
is with you. In the Kingdom of God comes such a majestic peace
to us that it spreads out over all nature and homeland and
shows us...only one mediates in all things and over all things:
God."[17] Walter Grundmann also spoke of man as a bit of nature,
experiencing God as man feels the "great rhythm of nature."
This was the experience that Goethe spoke of, said Grundmann,
when he spoke of God moving the world from within.[18] In typical fashion, one KDC writer advised the German to be what he
ought: "a kernel, planted in the field of your Volk, that grows
and bears fruit and is worthy to be bound together in the
shocks when the Master reaps the harvest."[19] "There is," said
Grundmann, "a positive, unmediated, nature-bound piety, that is
based in the connection between man and nature."[20]

The pages of *Briefe an deutsche Christen* are filled with
testimony of how God had revealed himself in the German forests
and soil. "The resurrection powers of nature stream through
us, and we feel how we, the sons of our time, create a new life
out of the soil of the homeland, out of the sprouting and growing and pushing of the German plain, of the German forest." It
is the essence of real Christian faith, said Meyer-Erlach, that
one can see the grace and love of God behind natural happenings.[21] At various times, articles were devoted to accounts of
KDC congregations holding services outdoors. One account
stressed the advantage such services had for bringing together
the "earth-bound healthy soul" of the farmer with the restless
hearts of the city men. "Speakers and listeners find here by

themselves, the inner way to one another by experiencing the
natural celebration sounds of the forest."[22]   In an issue of
their newspaper that was completely taken up with agricultural
and natural imagery, another service in the forest was report-
ed:

> It became a reality, what we had long yearned for.
> Our small congregation that had grown together in
> months-long study and joyous services, celebrated its
> first divine service in the forest [*Waldgottesdienst*].
> Catholics and Protestants together in the cathedral
> which the Heavenly Father himself has built. Grave
> high rock walls, venerable old trees of the forest,
> gently sloping meadows, are the living walls, columns,
> floor and ceiling of our cathedral! The rustling
> of the trees our organ, the lovely singing forest
> birds our church choir....As we are all the creatures
> of the Almighty Creator and became his children
> through our Savior, we ought to be also joyous and
> trustful that he will help us to fulfill the task
> which he put in the soul of our Volk as its task from
> earliest times: to realize a little piece of the
> Kingdom of God on earth as a German Christian con-
> gregation indissolubly bound as one in faith and
> love, that in obedience and faithfulness bravely and
> joyfully goes its way.[23]

The praise of the farmer stressed his purity, simplicity,
and piety. These KDC emphases reflect the KDC view of the
basic goodness of man. One stanza of a poem about the farmer,
printed as the first page of a 1934 issue of their newspaper,
crystallized the KDC view: "The German farmer brings the harvest in. His look is proud! For every kernel is sweat and a
high service in this eternal cycle of becoming! No service can
be more pure! And no endeavoring on earth is so burningly
strong, as the will and diligence of the farmer."[24]   The emphasis was on simplicity. No doubt it was the farmer that Leutheuser had in mind when he talked of the "simple German Volk-
man who still bore in him the memory of the primeval community-
principle." Leutheuser called for a new German church that
would speak to the needs of the "simple man, the simple woman,
the simple Volk."[25]   The essence of the farmer was his eternal
nature. "*Bauerntum*," said Wilhelm Bauer, "is eternal."
Through the hardships of harsh manorial taskmasters who made
him almost into a slave-animal, through wars which burned his
villages, killed his cattle, devastated his fields, through
plagues and epidemics, and even through the persecutions of

modern merchants, taxes, and interest slavery, the farmer en-
dured.[26] Some writers felt that the farmer was thus the repository of the eternal virtues upon which Germany would be
rebuilt.

> In the upheaval of our time the farmer and
> *Bauerntum* stand on the front line. It could scarcely
> be otherwise! Where a new age must create new bases
> of Volkish and state life, there the farmer must be-
> come the first, as the original class of Volkish be-
> ing, whose essence is formed anew....One thing is
> clear to me: only the farmer can comprehend its [the
> new Nazi order's] deep meaning, he who feels himself
> to be a part of the home soil, of the earth which he
> tills...who knows he comes from the dust of the
> mother earth and knows of the power that flows from
> holy mother earth....The farmer must be the most
> pious man on the entire earth...[27]

In the Third Reich, the KDC hoped the farmer would again be
given his rightful place equal to, or above, the secondary
powers of industry and the city. "The time of the 'dumb farmer' is past. People realize again that the farmer and agri-
culture are not only the basis of our economic life, but that
here also lie all the roots of our spiritual life."[28]

"We always thought organically," Leffler wrote, "just as
God works organically out there in nature and in the Volk
life."[29] One of the results of thinking "organically," was an
acceptance at face value of the Nazi revolution. Whether one
thought, as Bauer did, in terms of concentric circles of religious, natural and national life, or in terms of the "rhythm"
of nature and of historical events as Grundmann did, the natural religious experience included political events.

But more important was the religious view that this kind
of nature and farmer worship evoked. It attracted people who
were not attracted by the other German Christian groups. Farmers were attracted, of course, by the KDC praise of the farmer,
anti-city bias, and lack of complexity. Others were probably
attracted by its idyllic presentation of German natural environment and the life of the farmer which, along with faith,
had been lost in the secular age. Christianity came close for
the KDC to being nature worship or a new kind of pantheism, or
something that could be characterized as a simple struggle between the natural and unnatural, light and darkness, "Northern"

religion and "Southern" religion. Nevertheless, it fulfilled
the religious needs of a group of German Protestants who saw no
need, in the Third Reich, to build the church on orthodox principles, as the *Christlich-Deutsche Bewegung* did, nor to play
politics, as the *Glaubensbewegung Deutsche Christen* did.

NOTES

1. For a short analysis of the youth movement, see George L. Mosse, *The Crisis of German Ideology: Intellectual Origins of the Third Reich* (New York: Grosset & Dunlap, 1964), pp. 171ff.

2. Leffler, *Christus im dritten Reich*, p. 19.

3. *Ibid.*, pp. 142-43.

4. Meier, *Deutschen Christen*, pp. 2-3.

5. Leffler, *Christus im dritten Reich*, pp. 2-3.

6. Bauer, *Im Umbruch der Zeit*, p. 7.

7. *Ibid.*, p. 117.

8. Paul Berglar-Schröer, "Das Sterben eines Dorfes: Die Tragödie von Runstedt," *BDC*, III, No. 13 (November, 1934), 205-06.

9. Leffler, *Christus im dritten Reich*, p. 16.

10. Bauer, *Im Umbruch der Zeit*, p. 120.

11. Max Jungnickel, "Brot oder Maschine?" *BDC*, IV, No. 9 (May 1, 1935), 99.

12. Leffler, *Christus im dritten Reich*, p. 14.

13. *Ibid.*, p. 130-31.

14. Berglar-Schröer, "Das Sterben eines Dorfes," *BDC*, p. 205.

15. Grundmann, *Völkische Theologie*, pp. 3-6, in his discussion of Ernst Krieck's Volkish-political anthropology, and Leffler, *Christus im dritten Reich*, p. 8.

16. Leffler, *Christus im dritten Reich*, pp. 14-15.

17. *Ibid.*, pp. 44-45.

18. Grundmann, *Völkische Theologie*, p. 15.

19. G. B., "Ernte," *BDC*, IV, No. 16 (August 15, 1935), 185.

20. Grundmann, *Völkische Theologie*, p. 15.

21. Wolf Meyer-Erlach, "Der Sieg des Lebens," *BDC*, IV, No. 8 (April 15, 1935), 86.

198

22. Jacobi, "Deutsch-christliche Feierstätten," *BDC*, IV, No. 12 (June 15, 1935), 141.

23. "Unser Waldgottesdienst," *BDC*, IV, No. 16 (August 15, 1935), 191.

24. Poem by W. Otto Ullmann, *BDC*, III, No. 7 (July, 1934), 115.

25. Leutheuser, *Die deutsche Christusgemeinde*, pp. 9-10.

26. Bauer, *Im Umbruch der Zeit*, p. 119.

27. [Pastor?] Schroeter, "Bauerntum," *BDC*, IV, No. 19 (October 1, 1935).

28. Book review, *BDC*, IV, No. 20 (October 20, 1935), 247.

29. Leffler, "Die kirchliche Lage," *BDC*, IV, No. 19 (October 1, 1935), 228.

CHAPTER X: THE NON-DENOMINATIONAL GERMAN CHURCH

The *Kirchenbewegung Deutsche Christen* came out of an Evangelical-Lutheran (i.e., Protestant) background, as did the other German Christian groups. But, unlike the other groups, it
hoped to erase the lines between the Catholic and Protestant
denominations or confessions in Germany and base a new church
on all Christian Germans. As with all ideas of the KDC, this
attempt had its attractive and unattractive sides. On the one
hand, it was as ecumenical an idea as a Third Reich church
group could hope to hold; it arose out of the KDC dissatisfaction with internecine quarrels that have always existed within
what is supposedly a universal church, and it reflected the
basic optimism of the KDC members about the goodness of man.
On the other hand, the concept was limited to German participation, did not really recognize the possibility of legitimate
theological difference of opinion that might be reflected in
different church organizations, and was necessarily based on
fluid and undogmatic principles. The idea was, however, a
revolutionary one because it broke radically with the established churches both in its ideological and organizational
goals.

The old denominational churches (usually meaning the
Evangelical-Lutheran churches) had not escaped certain sins,
thought KDC writers. One of the sins was intellectualism.
Hans Buchheim has pointed out that Leffler and Leutheuser viewed systematic theology as a sign that the body and soul were at
odds and that the "official Christianity" of the church, insofar as it relied on systematics, had lost contact with the
Volk.[1] Leffler claimed theological debates had little practical value.

> No one wants to touch freedom of research or muzzle
> the scientific drive. But how can the pastors out
> there in the village and city maintain a community
> in their practical struggle for the soul of the Volk
> when they already in the university do not strive in
> one direction, but rather have become learned in
> compartmentalizing and separating themselves off by
> thinking in terms of liberal or orthodox or positive![2]

"No, good friend," said Leffler, "piety is not situated in the brain and in understanding, but in the heart."[3] Anti-intellectualism was even expressed by Wolf Meyer-Erlach, Professor of Practical Theology at Jena: "There is original sin in the church, the death-sin of theologians, intellectuals and Pharisees, who again and again kill and crucify life and truth in print."[4] Meyer-Erlach asserted that those who thought along KDC lines could eliminate much of the worthless dogmatism of theology. "We have a different God than do the intellectuals, the theologians of the study. We have the God of our fathers, the God of those men whose beginning, middle, and end was Christ and who knew that they were born as Germans and would live for Germany."[5]

Leffler associated modern systematic theologians with the Pharisees of Christ's time who argued about the coming of the Messiah while the Savior was among them.

> They, the complicated theologians, were annoyed that God should be revealed to men so simply as a child without going the traditional route through theology. But it is certainly still the same as 2000 years ago: if Christ the Master would go today through Germany in the flesh and blood, there would again be Pharisees and free-thinkers, whether they be of the Marxist or Nordic strain, who would nail him to the cross.[6]

Another writer noted that it was not the educated class, but the Volk who had an "instinct" for what was right in religion. This writer also compared the Biblical Pharisees to the modern day educated people and philosophers with their heads in the clouds never bothering to look below, to the cultured class with their beautiful books, and to the proletariat in the cities who had lost all faith. But they are not the "real" people, he said. "They are but the dead branches of the Volk-tree."[7] Finally, Leutheuser compared true Christianity with National Socialism in that both were not "the result of a clever understanding, but rather a concern of the heart."[8] The KDC writers saw no value in being orthodox for its own sake.

> All dogmatic questions are, for our movement, of secondary importance. Only thus is it possible that a religious coming-together and unity in the name of Christ can be accomplished....The forms of church acts and services and their symbolic meaning have become, in most cases, incomprehensible...[9]

In addition to being overly intellectual, the old churches were overly bureaucratic, said KDC writers, because in 1933 they were really only political power structures. Leffler attributed this to the dual influences of the world outlook of the Jewish people which he believed had insinuated itself into the church, and the church's desire to establish an international political organization.[10] If millions of Germans could no longer sustain faith, said Leutheuser, they were not to blame. It was the church as a bureaucratic institution that was guilty.[11]

Church politics was another area in which the KDC ideologists were impatient. Leffler, who had to deal with other church groups, was constantly berating them for playing politics. Whether one looked at the reactionary course of Martin Niemöller's "Pastor's Emergency League," or the blatantly political operations of the German Christians under Hossenfelder, 1933 had been, said Leffler, "a sad chapter in evangelical church history."[12] The KDC, however, had tried to base all its actions on the principle of love and tolerance. "Not a single pastor was deprived of his office by our church government for his beliefs or inner tenets."[13] The tragedy of the German Christian movement in general (excluding the KDC) was laid to its over-emphasis on church politics resulting in a public image as a church political group next to other groups rather than as the representation of all Christians in the Reich.[14] Leffler considered himself a peacemaker for the German Christian movements. In his explanation of the final break-off of attempts to affiliate with the "Berlin" German Christians (the *Reichsbewegung Deutsche Christen*) in 1935, he noted: "I could only counsel them to do one thing: separate from all church-political involvements and obligations, return to the ground and starting point of their power, return to the simple faith in the one Christian congregation of all Germans."[15]

In addition to the failings of the established churches and the misuse of church politics, the KDC also tried to point out the fallacy of confessional differences within Christianity. Confessionalism seemed to some writers to undermine the work of unity in the political sphere. "Christianity in Germany stands by today powerlessly, broken up into parties, and

offers to the world a horrible spectacle, and that in a time
when the German nationals prepared to become a unified Volk in
a unified Reich of all Germans under the unique Führer."[16] In
addition, confessionalism opened old religious civil war wounds
that had been nonsense in the first place. "We have had enough
of the criminality of the Thirty Years War which in the name of
God changed Germany into a graveyard. We do not wish to know
anything of that false God in whose name man became the murder-
er of man, instead of his brother, his Savior."[17] One KDC
writer, who described himself as a long-standing ecumenist,
told why he thought confessionalism was equal to stupidity:
"all confessional theology is antithetical theology...Catholic
as well as Reformed." It is sheer nonsense, he continued, that
Christian theologians of all sorts have not been able to come
to any common understanding. The really pious among the laity
are astounded by this. The author noted how he always asked
the advocates of confessionalism: "now, to which singularly
blessing-empowered [alleinseligmachenden] church do you belong?" Only the Thuringians, he said, were able to see the
correct way without paganization or reaction--"Very simple!
Christ and Germany!"[18]

One's Germanness had become a closer bond than theological
differences because of the experiences of recent German history. Leffler wrote:

> We cannot believe that the German brothers and sisters
> who travelled together through the suffering of the
> World War and through the grace of God's leadership,
> ought to be separated eternally in their worship of
> God. Therefore we believe that German Catholics and
> German Protestants could find each other in a German
> congregation of God in which the spirit of the Savior
> would live as love to one another, forgiveness for
> one another and common readiness to sacrifice for
> Germany.[19]

Professor Meyer-Erlach also linked the end of confessionalism
to the war experience. "Protestants, Catholics marched next to
each other through Hell. Rain and snow, hunger and cold,
grenades, mines, and machine guns did not ask, are you Catholic, are you Protestant."[20]

The way in which the confessionalism of the old churches
could be overcome was through the establishment of a new church

embracing all Christians in Germany. At times, it seemed that the German Church was to be only a spiritual, and not an administrative, concept. For example, at one point, Leffler counseled Germans to work from within the framework of the two great confessions. "The Confessional Churches are as two arms on one and the same body."[21] But his comments elsewhere, as well as the sentiments expressed by other KDC writers, left little doubt that the actual combination of Germans into one church was both desirable and possible. For the German of the Third Reich, said Leutheuser, the "National Church" is the most sacred of longings.[22] Indeed, the desire for the "German Christian National Church" to "encompass the entire Volk" was a prominent point of the KDC program which concluded with the cry: "one Volk!--one God!--one Reich!--one Church!"[23] In response to attacks on the theology of the KDC, Leffler, in July of 1934, noted that "it is false to assert that it would be a compromise of the Gospel if all Germans of Catholic and Protestant background came together in one congregation of German Christians in order to fulfill Christ's commandment: 'love one another.'" But Leffler continued by denying that the KDC desired to wage war with the Catholic Church to replace it with the Protestant or some other third church. However, he continued, "*it is true* that we intend to further the reconciliation of the confessions through the congregation of 'German Christians,' in order to achieve the cathedral of the Germans out of the spirit of Christ."[24]

Perhaps the lack of the immediate probability of the overcoming of organizational differences between the Catholics and Protestants allowed for the lack of clarity and seeming contradiction in KDC comments about the national church. "We never have sunk to saying," noted Leffler, "that all Protestants ought to become Catholic, or, vice-versa, that all Catholics ought to become Protestants. We only know that Germany needs a true congregation of Christ in which men experience how the Kingdom of God can be opened up."[25] In a speech given at the 1935 Thuringian Church convention, Leffler said, "when we say 'National Church,' we mean the heartfelt unity of all Germans in Christ."[26] At the second national convention of the KDC in October of the same year, he said, "we believe passionately in the quiet Christ-congregation of Germans, in which there may and will be different marks of faith and cult forms, but in which nothing separates us as German brothers of the heart."[27]

Other KDC writers seemed to have had a more concrete interpretation of the coming National Church. A pamphlet, circulated at the first national convention in 1934, stressed that religious union would have to follow as a natural consequence of the political union of the Third Reich. The goal of the KDC was to aid in the "reconciliation of the confessions through a return home to the one Savior..." and the one task was the unity of the German nation.[28] The theologian Erich Fascher of Jena also spoke of the "Christian congregation of Germans."

> Just as in politics [the Nazi revolution], the different world views were welded into a single one, so also in religion the confessions...will be welded together. In the Christ-congregation of Germans, the indivisible Christ rules over men who have awakened as National Socialists to their German character. Essentially there will no longer be confessions that divisively cut across the nations. If every Volk is "a thought of God," then the German Volk can conceive of and honor its Savior in a German way. For us, that is the completion of the Germanization of Christianity and the Christianization of the Germans..."[29]

The anticipated German National Church was to be based on a theology of sorts. Personal theology was to be flexible, and toleration the rule. Professor Meyer-Erlach, while noting his own position as an "orthodox Lutheran," welcomed the fact that the KDC included men of the most different positions. This, he believed, would eventually result in a new German theology which he defined simply as the recognition of Christ and Germany as the sources and content of life.[30] Systematic theology was not considered a necessary part of the National Church's theology. Leffler said that nothing was further from his mind than a polished theological position, and that colleagues would have sufficient time to elaborate on theology later. The member who looked for a favorite scientific theological commentary in the KDC, said Leffler, would be deceiving himself. "I counsel him not to begin first with readings, because their preconceived notions will make him blind to things as they really are. It is time in the church as everywhere that we move toward the simple life in God as the mid-point of our outlook,

and testify to his honor."[31] In a series of articles, Erich
Fascher tried to define some of the basic theological positions
of the KDC. It did not bode well for his attempts when he introduced his discussion with the following statement:

> The attack that we have no well-defined theology shakes
> us even less since we know our Reformer Luther also
> had no finished theology in the beginning, but rather
> a religious experience....Our answers will not have
> been previously programatically constructed at a writ-
> ing desk, but will grow partly from within through
> the further development of our movement, and partly
> from without through debates with our opposition.[32]

For the time being, simple piety and instinct would be
more highly valued than dogma. The accent for us, said
Fascher, is on the "experiencing of a relationship to the living Master." The written Word and resultant strife over what
it means was not to be emphasized by the KDC, "rather the living experience, about which this Word speaks in more or less
certain terms."[33] Leutheuser noted that in the German Volk
there were two strains of Christianity: an orthodox strain that
stressed form and the sacredness of "the Word," and a "religion
of the heart" (accepted by the KDC) that stressed decision and
the sacredness of the "spirit of the Word."[34] Ludwig Müller,
who by the second half of the 1930's was associating himself
with the KDC activities noted: "More important than the 'confession' is the 'confessing.' More important than the witnessing word is the witnessing deed."[35]

It is not easy to find theological positions that were
well-developed by the KDC ideologists. With simplicity as the
goal, God and Christ were defined only vaguely. Pastor Erich
Fromm, in an introduction to some of the work done for the "Institute for the Study of Jewish Influences on German Church
Life," summarized, in 1940, KDC systematics concerning God's
message to man. God's love, he said, appeared bodily in
Christ, who was the prototype (*Urbild*) of what men ought to be.
God was to be seen simply as "the Father." A complicating concept such as "justification by faith alone," though useful to
Luther for breaking the German slavery to Rome, was described
as just so much extra baggage.[36] Walter Grundmann, in his KDC
period, was not quite so barren with his theologizing, but that
was because he was trying to establish a theology based on

Volkish anthropology. Nevertheless, when it came to traditional or orthodox interpretations of Christianity, he too threw
over what he thought were non-essentials. Reflecting the KDC
optimism about the basic nature of man, and rejecting the "Adam
myth" as contrary to the New Testament message, Grundmann
noted, "just as certainly as the creation is more important
than guilt, so the [message about] being the children of God is
more important than the forgiveness of sins."[37] These concepts
in themselves reflect the revolutionary steps that KDC thinkers
were willing to take in rejecting orthodox Christianity, especially of a Lutheran sort.

KDC writers, in their rejection of systematic theology,
embraced a sort of "Christian activism," as one recent historian has put it.[38] Meyer-Erlach's inaugural lecture at Jena
when he became Professor of Practical Theology, spoke of a "socialism of the deed" that arose out of both the German and
Christian spirit and was antithetical to the attitude of Karl
Barth who hid behind his "cloister walls" and acted "as if
nothing had happened."[39] One KDC pastor alleged that a total
misunderstanding of St. Paul's teaching had led the Reformation
churches into falsely rejecting salvation through good works.[40]

The new German National Church was to be the "life-order"
of the Volk,[41] and would "strengthen the heart of the Volk with
the power of the prophetic-apostolic Word."[42] In saying these
things, the KDC writers were stressing the National Church's
service to the German Volk. An important way that the KDC
writers believed they could be of service was to make the Bible
more understandable to modern Germans by putting its messages
into modern terms. Pastor Fromm noted that Luther's work and
spirit had to be carried on, and that Luther himself had not
meant for his translation of the Bible to be understandable in
all times. Fromm was of the opinion that wider and wider
circles of Germans not only no longer could understand Luther's
language, but actually were led to misunderstand the Biblical
message.[43] Wolf Meyer-Erlach may also have been thinking of a
new editing of the Bible--at least of the Old Testament--when
he talked about how Luther had been able to take certain "judaized" parts of the Bible and translate them into German words
and concepts without betraying the central messages.[44] The

most telling example of what it meant to the KDC ideologists to
make the Bible relevant to modern Germans may be seen in Ludwig
Müller's "Germanization" (*Verdeutschung*) of the Sermon on the
Mount.

In an article in *Briefe an deutsche Christen*, Müller explained why he undertood the *Verdeutschung* of Christ's most
famous sermon. He noted how in the years of his ministry he
had talked with uncounted people--both educated and uneducated
--who could not understand the language of the Bible. Müller
estimated that 80 to 90 per cent of the German Volk felt alien-
ated from Luther's version of the Bible. As a start, Müller
decided to rework the Sermon on the Mount into language to
which the simple man could relate. He was not exactly trying
to "better" Luther's German, he said. "But what good to me is
the best, most beautiful, purest, most sonorous German if it no
longer speaks to men!" Müller claimed that the inability of
Germans to understand Luther was a purely linguistic matter.[45]
But the latter statement was really not true, as evidenced by
his further explanation of what he had in mind when undertaking
the new "*Verdeutschung*."

> I have permitted myself to present his [Christ's]
> challenges as they really are: the simplest challenges
> of cameraderie [*Kameradschaft*], of Volk community
> [*Volksgemeinschaft*], and the preservation of such
> bearing--yet with the result, that S. A.-men and
> Hitler-Youth admitted astoundedly that certainly
> these were the elementary challenges the fulfillment
> of which they struggled for in their own circles.
> ...Our Volk has said "yes" to the great venture of
> faith in a politics of which, I can dare say, it is
> characterized by the spirit of the Sermon on the
> Mount and with which the *Führer* is trying to save
> Europe from the edge of the precipice.[46]

Müller's new presentation of the Sermon on the Mount was not,
then, "purely a linguistic thing." The following excerpts from
Müller's project, compared with the corresponding passages in
the Luther Bible (starting with Matthew 5:3), show how much the
Nazi or German Christian world-outlook altered the ideas themselves of the Sermon.[47]

Luther's Sermon on the Mount	*Müller's Sermon on the Mount*
Blessed are [*Selig sind*] they who are spiritually poor, for theirs is the Kingdom of Heaven.	Benevolence to him [*Wohl dem*] who in Child-like simplicity trusts in God. He has communion [*Gemeinschaft*] with God.
Blessed are they who bear suffering, for they shall be comforted.	Benevolence to him who bears his suffering manfully. He will find the power to never doubt uncourageously.
Blessed are the meek, for they shall inherit the earth.	Benevolence to him who always maintains good comradeship [*Kameradschaft*]. He will get on well in the world.
. . .	. . .
Blessed are the peacemakers for they shall be called children of God.	Benevolence to those who maintain peace with the members of their Volk, they do God's will.
Blessed are they who are persecuted for the sake of justice, for theirs is the Kingdom of God.	Benevolence to those who live honorably and faithfully, and work, but who have been nevertheless persecuted and slandered--they keep communion with God.
. . .	. . .
You ought not to think that I have come to destroy the law or the prophets. I have not come to destroy, but to fulfill.	You ought not think that I want to change or dissolve the divine truths and challenges that you have received from your fathers. I intend to fulfill them.
. . .	. . .
You have heard how it was said to the ancients: Thou shalt not kill; but he who kills shall be due judgment.	You carry it in your blood and your fathers have taught you: You shall not commit assassination--such a murderer is guilty and must be sentenced to death. You must, however, recognize and make it clear to yourself that murder is the result of an inner development that begins with jealousy, envy and hate. He who allows such a mentality in himself is already guilty. But he who insults and
But I say to you: he who is angry with his brother is worthy of judgment. But he who says to his brother: Raca, is answerable to the council. But he who says: you fool, is in danger of hellfire.	

209

persecutes his fellow Volk
members out of such a mentality makes himself even more
guilty.

But he who seeks moral destruction or threatens vio-
lently, destroys the Volk
community and makes himself
due before God and man for
the most harsh of penalties.

. . .

You have heard further that
which was said to the an-
cients: you shall not give
false oaths, and shall not
give oaths by God. But I
say to you that you should
not swear at all, neither by
heaven for it is God's throne;
nor by the earth, for it is
his foot-stool; nor by Jerusalem, for it is a great
king's city. Also you should
not swear by your head for
you cannot make a single hair
white or black.

Let your speech be: Yes for
yes, no for no; anything beyond that is evil.

Further, you have as a Volk
law the holy tradition that
you must hold to a sworn oath
and that perjury is a crime.

I say to you: you must hold
the honor of God, of your
Volk and your own honor so
high and sacred that you do
not swear to every little
thing. You ought to so live
with each other that one's
word given as a man is of
value.

Then yes is yes, and no is
no. All ambiguity is dis-
honorable and untrue.

. . .

But I say to you that you
should not resist evil, but
if anyone should strike you
on the right cheek, turn the
other one also.

I say to you: it is better,
so to live with other members
of your Volk that you get
along with each other. Volk
community [Volksgemeinschaft]
is a high and sacred trust
for which you must make sacrifice. Therefore come out
to meet your opponent as far
as you can before you completely fall out with him.
If in his excitement your
comrade hits you in the face,
it is not always correct to
hit him back. It is more
manly to preserve a reflective calm. Then will your
comrade be truly ashamed of
himself.

. . .

. . .

210

You have heard how it is said: you should love your neighbor and hate your enemy.

But I say to you: love your enemy, bless those who curse you, do good to those who hate you, pray for those who offend and persecute you.

. . .

No one can serve two masters, either he will hate the one and love the other, or will stay with one and despise the other. You cannot serve God and Mammon.

. . .

If you, being evil, could nevertheless give your children good gifts, how much more will your father in heaven give good things to them who ask him?

Therefore, whatever you want that men should do to you, do so to them; that is the law and the prophets.

. . .

A message from ancient times says: "Love your friend and hate your opponents."

I say to you: if you wish to be God's children you must take a different stance toward your fellow Volk-members and your comrades. Be comrade-like not only to your friend, but also to those who oppose you. Be calm and composed toward those who are hateful for the moment; take pains yourself to attain a noble and calm attitude toward an offender and persecutor.

. . .

It is a simple truth that no one can serve two masters. He can only serve one with his whole effort, and not the other in the same way with the same joyfulness. Thus you cannot serve both God and the demon of Gold.

. . .

If earthly men now give their children good gifts, will not the eternal God help much more those who in concern for their inner life ask for his strength and power?...

And now I tell you the great secret of true *Volksgemeinschaft* and real comradeship: a truth which most men pass over without noticing and which could still help them so much in their daily lives. It is a divine truth that lies deep in your blood and which your fathers have passed on to you. A simple truth that nevertheless embraces all of God's greatness.

And this truth is: everything that you would wish men to do to you, do also to them!

. . .

Müller's edition of the Sermon on the Mount was more than
an updating of linguistic style. Every time the Luther version
used the word "brother" or "neighbor," Müller substituted "comrade" or "members of the Volk" [*Volksgenossen*]. He made the
sections dealing with peace or turning the other cheek into examples of manly self-control. All references to the prophets
or the law were deleted or changed to "the ways of our fathers."
There is undoubtedly some value in updating Biblical language
to allow the readers to understand better, but in Müller's
case, the meaning itself was often willfully altered to suit
the needs of the projected German Church.

As a way of comparison to other German Christian groups,
the KDC position on anti-Semitism should be noted. Anti-
Semitism was more developed among KDC ideologists than it was
in the *Christlich-Deutsche Bewegung* but was not of central importance as with the *Glaubensbewegung Deutsche Christen*. There
was no anti-Semitism in the 1933 platform of the KDC except
perhaps indirectly in the explanation of the position to be
taken regarding the Old Testament as "an example of divine Volk
education."[48] The 1937 program for the National Church Movement, successor of the KDC, also took no direct position on the
Old Testament.[49] Individual members of the KDC varied somewhat
in the degree of their anti-Semitism. Leutheuser said that
Jews prayed to mammon as the prince of the world, while Germans
believed in a future eternal world.[50] Ludwig Müller, in his
KDC stage in the late 1930's, carried over a more strident
anti-Semitism from his *Glaubensbewegung Deutsche Christen* days,
which was reflected in his elimination of all words and concepts that could be considered "Jewish" at all in his version
of the Sermon on the Mount. Pastor Erich Fromm denied that
Jesus was racially or intellectually Jewish, and asked that
German Christians tend to use the Gospel of John rather than
the other three Gospels which he thought were more Jewish in
emphasis.[51]

Generally, however, the question of the elimination of
the Old Testament (the logical result of, for instance, the
anti-Semitism of the *Glaubensbewegung Deutsche Christen*) did
not arise as a serious possibility for the KDC. At one point,
Leffler did ask that certain "Jewish concepts and words" not be

used in German churches, his reason being that he did not like
to make a "fetish" of words spoken "in the desert or some such
place, in Babylonia, in the temple, and in the synagogue..."[52]
But elsewhere, Leffler referred to both the New and Old Testaments when saying that the KDC would use only those "eternal
truths and sacred wisdoms" that spanned the ages.[53]

Although anti-Semitism existed among KDC members, KDC
writers continued to use Old Testament examples in their articles (which *Glaubensbewegung Deutsche Christen* members would
never have done). "We confess the God who spoke through the
prophets..." said the KDC shortly after the Krause affair.[54]
There is, in addition, more than a little evidence that the KDC
compared themselves (or the German nation) to the Biblical
Jews. This is not unrelated to their interpretation of German
history as God's revelation. Even when KDC writers engaged in
anti-Semitic journalism--e.g., when Leffler wrote: "the world
must choose between Israel and Germany,"--there was a certain
respect for the Jews as the one people that provided for all
times a record of how God worked in the world.[55]

KDC anti-Semitism became more intense as the years passed,
and was especially evident after about 1937. There were several possible reasons for this. No doubt Nazi national policy
was becoming more strident against the Jews and it was a natural and easy thing for the KDC to follow suit. In addition,
after 1937, numerous other types of German Christians were in
close contact with the original KDC ideologists as they all
joined together in the National Church Movement. Finally, the
outbreak of war apparently played some part in making anti-
Semitism more important for the KDC. Writing in 1940 for the
"Institute for the Research of Jewish Influences on German
Church Life," Meyer-Erlach combined hatred of Jews with hatred
of the English and produced a study that could hardly have been
more scurrilous. The interesting point that he made, however,
in lumping Jews and Englishmen together was his thesis that one
did not have to be racially Jewish to have all the hated Jewish
characteristics.[56] Thus even the most strident of KDC anti-
Semitism did not direct its venom solely against Jews!

KDC activities revealed a very high degree of pietistic
Christianity. It was, in fact, the formlessness of their

beliefs that gave the Thuringian German Christians their revolutionary character, explicitly directed against traditional,
conservative, systematic, or orthodox theology. "The...fact
that [Thuringian] German Christianity is in the first instance
a matter of the heart and not of the understanding," said
Leffler in January of 1935, "explains why the movement has had
to, and will have to, overcome its strongest opposition not in
the German people, but in the theologians."[57] This sentiment
about the "religion of the heart," which has been the central
concept of German pietism, was echoed a year later by Leutheuser who extended it to National Socialism which he said
sought "not only an outer orientation, but also lives again and
again on the inside."[58] One KDC pastor traced the history of
German pietism and reflected the revolutionary character of its
intellectual activity: "In the age of so-called 'pietism' at
the end of the 17th century when all church orders were thrown
over in favor of the unfolding of personal piety, the connection of the totality of the Christian congregation stepped back
before the subjective confessing of children to the bond which
God concluded with them as individuals in baptism." Later, he
said, the "children's belief" became the faith of the fathers.
The author hoped that youth would continue to question the old
truths: "May the young generation come to the old truths with
new questions..."[59]

Ideologically, the KDC writers were revolutionary, holding very few of the traditional German Protestant beliefs to be
sacred. There were no firm, unalterable, dogmatic foundations
except for one's feelings.[60] The KDC was therefore led into
affirming Hitler and Nazism in the most blatantly religious
terms. Here, as with the other German Christian groups, a
peculiar type of Protestant religiosity could find a home.

NOTES

1. Buchheim, *Glaubenskrise*, p. 49.

2. Leffler, *Christus im dritten Reich*, p. 113.

3. Leffler, *Unser Weg*, p. 23.

4. Meyer-Erlach, *Kirche oder Sekte*, p. 7.

5. Meyer-Erlach, "Deutsche Christen," *BDC*, III, No. 8 (August, 1934), 138.

6. Siegfried Leffler, "Unser Ziel," *BDC*, III, No. 11 (October 15, 1934), 176.

7. M. Dietze, "Jesus der Heiland," *BDC*, VI, No. 2 (January 15, 1936), 14.

8. From a speech by Leutheuser paraphrased in *Ibid.*, p. 21.

9. Siegfried Leffler, "Die Kirchenbewegung Deutsche Christen," *BDC*, IV, No. 12 (June 15, 1935), 136.

10. Leffler, *Unser Weg*, p. 17.

11. Leutheuser, *Die deutsche Christusgemeinde*, p. 9.

12. Leffler, *Christus im dritten Reich*, p. 105.

13. Siegfried Leffler, "Der Weg der Kirchenbewegung der 'Deutschen Christen!'" *BDC*, III, No. 12 (October, 1934), 195.

14. Leffler, "Die Kirchenbewegung Deutsche Christen," *BDC*, IV, No. 12 (June 15, 1935), pp. 134-35.

15. Siegfried Leffler, "Der Weg der Deutschen Christen: Kirchenpolitischer Verein oder geistige Bewegung--Der endültige Bruch mit den Deutschen Christen Berliner Richtung," *BDC*, IV, No. 18 (September 15, 1935), 210.

16. Lehnert, "Das Reich Gottes steht nicht in Worten, sondern in Kraft," *BDC*, IV, No. 21 (November 5, 1935), 251.

17. "Aufruf der Landgemeinde Thüringen der Deutschen Christen zur kirchlichen Lage," in Duhm, *Kampf*, pp. 122-23.

18. Pastor K. Veller, "Christus und Deutschland," *BDC*, V, No. 1 (January 1, 1936), 7.

19. *BDC*, III, No. 7 (July, 1934), 129.

20. Meyer-Erlach, "Die Toten erwachen," *BDC*, IV, No. 6 (March 15, 1935), 61.

216

21. Leffler, *Christus im dritten Reich*, p. 98.

22. Leutheuser, *Die deutsche Christusgemeinde*, p. 3.

23. Beckmann, *Kirchliches Jahrbuch*, p. 33.

24. *BDC*, III, No. 7 (July, 1934), 129.

25. Siegfried Leffler, "Grundsätzliches über die Kirchenbewegung der Deutschen Christen," *BDC*, III, No. 9 (September,
1934), 160.

26. Leffler, "Die Kirchliche Lage," *BDC*, IV, No. 19
(October 1, 1935), 228.

27. Siegfried Leffler, "Rede zur Zweiten Reichstagung
der Kirchenbewegung 'Deutsche Christen,'" *BDC*, IV, No. 21
(November, 1935), 258.

28. *BDC*, III, No. 12 (November, 1934), 190.

29. Erich Fascher, "Die theologische Grundhaltung der
Kirchenbewegung Deutsche Christen," *BDC*, IV, No. 15 (August 1,
1935), 176.

30. Quoted in Heinrich Weinel, "Thüringen und der Friede
in der Kirche," *Die Christliche Welt*, XLVIII, (February 17,
1934), 170-71.

31. Leffler, *Christus im dritten Reich*, p. 7.

32. Fascher, "Die theologische Grundhaltung der Kirchenbewegung Deutsche Christen," *BDC*, IV, No. 13 (July 1, 1935),
147-48.

33. Erich Fascher, "Deutsche Christen und die Theologie
der Gegenwart," *BDC*, IV, No. 7 (April 1, 1935), 78.

34. Julius Leutheuser, "Dogmatisches Christusglauben oder
deutsche Christusglaube," *BDC*, V, No. 7 (April 1, 1936), 86.

35. Ludwig Müller, *Was ist positives Christentum?* (Stuttgart: Der Tazzelwurm Verlag, 1939), p. 97.

36. Erich Fromm, *Das Volkstestament der Deutschen: Ein
Geleitwort zu der vom "Institut..." herausgegebenen Botschaft
Gottes* (Weimar: Verlag Deutsche Christen, 1940), pp. 16-18.

37. Grundmann, *Völkische Theologie*, p. 10.

38. Cochrane, *Church's Confessions*, p. 76.

39. *BDC*, III, No. 8 (August, 1934), 147.

40. Pastor K. Veller, "Christus und Deutschland," p. 7.

41. Grundmann paraphrased in *Die Christliche Welt*,
XLVIII, No. 7 (April 1, 1934), 326.

42. "Aufruf der Landgemeinde Thüringen der Deutschen Christen zur kirchlichen Lage," in Duhm, *Kampf*, p. 123.

43. Fromm, *Volkstestament*, pp. 9-10.

44. Meyer-Erlach, *Kirche oder Sekte*, p. 11.

45. Ludwig Müller, "Warum ich die Bergpredigt 'verdeutschte,'" *BDC*, V, No. 8 (April 15, 1936), 82.

46. *Ibid.*, p. 83.

47. Ludwig Müller's version is from *Deutsche Gottesworte: Aus der Bergpredigt verdeutscht* (Weimar: Verlag Deutsche Christen, 1936), pp. 9ff. Obviously, I am not concerned here with the likely possibility that Luther's translation also was influenced by his cultural-historical circumstances.

48. Beckmann, *Kirchliches Jahrbuch*, p. 33.

49. A more detailed discussion of the KDC attitudes toward the Old Testament may be found in Nicolaisen, *Auseinandersetzungen*, pp. 84ff.

50. Leutheuser, *Die deutsche Christusgemeinde*, p. 15.

51. Fromm, *Volkstestament*, pp. 23-24, 29-33.

52. Leffler, *Christus im dritten Reich*, p. 61.

53. Leffler, *Unser Weg*, p. 23.

54. Duhm, *Kampf*, p. 123.

55. Leffler, "Ein Gott-ein Volk!" *BDC*, IV, No. 8 (April 15, 1935), 89-91.

56. Wolf Meyer-Erlach, "Der Einfluss der Juden auf das englische Christentum," in Grundmann, ed., *Christentum und Judentum*, pp. 3ff.

57. Siegfried Leffler, "Im Glauben vorwärts," *BDC*, IV, No. 1 (January 1, 1935), 3.

58. "Rednertag in Friedrichroda am 3. und 4. Januar 1936," *BDC*, V, No. 2 (January 15, 1936), 21.

59. [Pastor?] Propp, "Jugend reiht sich ein!" *BDC*, V, No. 8 (April 15, 1936), 85-86.

60. The revivalist, emotional, irrational content of KDC activities was scornfully noticed even by Nazi surveillance agents who attended a KDC (National Church Movement) convention at Eisenach in October of 1937. They commented on "a certain impression of theatrics," and took a great deal of satisfaction in reporting how a service on the Wartburg was ruined by a downpour: "Those who still went up the Wartburg stood there feeling chilly and wet and seemed only to have one wish--

218

that the service might end soon." Leutheuser was described as having begun his speech by working himself into a kind of trance. The Nazi observers concluded: "National Socialism must renounce the well-meant attempts from this [KDC] side to complete the revolution religiously." Document 43 in Friedrich Zipfel, *Kirchenkampf in Deutschland 1933-1945* (Berlin: Walter de Gruyter & Co., 1965), pp. 435-36, 442.

CONCLUSION

There were basic ideological differences within the greater "German Christian" phenomenon. What was presented above showed three basic types of German Christian positions different enough to attract quite a wide variety of people and therefore collectively able to span a wide spectrum of German Protestantism. Virtually none of the ideological or political stances or social positions in German Protestantism was immune to the attractions of at least one of the German Christian groups.

Organizationally, the German Christians showed a development over the years that paralleled the attractiveness of their ideas. The *Christlich-Deutsche Bewegung* attracted conservative types, types who were not looking for revolutionary answers to the ills which they saw around them in the Weimar Republic. In the early 1930's, these people were still pinning their hopes on the German Nationalist Party (DNVP) and on a return to the morals and politics with which they had been familiar before the end of the Hohenzollern monarchy. The attempt by the members of the CDB to reserve judgment concerning the Nazi Party and the CDB failure to support the Nazis actively before 1933 reflects the unrevolutionary nature of the movement, as well as its upper-class distrust of the rabble who made up the cadres of the Nazi Party and the Storm Troopers. Most of those associated with the CDB supported Hitler as only one of the possible nationalist-Volkish alternatives to the Weimar democracy. Those who did seek a closer identification with the Nazi Party abandoned the CDB in 1933 and adhered to the *Glaubensbewegung Deutsche Christen* which was founded in 1932 at the instigation of the Party, and which put more emphasis on racial thinking.

The GDC provided, in addition to more definitely Nazi principles, an organizational roof under which virtually all German Christian groups were united in 1933 during the decisive months when Hitler came to power and consolidated the broadest basis of popular support. Organizationally, it is important to remember that the German Christians did feel it

possible to be united for a short time in the flush of national renewal during the first year of the National Socialist regime. However, at the end of 1933, the degree of racial anti-
Semitism in the GDC had reached unacceptable proportions for
many German Christians (especially those who had been associated with the conservative wing) and the interest of leading
GDC members in church-political maneuvers brought the end of a
united German Christian effort.

The Conservatives were by that time defunct organizationally, but the more radical branches of German Christians reestablished their autonomy. The most notable of the radical
groups was the *Kirchenbewegung Deutsche Christen*, or "Thuringian" German Christians, who had the significant social character at first of being based in rural areas. In the mid-
1930's, the KDC lack of interest in church politics, as well
as a radical affirmation of certain ideological stances, helped the KDC to gain adherents in proportion as the successors
of the GDC lost membership. In the late 1930's, the KDC was
the center of a renewed national German Christian organization.
However, after 1933, the Nazi Party did not support German
Christians as against other patriotic Protestant groups, and
the German Christians around the KDC cannot be said to have
wielded much political power in the Third Reich.

The ideas of the German Christian groups also showed a
great deal of variety. Orthodox or conservative churchmen
could find a home in the *Christlich-Deutsche Bewegung* (later
also in the *Reichsbewegung Deutsche Christen* and *Luther-
Deutschen*) with its old-style "Prussian" patriotism, emphasis
on Luther's teachings and a Christian militaristic bearing,
and lack of emphasis on strident racial anti-Semitism. The
CDB acceptance of National Socialism was the result of the
hope for a return to more traditional German ways that had
been subverted by the Weimar Republic. CDB ideology did not
demand so extreme a nationalism as Nazism offered; more traditional forms of political order would have sufficed. But the
CDB was of service to the establishment and consolidation of
the Nazi regime nonetheless. There were dangers, then, in being a conservative German nationalist in the early 1930's.
Conservative German Christianity helped bolster Nazi aims

without providing for their control. The conservatives were
the first German Christian movement to become disillusioned,
and many ceased their efforts in the German Christian direction as early as the fall of 1933. Ironically, conservative
Protestant ideas, the firm unalterable orthodoxy professed by
most CDB members and used to undermine allegiance to the Weimar
Republic, comprised also, in hindsight, the best Protestant
theological stance for avoiding the excesses of German Christianity and, one would like to believe, for avoiding the excesses of National Socialism itself. The members of the CDB
were not always unattractive personalities (while members of
the *Glaubensbewegung Deutsche Christen* almost always appear to
be). They were not vindictive, their anti-Semitism was almost
always relatively controlled, they were not taken in by the
Nazi racial pseudo-sciences. Human judgment, even with the
best of intentions, is far from infallible. Taking into consideration the aristocratic, traditionalist, social base of the
CDB ideologists, as well as their educational background and
their ability at least to attempt to test ideas in a formal
context, one cannot simply condemn them for the politics that
arose out of their ideology.

The *Glaubensbewegung Deutsche Christen*, however, cannot
hold up under the same kind of standards. Partly as a result
of its organizational nature, but more because it embraced individuals who were politically opportunistic, the ideology of
the GDC provided no firm intellectual or moral bases for action. "Positive Christianity," in the final analysis, was
nothing more than a shibboleth to cover over a complete lack of
theological content. The *Führerprinzip* was appropriated from
the political sphere and, for all the GDC claims to the contrary, it had no basis in the Christian religion. The same was
true for the GDC interpretation of German Protestant unity
which was based on force, uniformity of belief, and a desire to
complete the Nazi revolution in the church arena. Finally,
anti-Semitism was made a pillar of GDC beliefs, proving that
even in the 20th century religious anti-Semitism could thrive.
A religion that can only unite its forces by concentrating on
hatred cannot hope to give advice on how to live as a good person. The opportunistic nature of the GDC, the willingness of

its thinkers to bend or ignore theology for the same of organi-
zation-building makes it a very unpleasant group to consider.

Another special type of German Christian ideology was
represented by the *Kirchenbewegung Deutsche Christen*. It was
characterized by lack of dogma and by a pietistic religion of
the heart by which its members were led naively into the most
revolutionary of ideas that could be considered German Christian. German history was, for them, completely confused with
sacred canons and led into a *Heilsgeschichte* viewpoint of their
own national destiny that bordered on unbelievability. This,
along with their interest in the religious possibilities of nature and in the all-embracing non-denominational National
Church, made them religious revolutionaries. Perhaps it would
be more correct to see them as revolutionary visionaries, for
all of their ideas have a sort of unreal, millenaristic character about them. The historian, at the point at which he is
asked to pass judgment on his topic, is here faced with an interesting group. It is not easy to judge ideas that are basically informed with self-conscious irrationalism. Yet there are
reasons to give, conditionally, some positive judgments to the
KDC writers. They were not generally so involved with church
politics as to let it influence their ideological stances.
This situation may have changed somewhat after about 1937, but
through most of the mid-1930's, major KDC writers voiced only
scorn, probably sincere, for political maneuverings in the
churches. In addition, although anti-Semitism was certainly
present in their writings, it was not a necessary bulwark of
their thought, and played a secondary role. Also, the concept
of eliminating the useless forms that divide Christendom and
have historically been the source of internecine persecutions
was a sincere attempt (albeit limited to Germany) to fulfill
the centuries-old concept of the one Christian church. The
lack of orthodoxy so evident in KDC ideas reflected not a lack
of religious feeling, but an affirmation of the belief that
every man has a right to his unmediated relationship to God.
Finally, the glorification of nature reflected the KDC member's
joy in life as well as his uncertainty about his position in an
urbanized, technological age--both are sentiments that are
still alive today in the minds of many well-meaning people.

Nevertheless, one cannot deny that the KDC ideologists were
firm believers in Hitler. Their unbridled lack of dogma allowed for no check on affirmation of Nazism.

The German Christian movements fit into the larger structure of 19th and 20th century German national-Volkish thought.
All three groups had their roots in the 19th century--even
more than in the Reformation days of the 16th century. In all
three groups, the ideas of nationalists such as J. G. Fichte,
Ernst Moritz Arndt, and the more patriotic utterances of
Friedrich Schleiermacher, appeared over and over. Certain nationalistic forbears were the common intellectual property of
all the German Christian writers. But the differences in outlook in the German Christian ideas reflected some difference
of ideological models. The *Christlich-Deutsche Bewegung* was
in line with the Prussian nationalist ideology which came to
fruition in the Bismarckian Reich. Its members would have
been content to go back to pre-1918 Hohenzollern, Prussian,
Protestant Germany with its certainty of class divisions, close
relationship of the Protestant churches to the government, and
the alleged stability of the government based on the monarchical principle. It is significant that unlike other German
Christian groups, the CDB did not trace the origins of problems
of modern life--industrialization, the breakdown of class differences, the phenomenon of mass movements--back to the 19th
century. They recognized these problems as part of the trai-
torous and godless synthesis of 1918. The ideas of the CDB
took on a general significance that reflected their historical
position in the conservative line. They could not think of
Germanness without thinking of alleged Lutheran Protestant
ideals. They did not think in terms of neo-paganism as did
other German Volkish groups, yet they gave certain Volkishly-
desired German characteristics--strength of character in the
militaristic sense, belief in the leadership principle, the
Kämpfer spirit--a kind of respectable Lutheran backing that
these ideas did not perhaps otherwise deserve. The same was
true of the conservative German Christian position on the need
for political order. The allegedly Lutheran-Reformation bases
of political science were evoked to subvert the Weimar democracy and help usher in the Nazi period. All of this was

supported by the CDB glorification of war and the strengthening of the spirit of militarism by the antagonistic position of the CDB toward the possibility of Christian pacifism. The long-range significance of the *Christlich-Deutsche Bewegung*, then, was its continuance of a tradition of conservative Prussian-nationalism that, albeit partly unwittingly, gave the Nazi efforts in 1933 the respectability and support of a large segment of German Protestantism.

The *Glaubensbewegung Deutsche Christen* found its intellectual forbears in a somewhat different strand of the 19th century German ideological fabric. Its social make-up (lower middle class) as well as its "pathological dissatisfaction," as Hans Buchheim puts it, made the GDC the descendant of such thinkers as Adolf Stoecker, Houston Stewart Chamberlain, and Paul de Lagarde. In fact, de Lagarde's particular prejudices were obviously of importance in the formulation of GDC ideas. He had little use for the formation of the Bismarckian Reich because he believed that it was an artificial construct that accommodated precisely those ills--industrial and modern--that could only be overcome by basing German renewal on the Volk-nation rather than on the state. It was necessary, de Lagarde believed, to establish a Germanic faith that would be an amalgam of a romantic German mysticism and an unorthodox Christianity. The GDC writers also consciously looked for a break with the past. They too stressed the Volkish-nation rather than the Reich built by Bismarck. De Lagarde's anti-Semitism, with such elements as his rejection of the "legalism" of St. Paul and his identification of Judaism with modern liberalism, was also reflected in the ideas of the GDC. The significance, then, of the GDC was that it continued a line of Volkish thought that had its roots in certain culturally despondent and anti-Semitic people of the second half of the 19th century. Like the conservatives, the ideologists of the GDC rejected the Weimar Republic, but the GDC saw the roots of modern evils in the Bismarckian empire and thus were looking for a new solution to German fate, which they specifically identified with the Nazi Party. Their close connection with the Nazi Party put the stamp of opportunism on all their ideas and GDC writers thought of Party principles first and Christian principles second.

Therefore, they devoted much of their time analyzing "positive Christianity"--the officially accepted Nazi position on religion according to the Party program--and interpreted the term in widely varying definitions, according to the impression they desired to convey. In this way, German Protestants were assured that Nazism was in some way acting on Christian principles. The GDC attempt to find legitimate Christian bases for the *Führerprinzip* largely failed, but here again the attempt to bring the church into correct coordination with the Nazi regime was the desired goal. The most insidious of the ideas of the GDC was its attempt to bolster cultural and political anti-Semitism with religious hatred of the Jews. The GDC appealed to those who were interested in political positions in the church, who wanted to justify Nazism on Christian grounds, and who focused their disappointments in hatred of the Jews.

The third group, the *Kirchenbewegung Deutsche Christen*, also had its peculiar ideological ancestors. It was the most extreme in its rejection of modern industrialized society which included for them the Bismarckian Reich as well as the Weimar Republic. Therefore the early 19th century romantics and such people as de Lagarde, Julius Langbehn, Moeller van den Bruck, and Friedrich Nietzsche were lauded as representatives of the eternal German spirit fighting battles for the Volk. The leaders of the KDC came out of the German Youth Movement and continued the ideals of their *Wandervögel* youth by stressing the German countryside and the eternal values of rural life. Most importantly, the KDC ideologists represented the familiar element of German Protestant pietism, which on the Protestant spectrum, put them theologically at the opposite pole from the CDB. The pietistic framework has contributed to an enthusiastic nationalism, as Koppel Pinson has pointed out effectively in dealing with early 19th century German pietistic thought. When the KDC member looked at German history in *Heilsgeschichte* terms, confusing secular and religious history completely, or when he identified German natural and agricultural scenery as the matrix of Christianity, he was putting Germany in the place of God, and, by extension, putting a religious content into Nazism--the contemporary result of German sacred history, as he saw it. Certainly, the Nazi leaders themselves had only

thinly-veiled scorn for the KDC ideas, but the KDC had its
significance in giving a thoroughly religious interpretation
to Nazi actions.

It was thus a very wide spectrum of people attracted to
the various German Christian movements. It is impossible to
make a final judgment or blanket condemnation of all German
Christians. One conclusion that results from this study is
that it was possible for a German to ally with National Socialism from almost any church position or ideological presuppositions. Excluding *Glaubensbewegung Deutsche Christen* opportunism, one can also say that Christian beliefs concerning very
important daily issues were not considered by sincere Christians to be antithetical to Nazi theology. Ideas which today
may appear to be essentially unchristian were considered by
sincere people in the decade of the 1930's to be at the basis
of right belief. This has continuing relevance. The issues
of war, race, and nationalism remain major issues that the
churches continue to deal with.

Was there any general German Christian ideological tendency that tied all the movements together? There was really
only one--the more or less ready acceptance of national renewal
embodied in Hitler and National Socialism. Although the various issues sometimes overlapped the borders of the movements,
the groups were ideologically distinct. One additional trait
characterized all German Christian movements--the inability to
maintain a balance between, on the one hand, the firm retention
of some basic theological and moral positions and, on the
other, the allowance for a responsible flexibility to face life
in the world.

APPENDIX

BIOGRAPHIES OF MAJOR FIGURES IN THE
GERMAN CHRISTIAN MOVEMENTS

This information was gathered from a variety of sources, including J. S. Conway, *The Nazi Persecution of the Churches*, Kurt Meier, *Die Deutschen Christen*, standard reference books such as the various editions of *Wer ist Wer*, and also various German Christian writings.

Paul Althaus - born 1888 in Obershagen near Hannover; educated at Tübingen and Göttingen; lecturer, University of Göttingen, 1914; served in World War I; professor at Rostock until 1925; since then at the University of Erlangen; member of the CDB; conservative Lutheran authority on pacifism and political authority; died 1966.

Heinrich Bornkamm - born at Wuitz near Zeitz, 1901; educated at Jena, Tübingen, and Berlin; taught at Tübingen, Giessen, Leipzig, and Heidelberg; President of the Evangelical Union; interested in the relationship of Luther and the German mystics.

Bruno Doehring - born 1879 at Mohrungen, East Prussia; studied at Halle, Berlin, Königsberg; 1912, Director of preacher seminar at Wittenberg (West Prussia); 1914, court preacher in Berlin; until 1923 a tutor; 1923-27, President of the Evangelical Bund; 1924-27, co-editor of *Neue Tägliche Rundschau*; one of the founders of the *Christliche-Deutsche Bewegung*.

Cajus Fabricius - born 1884 at Graudenz (after 1919 a part of Poland); studied theology at Heidelberg, Göttingen, Berlin; 1911, *Privatdozent* in systematic theology at Berlin; 1921-1935, Professor of Systematic Theology at Berlin; 1935-1942, the same at Breslau; member of the NSDAP, 1932-1940; described himself as an early founder of a student labor-service corps; author of *Positive Christianity in the New State* (1936); died 1951.

Erich Fascher - born 1897 in Göttingen; educated at Göttingen; 1926-1930, lecturer at Marburg; after 1930, a Professor at Jena in New Testament theology; a prolific writer for the KDC.

Friedrich Gogarten - born 1887 at Dortmund; educated at Berlin, Jena, and Heidelberg; served pastorates at various places until 1931; after 1931 Professor at Breslau; associated for a time with the dialectical theology and with Karl Barth's journal, *Zwischen den Zeiten*; conservative formulator of Protestant state-teachings theories; Professor of Systematic Theology at Göttingen after 1935.

Walter Grundmann - born 1906; ordained 1932; member of the Saxon German Christian movement; at the end of 1933 he wrote the "Twenty-eight Theses of the Saxon German Christians," which

230

was adopted as the platform of the *Reichsbewegung Deutsche Christen*; 1936, joined the NKBDC (Leffler's National Church Movement) and wrote articles for *Briefe an deutsche Christen (Die Nationalkirche)*; 1938, Professor of New Testament and Volkish Theology at the Nazified University of Jena; 1941, General Secretary of the "Institute for Research of Jewish Influences on German Church Life" based at Eisenach; after 1954, Professor of New Testament on the Eisenach Theological Faculty.

Emanuel Hirsch - born 1888 at Bentwisch, West Priegnitz; student of Karl Holl; Luther and Kierkegaard the two most important influences on his ideas, but also had strong neo-Fichtean interests; 1915, lecturer at Bonn; 1921, Professor of Church History at Göttingen; also known after 1935 as a systematic theologian; although an early member of the CDB, he joined the GDC in 1933 and, unlike other conservatives, maintained his allegiance to the German Christians until 1945; strongly opposed dialectical theology; dismissed in 1945 from his position at Göttingen.

Joachim Hossenfelder - born 1899 at Kottbus; his father (of Silesian peasant stock) was a principal in a Kiel commercial school; his mother was the daughter of a seminary director; after taking his high school exams, he enlisted in the army in 1917 and was a non-commissioned officer with the field artillery; saw action at the Somme and Verdun; after the war, studied theology at Kiel and Breslau; because of boredom, joined the border defense *Freikorps* in the summer of 1919 and in 1921 participated in fights along the Polish border and in Upper Silesia; returned to school but took out a quarter to work at the Kiel gas works; ordained, 1923; with his young wife went to his first pastorate at Siemenau, Upper Silesia where some of his parishioners lived in Polish territory; after three years of marriage, his wife died of tuberculosis, leaving him with a daughter; 1927, second pastorate in Alt-Reichenau; remarried; joined Nazi Party, April 1, 1929; 1931, pastorate in Berlin; May, 1932, became *Reichsleiter* of the GDC and published his platform June 6; known as a good orator and good organizer; August, 1933, Prussian Synod named him Bishop of Brandenburg; after the *Sportpalast* debacle of November of 1933, was forced to give up his church and GDC offices; tried a comeback in 1935 with a new organization, the *Kampf- und Glaubensbewegung Deutsche Deutsche Christen*; after the war, was de-Nazified and made pastor at Ratekau, Schleswig-Holstein.

Christian Kinder - born 1897 at Plön, Schleswig-Holstein; 1914, enlisted in army where remained until the end of the war; legal studies after the war; used his law background working for Schleswig-Holstein State Church, where he became vice-president in the spring of 1933; member of the S. A. and on the *Führerrat* of the state leadership of the Schleswig-Holstein German Christians; December 21, 1933, became *Reichsleiter* of the *Reichsbewegung Deutsche Christen*.

Gerhard Kittel - born 1888 at Breslau; studied at Leipzig, Tübingen, and Berlin; between 1913 and 1926, taught at Kiel, Leipzig, and Greifswald; after 1926, Professor of Theology at Tübingen, and between 1939 and 1943, at Vienna; conservative

Lutheran; joined GDC though resigning in November, 1933; after
1935 closely connected with Walter Frank's racial-political
pseudo-scientific history institute; allegedly an expert on
oriental and old-Jewish-Christian groups as well as of ancient
Judaism; in the tradition of the Christian anti-Semitism of
Stoecker, wrote numerous polemical works on the character of
Judaism; died 1948.

Helmuth Kittel - born 1902 at Potsdam; educated at Tübingen and
Berlin; professor at Greifswald (later at Münster); once interested in dialectical theology; member of the GDC until November
of 1933, after which he continued to support *Reichsbischof*
Müller but rejected Hossenfelder; conservative; ideologically
close to the *Luther-Deutschen*; 1940, signed the Godesberg
Declaration, though he denied it after 1945; at Osnabrück after
1946.

Julius Kuptsch - one time Latvian Minister of Cults; during the
early 1930's, wrote a number of pamphlets and books alleging
the parallelism of Christian and Nazi concepts; affiliated with
both the GDC and the KDC.

Siegfried Leffler - born 1900; good friend of Julius Leutheuser
with whom he was involved in youth groups and *Freikorps* after
World War I; along with Leutheuser, left the Bavarian Evangelical-Lutheran State Church in 1927, claiming that with his National Socialist beliefs he was in sharp conflict with Bavarian
church leadership; Leffler and Leutheuser moved to the Wiera
Valley of Thuringia and organized the KDC out of local circles
of pastors and teachers; after 1933, Leffler was a member of
the ruling council of the Thuringian *Volksbildungsministerium*,
and *Reichsgemeindeleiter* of the KDC (and later of the NKBDC);
after World War II, was de-Nazified, issued a statement rejecting the errors of his German Christian past, and went back into
the service of the Bavarian State Church; later pastor at
Hengersberg, Bavaria.

Johannes Leipoldt - born 1880 in Dresden; taught at Leipzig,
Kiel, and Münster; wrote anti-Semitic works based on his re-
search on the ancient Jews and on his analysis of Christ's
"Aryan" character.

Julius Leutheuser - born 1900; 1918, standard bearer in army;
after the war, studied theology while taking part in *Freikorps*
activities; 1920-1921, in *Freikorps "Oberland"* as an orator for
the Nazi Party; left Bavarian Protestant Church after two years
at Augsburg; went to Thuringia with Siegfried Leffler; after
1933, a *Kirchenrat* in Thuringian State Church and a leading
functionary of the KDC, specializing in ideas concerning God's
direct intervention in modern German history; killed at Stalin-
grad on November 24, 1942.

Wolf Meyer-Erlach - born 1899; war service and *Freikorps* service in Bavaria against Communist forces; radio pastor in
Bavaria, 1931; after 1933 taught practical theology at Jena,
where he became Rector in 1935; never received academic degree;
associated with the KDC and wrote articles for *Briefe an
deutsche Christen*; in 1961, received the *Bundesverdienstkreuz*

first class from the Federal Republic for his anti-Communist efforts; lately the vicar of Wörsdorf, Ilstein, Hessen.

Ludwig Müller - born 1883 at Gütersloh into a pietistic family surrounding; studied at Halle and Bonn; his first pastorate was at Rödinghausen bei Bünde, said, by a GDC writer, to be a congregation that "combined the united Lutheran church concept with pietistic innerness"; as a Marine chaplain, he saw service in Flanders and the Dardanelles during World War I; 1926, joined Nazi Party in Königsberg and met Hitler when the latter visited Königsberg in 1926 and stayed as a guest with Müller; 1933, named as Representative of the Reich Chancellor for Church Affairs; August, 1933, elected State Bishop of Prussia; September of 1933, officially designated *Reichsbischof* of the German Evangelical Church; after mid-1934, his church powers were largely taken away from him; died 1945.

Heinrich Rendtorff - born 1888 at Westerland (Sylt), which was once Danish; father was a pastor and later President of the *Gustav-Adolf Verein*; much of his childhood spent with the son of Prince Heinrich of Prussia (the latter Kaiser Wilhelm II's brother); educated at Kiel and Tübingen where his uncle, Adolf Schlatter, was a well-known New Testament scholar; 1924-1926, director of the theological preaching seminar at Preetz (Holstein); 1926-1930, Professor of Practical Theology at Kiel; 1930-1934, Bishop of Mecklenburg Lutheran Church; 1934-1945, pastor at Stettin; since 1945, professor and (in 1948-1949) Rector at Kiel; founder of the CDB; forced to resign his bishopric in 1934 after vicious attacks from the more radical GDC of Mecklenburg; died 1960.

Heinz Weidemann - born 1895 at Hannover; studied theology at Göttingen; an officer during World War I; after a short pastorate elsewhere, became the cathedral preacher of Bremen in 1926; 1934, became German Christian State Bishop of Bremen with the help of the local S. A.; later, in 1935, separated from the RDC and founded his own German Christian organization known as "*Kommende Kirche*"; convicted in 1944 of suborning a nineteen-year-old girl to perjure herself after he was named co-respondent in divorce proceedings; sent to prison.

Friedrich Wieneke - born 1892 at Zahlendorf near Berlin; son of an author; studied at Berlin until August of 1914, when he enlisted in the army where he remained until 1919; received the Iron Cross second class; 1929, joined Nazi Party and was active in local party affairs at Soldin, Brandenburg; early a member of the CDB, but changed to the GDC with its more blatant racialism; GDC authority on educational questions and its self-styled theologian; vicar at Alt-Töplitz near Potsdam, 1950; died 1957.

BIBLIOGRAPHY

BIBLIOGRAPHY

Primary Sources

Allgemeine Evangelische-Lutherische Kirchenzeitung. Leipzig:
Verlag von Dörffling & Franke, 1932-33.

Althaus, Paul. *Christus und die deutsche Seele.* Gütersloh:
Verlag C. Bertelsmann, 1934.

————. *Die deutsche Stunde der Kirche.* 3d ed. Göttingen:
Vandenhoeck & Ruprecht, 1934.

————. *Evangelium und Leben: Gesammelte Vorträge.* Gütersloh: Verlag von C. Bertelsmann, 1927.

————. *Kirche und Staat nach lutherischer Lehre.* Leipzig:
A. Deichertsche Verlagsbuchhandlung, 1935.

————. *Politisches Christentum: Ein Wort über die Thüringer
"Deutschen Christen."* 2d ed. Leipzig: A. Deichertsche
Verlag, 1935.

————. "Thesen zum Gegenwärtigen lutherischen Staatsverständnis." *Kirche und Welt: Studien und Dokumenten,* No.
2 of *Die Kirche und das Staatsproblem in der Gegenwart.*
Berlin: Furche-Verlag, 1935.

————. *Theologie der Ordnungen.* 2d ed. Gütersloh: Verlag
C. Bertelsmann, 1935.

Andersen, Friedrich. *Der deutsche Heiland.* Munich: Deutscher
Volksverlag, 1921.

Barth, Karl. *The Epistle to the Romans.* Oxford: Oxford University Press, 1933.

Bauer, Gerhard. *Reich Gottes und drittes Reich.* Göttingen:
Vandenhoeck & Ruprecht, 1934.

Bauer, Wilhelm. *Im Umbruch der Zeit.* Weimar: Verlag Deutsche
Christen, 1935.

Beckmann, Joachim, ed. *Kirchliches Jahrbuch für die Evangelische Kirche in Deutschland.* LX-LXXI (1933-44).
Gütersloh: C. Bertelsmann, 1948.

Bornkamm, Heinrich. *Christus und die Germanen.* Berlin: Verlag
des evangelischen Bundes, 1936.

————. *Luther und der deutsche Geist.* Tübingen: Verlag von
J. C. B. Mohr, 1934.

————. *Der Totalitätsanspruch des Evangeliums.* Berlin:
Verlag des evangelischen Bundes, 1937.

Briefe an Deutsche Christen [after 1937, called *Die National-kirche*]. III-XI (1934-41).

Christentum und Wissenschaft [after 1935, called *Kirche im Angriff*; after 1939, called *Seelsorge*]. Dresden: Verlag C. Ludwig Ungelenk, 1925-39.

Die Christliche Welt. Gotha: Leopold Klotz Verlag, 1932-36.

Dannenmann, Arnold. *Die Geschichte der Glaubensbewegung "Deutsche Christen."* Dresden: Oskar Günther Verlag, [1933].

Deutsche Theologie. Stuttgart: W. Kohlhammer Verlag, 1935, 1939, 1940.

Deutsches Volkstum: Monatsschrift für das deutsche Geistes-leben. Edited by Wilhelm Stapel and Albrecht Günther. Hamburg: Hanseatische Verlagsanstalt, 1920-36.

Doehring, Bruno. *Gott, das Leben und der Tod: Drei Kriegs-vorträge...gehalten im Dom zu Berlin*. Berlin: Verlag von Reuther & Reichard, 1914.

Duhm, Andreas. *Der Kampf um die deutsche Kirche: Eine Kirchen-geschichte des Jahres 1933/34, dargestellt für das evan-gelische Volk*. Gotha: Leopold Klotz Verlag, [1934].

Das Evangelium im dritten Reich: Sonntagsblatt der Deutschen Christen. Berlin: 1932-35.

Fabricius, Cajus. *Positive Christianity in the Third Reich* (English edition of *Positives Christentum im neuen Staat*). Dresden: Hermann Puschel, 1937.

Fascher, Erich. *Grosse Deutsche begegnen der Bibel: Eine Weg-weisung für Deutsche Christen*. Weimar: Verlag Deutsche Christen, 1935.

Franks, Walter. *Deutsches Christentum und deutsche Reichs-kirche als Forderung der Gegenwart*. Frankfurt am Main: Verlag Moritz Diesterweg, 1933.

Fromm, Erich. *Das Volkstestament der Deutschen: Ein Geleitwort zu der vom "Institut zur Erforschung des jüdischen Ein-flüsses auf das deutsche kirchliche Leben" herausgegebenen Botschaft Gottes*. Weimar: Verlag Deutsche Christen, 1940.

Glaube und Volk: Christlich-deutsche Monatsschrift. Küstrin: Verlag Deutscher Osten, 1932-33.

Gogarten, Friedrich. *Einheit von Evangelium und Volkstum?* Hamburg: Hanseatische Verlagsanstalt, 1933.

_____. *Ist Volksgesetz Gottesgesetz? Eine Auseinander-setzung mit meinen Kritikern*. Hamburg: Hanseatische Ver-lagsanstalt, 1934.

_____. *Politische Ethik*. Jena: Eugen Diederichs, 1932.

Gogarten, Friedrich. *Die Schuld der Kirche gegen die Welt.*
2d ed. Jena: Eugen Diederichs Verlag, 1930.

Grossmann, Constantin. *Deutsche Christen--Ein Volksbuch: Wegweiser durch die Glaubensbewegung unserer Zeit.* Dresden: Verlag E. am Ende, 1934.

Grundmann, Walter, ed. *Christentum und Judentum: Studien zur Erforschung ihres gegenseitigen Verhältnisses--Sitzungsberichte der ersten Arbeitstagung des Instituts...vom 1. bis 3. März 1940 in Wittenberg.* Leipzig: Verlag Georg Wigand, 1940.

_____. *Gott und Nation: Ein evangelisches Wort zum Wollen des Nationalsozialismus und zu Rosenbergs Sinndeutung.* 2d ed. Berlin: Furche-Verlag, 1933.

_____. *Völkische Theologie*, No. 1 of *Schriften zur Nationalkirche*. 2d ed. Weimar: Verlag Deutsche Christen, [1937].

Handtmann, Superintendent. *Die Stellung der Kirche zu Volk und Staat*, No. 4 of *Glaube und Volk: Schriftenreihe der Christlich-deutschen Bewegung*. Küstrin: Verlag Deutscher Osten, 1933.

Hirsch, Emanuel. *Deutsches Volkstum und evangelischer Glaube.* Hamburg: Hanseatische Verlagsanstalt, 1934.

_____. *Die gegenwärtige geistige Lage im Spiegel philosophischer und theologischer Besinnung.* Göttingen: Vandenhoeck & Reprecht, 1934.

_____. *Das kirchliche Wollen der deutschen Christen.* Berlin-Steglitz: Evangelischer Pressverband für Deutschland, 1933.

_____. *Die Liebe zum Vaterlande*, No. 12 of *Schriften zur politischen Bildung*. 3d ed. Langensalza: Hermann Beyer & Söhne, 1924.

_____. *Staat und Kirche im 19. und 20. Jahrhundert.* Göttingen: Vandenhoeck & Ruprecht, 1929.

_____. *Das Wesen des Christentums.* Weimar: Verlag Deutsche Christen, 1939.

Die Hochkirche [after 1934, called *Eine Heilige Kirche*]. Munich: Verlag von Ernst Reinhardt, 1932-40.

Hossenfelder, Joachim. *Unser Kampf*, No. 1 of *Schriftenreihe der "Deutschen Christen."* Berlin-Charlottenburg: Max Grevemeyer Verlag, 1933.

Jäger, August. *Kirche im Volk: Ein Beitrag zur Geschichte der nationalsozialistischen Rechtsentwicklung.* Berlin: Deutscher Rechts-Verlag G. m. b. H., 1936.

238

Kinder, Christian, ed. *Der Deutschen Christen Reichs-Kalender, 1935*. Meissen: Schlimpert & Püschel Verlag, 1935.

————. *Volk vor Gott: Mein Dienst an der Deutschen Evangelischen Kirche*. Hamburg: Hanseatische Verlagsanstalt, 1935.

Kittel, Gerhard. *Die Judenfrage*. Stuttgart: W. Kohlhammer Verlag, 1933.

————. *Kirche und Judenchristen*. Stuttgart: W. Kohlhammer Verlag, 1933.

Kittel, Helmuth. *Religion als Geschichtsmacht*. Leipzig: B. G. Teubner, 1938.

Klotz, Leopold, ed. *Die Kirche und das dritte Reich: Fragen und Forderungen deutscher Theologen*. 2 vol. Gotha: Leopold Klotz Verlag, 1932-33.

Kremers, Hermann. *Nationalsozialismus und Protestantismus*. 3d ed. Berlin: Verlag des Evangelischen Bundes, 1931.

Kúptsch, Julius. *Christentum im Nationalsozialismus*. Munich: Verlag F. Eher, 1932.

————. *Im dritten Reich zur dritten Kirche*, No. 1 of *Die christliche und kirchliche Revolution*. Leipzig: Adolf Klein Verlag, [1933].

————. *Mit Hitler zur Volksgemeinschaft und zum dritten Reich, mit Christus zur Glaubensgemeinschaft und zur dritten Kirche*. Heiligenbeil: Ostpreussischer Heimatverlag, 1934.

————. *Nationalsozialismus und positives Christentum*. 2d ed. Weimar: Verlag Deutsche Christen, 1939.

Leffler, Siegfried. *Christus im dritten Reich der Deutschen: Wesen, Weg und Ziel der Kirchenbewegung Deutsche Christen*. Weimar: Verlag Deutsche Christen, 1935.

————. *Unser Weg: Rede von Siegfried Leffler im Sportpalast in Berlin, 28. Mai 1938*. Weimar: Verlag Deutsche Christen, 1938.

Leipoldt, Johannes. *Antisemitismus in der alten Welt*. Leipzig: Verlag von Dörffling & Franke, 1933.

————. *Gegenwartsfragen in der neutestamentlichen Wissenschaft*. Leipzig: A. Deichertsche Verlag, 1935.

————. *War Jesus Jude?* Leipzig: A. Deichertsche Verlag, 1923.

Leutheuser, Julius. *Die deutsche Christusgemeinde: Der Weg zur deutschen Nationalkirche*. 2d ed. Weimar: Verlag Deutsche Christen, 1935.

Luthertum, [see *Neue Kirchliche Zeitschrift*].

Maurenbrecher, Max. *Der Heiland der Deutschen: Der Weg der Volkstum schaffenden Kirche*. 2d ed. Göttingen: Vandenhoeck & Ruprecht, 1933.

Meyer, Heinrich. *Wie stellst Du Dich, deutscher Christ, zum Nationalsozialismus?* No. 1 of *Schriftenreihe der Arbeitsgemeinschaft nationalsozialistischer evangelischer Geistlicher*. 2d ed. Leipzig: Adolf Klein Verlag, 1933.

Meyer-Erlach, Wolf. *Kirche oder Sekte: Offener Brief an Herrn Landesbischof D. Meiser*. Weimar: Verlag Deutsche Christen, 1934.

Müller, Hans Michael. *Der innere Weg der deutschen Kirche*. Tübingen: Verlag von J. C. B. Mohr, 1933.

_____. *Was muss die Welt von Deutschland Wissen? Nationale Revolution und Kirche*. Tübingen: Verlag von J. C. B. Mohr, 1933.

Müller, Ludwig. *Deutsche Gottesworte: Aus der Bergpredigt verdeutscht*. Weimar: Verlag Deutsche Christen, 1936.

_____. *Was ist positives Christentum?* Stuttgart: Der Tazzelwurm Verlag, 1939.

_____, and Kinder, Christian. *Die Deutschen Christen: Die Reden des Reichsbischofs und des Reichsleiters der deutschen Christen, Dr. jur. Kinder, im Berliner Sportpalast am 28. Februar 1934*. Berlin: Gesellschaft für Zeitungsdienst G. m. b. H., 1934.

Neue Kirchliche Zeitschrift [after 1934, called *Luthertum*]. Leipzig: A. Deichertsche Verlagsbuchhandlung, 1918-39.

Pflugk, Heinz. *Die Christliche-deutsche Bewegung*, No. 2 of *Glaube und Volk: Schriftenreihe der Christlich-deutschen Bewegung*. Küstrin: Verlag Deutscher Osten, 1931.

Die Religion in Geschichte und Gegenwart: Handwörterbuch für Theologie und Religionswissenschaft. 6 vols. 2d ed. Tübingen: J. C. B. Mohr Verlag, 1927-32.

Rendtorff, Heinrich. *Kirche im Kampf: Evangelische Rufe und Reden aus der Zeit des Kampfes um Deutschlands Erneuerung*. 2d ed. Schwerin: Verlag Friedrich Bahn, 1934.

_____. *Das Wort Gottes über das Volk*, No. 1 of *Glaube und Volk: Schriftenreihe der Christlich-deutschen Bewegung*. Küstrin: Verlag Deutscher Osten, 1931.

Sasse, Hermann, ed. *Kirchliches Jahrbuch für die evangelischen Landeskirchen Deutschlands*. LIX (1932). Gütersloh: C. Bertelsmann Verlag, 1933.

Schmidt, Kurt Dietrich. *Die Bekentnisse und grundsätzlichen Äusserungen zur Kirchenfrage des Jahres 1933, 1934.* Göttingen: Vandenhoeck & Ruprecht, 1934-35.

Schneider, Georg. *Deutsches Christentum: Der Weg zur dritten Kirche.* Stuttgart: Verlag von W. Kohlhammer, 1934.

Stapel, Wilhelm. *Der christliche Staatsmann: Eine Theologie des Nationalismus.* Hamburg: Hanseatische Verlagsanstalt, 1932.

_____. *Die Kirche Christi und der Staat Hitlers.* Hamburg: Hanseatische Verlagsanstalt, 1933.

_____. *Sechs Kapitel über Christentum und Nationalsozialismus.* Hamburg: Hanseatische Verlagsanstalt, 1931.

Die Theologie der Gegenwart. Leipzig: A. Deichertsche Verlagsbuchhandlung, XXIII-XXV (1929-31).

Theologische Blätter. Leipzig: Verlag der J. C. Hinrichs Buchhandlung, VIII, X, XII, XV, XVII (1929, 1931, 1933, 1936, 1938).

Thom, Pfarrer Dr. Martin. *Christenkreuz und Hakenkreuz.* Berlin: Kranzverlag, 1933.

Tügel, Franz. *Wer bist Du? Fragen der Kirche an den Nationalsozialismus.* Hamburg: Agentur des Rauhen Hauses G.m.b.H., 1932.

Völkischer Beobachter. May 28/29, June 21, July 19, 1933.

Weidemann, Landesbischof Lic. Dr. Heinz. *So sieht die kommende Kirche aus.* 3d ed. Bremen: Verlag Kommende Kirche, 1940.

Wieneke, Friedrich. *Deutsche Theologie im Umriss,* No. 5 of *Schriftenreihe der "Deutschen Christen."* Soldin: Druck und Verlag H. Madrasch, 1933.

_____. *Die Entwicklung des philosophischen Gottesbegriffs bei Ernst Troeltsch.* Soldin: Druck und Verlag H. Madrasch, 1929.

_____. *Die Glaubensbewegung "Deutsche Christen,"* No. 2 of *Schriftenreihe der "Deutschen Christen."* Edited by Joachim Hossenfelder. Soldin: H. Madrasch, 1933.

Zeitschrift für Theologie und Kirche. Tübingen: Verlag von J. C. B. Mohr, XIII-XIX (1932-38).

Secondary Sources

Baumont, Maurice; Fried, John H. E.; and Vermeil, Edmond, eds. *The Third Reich.* New York: Frederick A. Praeger, 1955.

Bonus, Arthur. *Religion als Schöpfung: Erwägungen über die religiöse Krisis.* Leipzig: Eugen Diederichs, 1902.

Bracher, Karl Dietrich; Sauer, Wolfgang; and Schulz, Gerhard. *Die nationalsozialistische Machtergreifung: Studien zur Errichtung des totalitären Herrschaftssystems in Deutschland 1933/34.* 2d ed. Cologne: Westdeutscher Verlag, 1962.

Buchheim, Hans. *Glaubenskrise im dritten Reich: Drei Kapitel nationalsozialistischer Religionspolitik.* Stuttgart: Deutsche Verlags-Anstalt, 1953.

Chamberlain, Houston Stewart. *Foundations of the Nineteenth Century.* Translated by John Lees. New York: John Lane Co., 1912.

Cochrane, Arthur C. *The Church's Confession under Hitler.* Philadelphia: The Westminster Press, 1962.

Conrad, Walter. *Der Kampf um die Kanzeln: Erinnerungen und Dokumente aus der Hitlerzeit.* Berlin: Alfred Töpelmann, 1957.

Conway, J. S. *The Nazi Persecution of the Churches, 1933-45.* New York: Basic Books, Inc., 1968.

Douglass, Paul F. *God Among the Germans.* Philadelphia: University of Pennsylvania Press, 1935.

Drummond, Andrew L. *German Protestantism Since Luther.* London: The Epworth Press, 1951.

Evangelische Theologie. Munich: Chr. Kaiser Verlag, 1958, 1962, 1963.

Evangelisches Kirchenlexikon: Kirchlich-theologisches Handwörterbuch. Göttingen: 1956-58.

Eyck, Erich. *A History of the Weimar Republic.* Cambridge: Harvard University Press, 1962.

Frey, Arthur. *Cross and Swastika.* Translated by J. Strathearn McNab. London: Student Christian Movement Press, 1938.

Götte, Karl-Heinz. *Die Propaganda der Glaubensbewegung "Deutsche Christen" und ihre Beurteilung in der deutschen Tagespresse: Ein Beitrag zur Publizistik im Dritten Reich.* Ph.D. dissertation, University of Münster, 1957.

Gurian, Waldemar. *Hitler and the Christians.* Translated by E. F. Peeler. London: Sheed & Ward, 1936.

Herman, Stewart W. Jr. *It's Your Souls We Want.* Philadelphia: Muhlenburg Press, 1943.

_____. *The Rebirth of the German Church.* London: S. C. M. Press, 1946.

Hermelink, Heinrich. *Das Christentum in der Menschheitsgeschichte von der französischen Revolution bis zur Gegenwart.* Tübingen: Rainer Wunderlich Verlag Hermann Leins, 1955.

242

Hermelink, Heinrich. *Kirche im Kampf: Dokumente des Widerstandes und des Aufbaues in der evangelischen Kirche Deutschlands von 1933 bis 1945*. Tübingen: Rainer Wunderlich Verlag Hermann Leins, 1950.

Hitler, Adolf. *Mein Kampf*. Boston: Houghton Mifflin Company, 1943.

Kohn, Hans. "Romanticism and the Rise of German Nationalism." *The Review of Politics*, XII (1950), pp. 443-72.

Krieger, Leonard. *The German Idea of Freedom*. Boston: Beacon Press, 1957.

Kupisch, Karl. *Zwischen Idealismus und Massendemokratie: Eine Geschichte der evangelischen Kirche in Deutschland von 1815-1945*. Berlin: Lettner Verlag, 1955.

Littell, Franklin Hamlin. *The German Phoenix: Men and Movements in the Church in Germany*. Garden City, New York: Doubleday & Company, Inc., 1960.

_____. "The Protestant Churches and Totalitarianism-- Germany 1933-1945." *Totalitarianism*. Edited by Carl J. Friedrich. Cambridge: Harvard University Press, 1954.

MacFarland, Charles S. *The New Church and the New Germany: A Study of Church and State*. New York: The Macmillan Company, 1934.

Mau, Hermann, and Krausnick, Helmut. *German History 1933-45*. New York: Frederick Ungar Publishing Co., 1963.

Means, Paul B. *Things That Are Caesar's: The Genesis of the German Church Conflict*. New York: Round Table Press, Inc., 1935.

Meier, Kurt. *Die Deutschen Christen: Das Bild einer Bewegung im Kirchenkampf des Dritten Reiches*. Göttingen: Vandenhoeck & Ruprecht, 1964.

Mosse, George L. *The Crisis of German Ideology: Intellectual Origins of the Third Reich*. New York: Grosset & Dunlap, 1964.

Neumann, Sigmund. *Permanent Revolution*. 2d ed. New York: Frederick A. Praeger, Publishers, 1965.

Neurohr, Jean F. *Der Mythos vom dritten Reich: Zur Geistesgeschichte des Nationalsozialismus*. Stuttgart: J. G. Cotta, 1957.

Nichols, James Hastings. *History of Christianity, 1650-1950: Secularization of the West*. New York: The Ronald Press Company, 1956.

Nicolaisen, Carsten. *Die Auseinandersetzungen um das Alte Testament im Kirchenkampf, 1933-1945*. Ph.D. dissertation, University of Hamburg, 1966.

Norden, Günther Van. *Kirche in der Krise*. Düsseldorf: Presse-verband der Evangelischen Kirche im Rheinland, 1963.

Oppenheimer, Heinrich. *The Constitution of the German Republic*. London: Stevens and Sons, Limited, 1923.

Pinson, Koppel S. *Pietism as a Factor in the Rise of German Nationalism*. New York: Columbia University Press, 1934.

Poliakov, Leon; and Wulf, Josef. *Das Dritte Reich und seine Denker: Dokumente*. Berlin-Grunewald: Verlags-GMBH, 1959.

Raab, Herbert, ed. *Kirche und Staat*. Munich: Deutscher Taschenbuch Verlag, 1966.

Schlemmer, Hans. *Von Karl Barth zu den Deutschen Christen: Ein Wort zum Verständnis der heutigen theologischen Lage*. Gotha: Leopold Klotz Verlag, 1934.

Schoenbaum, David. *Hitler's Social Revolution: Class and Status in Nazi Germany 1933-1939*. Garden City, New York: Anchor Books, Doubleday & Company, Inc., 1967.

Tilgner, Wolfgang. *Volksnomostheologie und Schöpfungsglaube: Ein Beitrag zur Geschichte des Kirchenkampfes*. Göttingen: Vandenhoeck & Ruprecht, 1966.

Tillich, Paul. "The Totalitarian State and the Claims of the Church." *Social Research*, I, No. 4 (November, 1934), pp. 405-33.

Toaspern, Paul, ed. *Arbeiter in Gottes Ernte: Heinrich Rendtorff. Leben und Werk*. Berlin: Christlicher Zeit-schriftenverlag, 1963.

Veit, Ludwig A. *Die Kirche im Zeitalter des Individualismus: 1648 bis zur Gegenwart*. Freiburg: Herder & Co., 1933.

Whiteside, Andrew Gladding. *Austrian National Socialism before 1918*. The Hague: Martinus Nijhoff, 1962.

Zipfel, Friedrich. *Kirchenkampf in Deutschland 1933-1945*. Berlin: Walter de Gruyter & Co., 1965.